Implementing Elliptic Curve Cryptography

Implementing Elliptic Curve Cryptography

MICHAEL ROSING

MANNING

Greenwich
(74° w. long.)

For electronic browsing and ordering of this and other Manning books,
visit http://www.manning.com. The publisher offers discounts on this book
when ordered in quantity. For more information, please contact:

    Special Sales Department
    Manning Publications Co.
    32 Lafayette Place   Fax: (203) 661-9018
    Greenwich, CT 06830   email: orders@manning.com

Library of Congress Cataloging-in-Publication Data
Rosing, Michael,   1954-
    Implementing elliptic curve cryptography / Michael Rosing
        p.   cm.
    Includes bibliographical references and index.
    ISBN 1-884777-69-4 (alk. paper)
    1. Computer security. 2. Data encryption (Computer science)
      3. Curves, Elliptic--Data processing.   I. Title
  QA76.9.A25R66 1998
  005.8'2--dc21   98-40461
                          CIP

Manning Publications Co.   Copyeditor: Katherine Antonsen
32 Lafayette Place   Typesetter: Dottie Marsico
Greenwich, CT 06830   Cover designer: Leslie Haimes

Printed in the United States of America
2 3 4 5 6 7 8 9 10 – CR – 01 00 99

To Joshua and Samuel

Live Free

contents

preface xii

author online and source code xiii

acknowledgments xiv

1   **Introduction 1**

    1.1   Some initial comments 2

    1.2   Why elliptic curves? 4

    1.3   Orders of magnitude 4

    1.4   About this book 7

    1.5   Why C? 11

    1.6   Comments on style 12

    1.7   References 12

2   **Basics of number theory 13**

    2.1   Large integer math header 14

    2.2   Large integer math routines 19
            Multiplication 21,   Division 23

    2.3   Large integer code example 27

    2.4   Back to number theory 29

    2.5   Greatest common factor 30

    2.6   Modular arithmetic 37

    2.7   Fermat's Theorem 39

2.8   Finite fields 40

2.9   Generators 43

2.10 References 44

3   *Polynomial math over finite fields 47*

3.1   Introduction to polynomials 48

3.2   All structures are polynomials 52
Polynomial addition 54,   Polynomial multiplication 55,   Polynomial division 58

3.3   Modular polynomial arithmetic 64

3.4   Inversion over prime polynomials 66

3.5   Polynomial greatest common divisor 67

3.6   Prime polynomials 68

3.7   Summary 72

3.8   References 72

4   *Normal basis mathematics 75*

4.1   What is a normal basis? 76

4.2   Squaring normal basis numbers 78

4.3   Multiplication in theory 78

4.4   Type I optimal normal basis 80

4.5   Type II optimal normal basis 85

4.6   Multiplication in practice 92

4.7   Inversion over optimal normal basis 97

4.8   References 102

5   *Elliptic curves 103*

5.1   Mathematics of elliptic curves over real numbers 104

5.2   Mathematics of elliptic curves over prime fields 108

5.3   Mathematics of elliptic curves over Galois Fields 109

5.4   Polynomial basis elliptic curve subroutines 114

5.5   Optimal normal basis elliptic curve subroutines 118

5.6   Multiplication over elliptic curves 120

5.7   Balanced integer conversion code 122

5.8   Following the balanced representation 125

5.9   References 126

6   Cryptography 129

6.1   Fundamentals of elliptic curve cryptography 131

6.2   Choosing an elliptic curve 132

6.3   Nonsupersingular curves 133

6.4   Embedding data on a curve 136

6.5   Solving quadratic equations in binary fields 137

6.6   The Trace function 138

6.7   Solving quadratic equations in normal basis 141

6.8   Solving quadratic equations in polynomial basis 148

6.9   Quadratic polynomials: the code 149

6.10   Using the T matrix 158

6.11   Embedding data using polynomial basis 161

6.12   Summary of quadratic solving 162

6.13   References 163

7   Simple protocols 165

7.1   Introduction 166

7.2   Random bit generator 168

7.3   Choosing random curves 171

7.4   Protocols 174
Diffie-Hellman 174,   ElGamal Protocol 180,   Menezes-Qu-Vanstone key agreement scheme 188

7.5   References 197

8   Elliptic curve encryption 199

8.1   Introduction to ECES 200

8.2   Mask generation function 202

8.3   Hash function SHA-1 203

8.4 Mask generation: the code 210

8.5 ECES: the code 212
Polynomial basis 212,   Normal basis 216

8.6 References 219

9 Advanced protocols, key exchange 221

9.1 Preliminaries for key exchange 222

9.2 Polynomial solution to $\gamma^3 = \gamma + 1$ 226

9.3 Massey-Omura protocol 234
Massey-Omura: the code 236

9.4 MQV: the standard 244
MQV: normal basis version 246,   MQV: polynomial basis version 250

9.5 References 254

10 Advanced protocols, signatures 255

10.1 Introduction to digital signatures 256

10.2 Message hash 259

10.3 Nyberg-Rueppel signature scheme 260
Nyberg-Rueppel signature: normal basis 261,   Nyberg-Rueppel: polynomial basis 267

10.4 Digital Signature Algorithm (DSA) 271
DSA in normal basis 273,   DSA: polynomial basis 278

10.5 Signatures: a summary 282

10.6 References 282

11 The bleeding edge 283

11.1 High-speed inversion for ONB 284

11.2 Faster inversion, preliminary subroutines 288
Faster inversion, the code 292

11.3 Security from cryptography 297

11.4 Counting points 298

11.5 Polynomials: base p 299

11.6 Hyperelliptic curves 299

11.7 References 300

12 A simple application 301

12.1 Personal security example 302

12.2 Security analysis 305

12.3 Putting it all together 305

12.4 References 307

index 309

preface

When I first posted elliptic curve cryptography (ECC) math to cipherpunks, I assumed it would help lots of people learn all the math associated with ECC. Only a few professors contacted me and wanted to know if their students could use it for their thesis work. After a while, it began to sink in that just posting code wasn't going to bring enlightenment to the engineers who needed to know ECC. So I decided to write this book.

What I originally wanted to do was to explain the code I posted. This was very limited in scope, because it only involved Type I optimal normal basis mathematics. Nor were there any protocols; it was just math. This also proved to be much too limited, so I figured I should learn all the Type II mathematics as well as polynomial basis mathematics.

Mathematicians consider everything in this book to be "trivial." The problems solved in excruciating detail are so basic that you won't find them discussed in any math texts, other than a sentence or two or possibly in a homework problem. Mathematicians don't have secrets, but they do have tricks of the trade, which are simply assumed available.

One of the most exciting aspects of elliptic curve cryptography (crypto) is the inability of mathematicians to solve the "discrete logarithm problem." ECC is really the most secure mathematical crypto method human beings presently know about. This alone makes learning elliptic curve crypto worthwhile.

There are some people who feel that the mathematics behind elliptic curve cryptography is too obscure and difficult. The main reason behind this book is to dispel that attitude. It is true that there are many aspects of elliptic curve mathematics currently on the cutting edge of mathematical knowledge. This is an exciting element of learning something that is state of the art. But you need no more than high school algebra to understand what this book is about. With luck, a few readers will be motivated to charge on and learn enough to push the edge of knowledge further.

For most of you, implementing state-of-the-art crypto for your present project (which is two months late) is the primary reason for picking up this book. You'll find complete subroutines that can be linked with your project to get the show on the road. (The IEEE P1363 draft was not finalized by the time this book went to press, so you may need to make a few changes to be fully compatible.) The mathematical descriptions throughout should help you understand the protocols in that standard.

Elliptic curve cryptography is "new," because it was first introduced in 1985. Public key cryptography was introduced in 1976, so by comparison elliptic curve crypto is "untested." These comparisons are not useful, because the fundamental mathematics behind integer factoring schemes proposed in the 1970s, as well as elliptic curve schemes proposed in the 1980s, are all hundreds of years old. The math problems have always been difficult; elliptic curve mathematics is just exceptionally more difficult to crack, but surprisingly easy to implement.

Since first suggested, a great deal of academic interest has spawned detailed investigation into elliptic curve cryptography. What is presented in this book is just the tip of the iceberg, but it includes the most efficient mathematics and highest security protocols found so far. The fact that the greatest minds in mathematics have trouble proving otherwise indicates that this is a good place to start to get the most out of crypto.

All the math in this book is easy. But there is a lot of it, so take your time. Unless, of course, you're six months behind!

author online and source code

Purchase of the *Implementing Elliptic Curve Cryptography* book includes free access to a private Internet forum where you can make comments about the book, ask technical questions, and receive help from the author and from other readers. To access the *Author Online* forum, point your Web browser to www.manning.com/Rosing. There you will be able to subscribe to the forum. This site also provides information on how to access the forum once you are registered, what kind of help is available, and the rules of conduct on the forum.

All source code for the examples presented in *Implementing Elliptic Curve Cryptography* is available to purchasers from the Manning Web site. The url www.manning.com/Rosing includes a link to the source code files. Each example is presented as a complete set of files which can be compiled and linked as a terminal application on any ANSI C compiler.

acknowledgments

Many people have helped me learn the math and improve the code in this book. Professor Neal Koblitz (U. Washington) answered many questions very early in my learning curve and has helped in more ways than he can imagine. Steve Albrect converted the first subroutines posted to cipherpunks, which allowed much wider distribution, and has read every draft of this text with great care, allowing it to be vastly improved. Professor Christof Paar (Worcester Polytechnic) has answered many questions and helped me to understand that there are more ways to do elliptic curve mathematics than I ever thought possible. Professor Richard Schroeppel (U. Arizona) spent a lot of time explaining his work to me, and Dave Dahm found the solution I never could that related the "almost inverse algorithm" to normal basis math. Professor Richard Pinch (Queen's College) explained that I was doing things the hard way and greatly improved the polynomial basis code described in chapter 6. I apologize for not having time to implement every suggestion received from these people. With more people writing more code, I fully expect to see many more improvements in a short time.

I thank Cameron Laird for pointing out obvious errors that others missed. In addition, he helped reword many passages in a very short time. The book is far more readable due to his efforts.

Thanks to Katherine for letting me disappear many hours to write this. Without her understanding and support this would not have been possible.

Special thanks to all the folks at Manning. It takes a lot of people to convert a good idea into a book. As always, the end result is my responsibility. But without all the help I received, this book would not exist in its present form.

C H A P T E R   1

Introduction

1.1 Some initial comments   2

1.2 Why elliptic curves?   4

1.3 Orders of magnitude   4

1.4 About this book   7

1.5 Why C?   11

1.6 Comments on style   12

1.7 References   12

1.1 Some initial comments

Public key cryptography is a relatively new field for engineers. Almost all books to date on the subject have been written by and for mathematicians. As an engineer, I appreciate what the mathematicians do, but making things work requires getting a job done. This book is for hardware and software engineers who were told today to get the job done last week. The goal here is to help you get the job done well using state-of-the-art knowledge. By the time you finish this book, you will be able to understand just about every mathematical argument that takes place on a standards committee and have the skills required to implement security patches.

I am going to discuss a particularly interesting and very useful implementation of public key crypto systems that utilizes the mathematics of elliptic curves. Don't look for a relation between elliptic curves and the geometric ellipses you know. Mathematicians labeled the former in the eighteenth century for reasons that hold little pertinence now. The basic arithmetic will be novel for most engineers. My purpose is to help computer programmers and software engineers develop state-of-the-art crypto systems that utilize minimal resources to get maximum security. Hardware engineers will have to do a bit more homework, but I hope the code that implements the math will be easy to convert to hardware-descriptive language.

Most everyone who deals with computers or cryptography has heard of the program PGP, or "Pretty Good Privacy." This utilizes both a public key and a secret key system (I'll explain those terms in more detail later). The security of the public key portion of PGP is based on the difficulty of factoring large numbers. The mathematics associated with elliptic curve public key crypto systems appears to be an even more difficult problem to solve, so fewer bits (and hence fewer resources in power, gates, and so on) lead to the same level of security.

Note that I say "appears to be" more difficult. As I write this, there are no known algorithms that take less than exponential time to crack certain elliptic curves. That does not mean there won't be algorithms developed in the future, but at present the resources needed to crack elliptic curve crypto schemes are *much* larger than the resources required to crack integer factorization schemes such as the one used in PGP.

Up to now, the mathematics of elliptic curve cryptography has been very difficult for any engineer to dig through. I've simplified the presentation in this book to avoid any proofs. The fact that the code works is proof enough. For those who want to improve the code, I strongly urge you to read the supplied references and delve deeper into the math.

I will repeat the following many times: Cryptography is not security. This book is about one particular type of cryptography. I will give you subroutines, which will help you implement secure systems, but it is the responsibility of the system designer to understand all the possible attacks. For example, many of the math functions implemented here follow different paths depending on bits being set or clear. This might allow a "timing attack." While this particular attack is exceptionally difficult to perform in reality, those who feel it is a real threat must modify the code included in this book to prevent it.

Security also depends on users and their attitude, as well as physical constraints. Users who tell someone their passwords over the phone completely defeat even the most secure system. An otherwise secure server placed in an unlocked closet may be read with an RF (radio frequency) tap. This may or may not be a problem, depending on how well the room is shielded to RF. The point is, this book is focused on a very specific topic of cryptography. You should read the references at the end of each chapter for more general security perspectives. A good place to start is [1].

Because some of you may be in a hurry to get the job done, you may jump to the end of the book and pull out all the subroutines needed to implement a signature scheme (for example). Inattention to details of the math leaves you open to hackers, though. To explain why, I'll give a simple (but possibly silly) analogy followed by a more sober attempt.

The silly comparison refers to the design of a car. There are lots of subsections to a car, just as there are lots of subroutines in any application. For my comparison, I'll take the mathematics to be similar to the engine, since that's what makes the crypto work.

Suppose you want to build a race car, and you can get a frame, an engine, and a suspension system for free. You might pick out the engine for a large dump truck because it has a huge amount of power, but you may not notice that it's larger than the frame and suspension! By learning the math, the choice of subroutines will be easier (and sensible) for any given application.

Another reason to dig through all the math is to ensure the final product will be secure. There are researchers all over the world pushing the state of the art. Every time one of them finds a weakness in an algorithm it is "big news" in the crypto community. These weaknesses are not always very easy to exploit, but by learning the math you can be sure you know the level of threat posed to your product every time a new problem is found.

Hackers will always try to find a way into a secure application. You cannot fully understand where cracks in the code might be hiding if you simply copy all the subroutines. You may have to modify the routines so they are perfect for your application. It may not seem to matter when you are in the nitty gritty of making something work, but in the long run understanding the math will allow you to confidently change subroutines correctly.

1.2 Why elliptic curves?

In 1985, Koblitz [2] and Miller [3] independently suggested that elliptic curves could be used for cryptographic public key schemes. At that time it was very difficult to perform the necessary calculations. The underlying math was not very efficient, and it was only an interesting academic exercise. Since then, a great deal of effort has gone into understanding efficient ways to perform the calculations. By the late 1990s, the implementations were ten times more efficient, and this allowed the performance of elliptic curve mathematics to take the same amount of time as implementations of integer factoring schemes (such as PGP) for the same number of bits. Since elliptic curves require fewer bits for the same security, there is a net reduction in cost, size, and time.

Since that original introduction, many people have tried to crack elliptic curve schemes. Many of the initial proposals turned out to be easy to crack, but a few have proven exceptionally difficult. Some are so difficult that companies such as Certicom (http://www.certicom.com) have issued a set of challenges with rewards as high as $100,000 for cracking them. What I will present in this book are the best schemes found so far that are the most resistant to attack. I do not describe schemes that have fallen out of favor due to possible attacks.

One of the most important benefits of elliptic curve cryptography is the lack of patents covering the published schemes. This means that exceptionally good crypto is available without royalties. A few patents have been filed for specific implementations of elliptic curve cryptographic schemes, and, as of summer 1998, a few more are in application. The most interesting schemes I'll discuss are the Nyberg-Rueppie signature scheme, which may be patented in Europe, and the MQV key authentication scheme, which may get a patent issued in Canada and the United States. This may limit the distribution of these particular algorithms, but there are enough other choices to create a high-quality, royalty-free crypto system. All other schemes are patent free, either because there is none or because the patents have expired (as in the Diffie-Hellman key exchange protocol).

I'll summarize: Elliptic curve cryptography is cheaper, faster, and more secure than competing methods.

1.3 Orders of magnitude

One of the important aspects of public key cryptography is understanding what it takes to crack a code. Implementing algorithms for cracking public key crypto systems requires a fantastic background in number theory. I do not present anything quite so deep here. What I can do is attempt to compare the results of various methods already known.

Before I get into specifics, I need to describe the terms "exponential time," "subexponential time," and "polynomial time." For something that is n bits long, a polynomial time algorithm will appear as:

$$\text{time}_{\text{polynomial}} \sim n^k \tag{1.1}$$

where k is a fixed number, independent of n. This type of algorithm is very fast. Most of the code in this book runs in polynomial time on the order of n^3 or less. This makes the task easy.

An exponential time algorithm appears as:

$$\text{time}_{\text{exponential}} \sim e^n. \tag{1.2}$$

If the time to crack an algorithm is fully exponential, and the time to compute it is polynomial, we have the best of all possible worlds. A subexponential algorithm is in between polynomial and exponential. The problem is difficult, but possible to do for many practical cases.

Integer factorization schemes (such as RSA used in PGP, see [1]) have well-known attacks. The basic problem for this type of public key cryptography is the difficulty in finding two large primes (p and q) whose product is one very large number N. It turns out that the time required to factor this type of number is roughly as follows:

$$\text{time}_{\text{factoring}} \sim \exp(c\sqrt[3]{(\log N)(\log\log N)^2}). \tag{1.3}$$

This is for one particular method (which, coincidentally, uses elliptic curves); there are other methods that take more or less time depending on the size of the number N. But as a rough estimate, we can see that the running time to crack this type of scheme is:

$$\exp\left((\log N)^{\frac{1}{3}})\right). \tag{1.4}$$

This falls under the classification of subexponential.

Factoring is a very old problem and has been studied for a long time. Since the late 1970s, many mathematicians have contributed to the methods that make the above estimate possible. Our understanding of elliptic curves is not yet nearly as mature.

Elliptic curve crypto systems use points or pairs of numbers to hide information. We'll get into all the details much later, but the basic idea is to have the total number of points available (m) be very large. This defines the space in which we can hide messages. The time required to find a particular point, or message, is roughly as follows:

$$\text{time}_{\text{elliptic}} \sim \exp(c\sqrt{m}). \tag{1.5}$$

This is fully exponential. It is very difficult to pin down any exact comparison, but the number of bits required to be compatible with RSA 1024 using elliptic curves is under 200 bits. So, although it takes two 200-bit elements to represent each point, the amount of hardware required to accomplish the mathematics (or equivalently the amount of processor time for general-purpose processors) is far less than that required for the same level of security using integer factorization methods.

The bottom line is that the good guys use less resources and force the bad guys to use more resources. This is the security reason for using elliptic curves for your crypto system.

The numbers associated with cryptography are huge. To attempt to guess an arbitrary key is ridiculous. The security of a crypto system does not depend on the ability to guess. It depends on the algorithms and number of computer cycles available to the cryptanalyst. To really appreciate the size of the numbers, let's look at a couple of astronomical examples. The purpose of these examples is to help you understand just how much more secure elliptic curves are compared to the alternatives.

We can estimate the number of protons in the sun by dividing the solar mass by the mass of a hydrogen atom. In orders of magnitude these masses are about:

$$M_{\text{sun}} = 2 \times 10^{31} \text{ kg} \tag{1.6}$$

and

$$M_{\text{hydrogen}} = 1.67 \times 10^{-27} \text{ kg}. \tag{1.7}$$

So we can estimate the number of solar protons to be roughly 10^{58}. This is about 2^{193}. Cracking an elliptic curve algorithm is the same as finding a specific proton somewhere in all the protons in the sun. Finding a needle in a haystack is really simple by comparison.

As another comparison, let's look at the number of cubic femtometers in the universe. This is the only way I can contrive real countable "things" for comparison to the numbers used in cryptography. Let's just assume the radius of the universe is on the order of 10 billion light-years. A femtometer is 10^{-15} meters (about the diameter of a proton). A light-year is about 10^{16} meters, so the number of cubic femtometers is roughly $10^{3(26+15)} = 10^{123}$, which is about 2^{408}. Elliptic curve crypto systems are in the range of astronomical. Integer factoring schemes require numbers that are more than twice as large in the exponent (being on the order of 2^{1024}) and make "astronomical" look tiny. This is the real difference between fully exponential and subexponential time.

These numbers only apply to public key crypto systems. Symmetric key crypto systems are always fully exponential. Symmetric key systems are based on the premise that there are no mathematical tools that can crack them. Only brute-force guessing will work. For these systems good security can be assured with 128 bits (or 2^{128} "things"). I'll get into the details eventually, but, as you learn the math, remember that we are developing a crypto system that is fully exponential to crack—even with mathematical tools.

1.4 About this book

The background required to understand the math presented in this book includes algebra and computer programming. Since most engineers have little background in number theory, I've tried to be as basic as possible and introduce only the concepts needed to understand why the code works. Many computer science graduates who have been exposed to number theory may be rusty. My hope is that many high school students will be able to follow along and be motivated to learn more.

A complete view of the book can be seen in figure 1.1. Notice the two columns titled "Mathematics" and "Cryptography." This indicates that chapters 2 through 5 describe the mathematics, and chapters 7 through 10 describe the cryptography. Chapter 6 is a bridge between these two concepts, and chapters 11 and 12 go over a lot of ground that just doesn't fit anywhere else. The arrows show how subroutines from specific chapters feed into the subroutines of following chapters.

Within each chapter you'll find a subroutine schematic similar to that shown in figure 1.2. This is a cross between a flow chart and a circuit schematic. I've tried to leave each chapter as its own "bus," so anyone who prefers to read things in a top-down approach can follow the book backwards. Subroutines within a chapter will be on the same bus, and subroutines from other chapters will be schematically referenced.

Each subroutine has a separate box, which gives its name and brief description. On one side is a small box with arrows going into it, which lists all the subroutines that are directly called by the described subroutine. In a slightly different font are global variables. The initialization routines have the global variables in a box with arrows leaving the subroutine name to show that they are outputs.

Routines that stand alone are usually at the top, and the "bus" then wraps around the remaining subroutines to show that they are all interlinked. In later chapters, there are many references to previous chapters. This overall flow can be found in figure 1.1.

Chapter 2 starts with very basic number theory. Basic ideas of addition, multiplication, and division are discussed. These may seem trivial, but when you have to multiply two numbers that are hundreds of bits long even simple things must be done with care. Modular arithmetic is described and so are basic concepts such as greatest common divi-

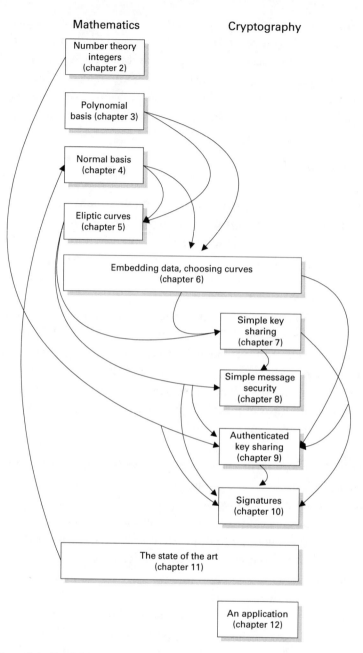

Mathematics   Cryptography

Number theory
integers
(chapter 2)

Polynomial
basis (chapter 3)

Normal basis
(chapter 4)

Eliptic curves
(chapter 5)

Embedding data, choosing curves
(chapter 6)

Simple key
sharing
(chapter 7)

Simple message
security
(chapter 8)

Authenticated
key sharing
(chapter 9)

Signatures
(chapter 10)

The state of the art
(chapter 11)

An application
(chapter 12)

Figure 1.1   Book layout

sor. Since the book is about code, every section illustrates mathematical descriptions with C listings. As you can see from figure 1.1, the code from chapter 2 isn't used until much later in the book. This chapter can be skipped by those who already have a number theory background.

In chapter 3, I introduce polynomial mathematics. This is where having a background in algebra becomes necessary. The basic number theory ideas from chapter 2, including multiplication, addition, and inversion, are generalized to polynomial mathematics. The basic concepts of Galois Fields are introduced, along with the mathematics that applies to them. Again, every section is a mixture of math and code. Because the subroutines in this chapter are fundamental to the whole book, it is probably a good idea to at least skim it to understand the code in the remainder of the book.

Chapter 4 discusses normal basis mathematics. This is a specialization of polynomial math that has particularly favorable computational performance on binary computers. Multiplication and inversion take up most of the chapter, because there are several types of normal basis representations and all need to be described for the code to make sense. This gives a lot more flexibility later on when choosing field sizes for specific applications.

As you can see in figure 1.1, chapters 3 and 4 feed directly into chapter 5. This forms the core of the mathematical subroutines in the book. The two mathematical methods of polynomial and normal basis then proceed in parallel throughout the rest of the book. My own preference is for the normal basis mathematics, because of its superior performance when setting up higher-level schemes. There are good reasons to

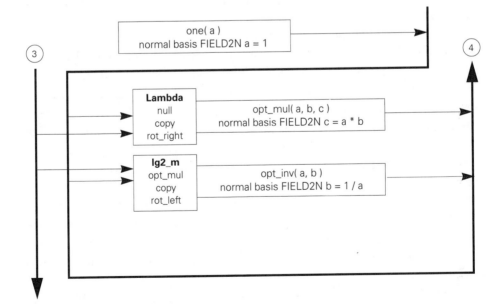

Figure 1.2   Subroutine schematic

choose one method over the other, depending on the application. You may find it worthwhile to try both methods and pick the best for your task.

Elliptic curves are introduced in chapter 5. I start with real numbers and explain with figures some of the basic concepts. From there I go into the finite field mathematics useful for computers. Code using both chapter 3 (polynomial basis) and chapter 4 (normal basis) versions of elliptic curve mathematics is given. The essential ideas are adding points and multiplication of integers and points.

As shown in figure 1.1, chapter 5 routines are called by every other chapter in the book. This is the core of the book. If you are in a hurry to find out what elliptic curve crypto is all about, chapter 5 is a good place to start reading. It may be worthwhile to skim it first to get a sense of what elliptic curve cryptography is all about before really delving into the details. Understanding the subroutines in chapter 5 is essential to understanding the rest of the book.

In chapter 6, the connection to cryptography is finally made. This chapter begins with code that embeds data onto elliptic curves. The importance of choosing the right hard-to-crack curve is explained, and several known good curves are given. Code that implements solutions to both polynomial basis (chapter 3) and normal basis (chapter 4) problems is given.

Simple cryptographic protocols are introduced in chapter 7, including elliptic curve versions of Diffie-Hellman and ElGamal. These routines only use the routines of chapters 5 and 6. Since all protocols can use either the polynomial or normal basis, examples of both are given. Only the MQV algorithm may have a patent on it, but the others in this chapter are free and clear.

In chapter 8, I describe the Elliptic Curve Encryption Scheme, which was originally proposed in the IEEE P1363 public key standard. This uses an additional hash algorithm, as well as the math of chapters 5 and 6. These routines are not patented.

Two key agreement schemes are described in chapter 9. One is from the IEEE standard, and the other is an elliptic curve version described in [4]. This utilizes integer math routines, along with the rest of the math described in chapters 2 through 5. The MQV algorithm may be patented, but the Massey-Omura scheme is not.

The IEEE crypto standard describes two elliptic curve signature schemes. Both are described in chapter 10. This chapter uses every subroutine in the book at least once. The DSA scheme is not patented, but the Nyberg-Rueppole scheme may be.

All the protocol chapters (7 through 10) have example routines along with their output. What is missing is real-world communications. The routines given are useful, but it remains the responsibility of the reader to combine them with other routines that actually move data around.

Chapter 11 ties together miscellaneous subjects that are interesting and likely to be useful. It includes a very fast inversion algorithm and many comments on what the future might bring. While only loosely linked to previous chapters, these are potentially important to readers. The arrow going back from chapter 11 signals that the inversion routine there can be used to replace the basic subroutine shown in chapter 3.

Finally, chapter 12 gives a sample application. There is no code or math. This chapter ties the real-world problems associated with security with the available crypto options presented in the book. The idea is to show you design decisions that go into a crypto application and how to pick code out of this book.

1.5 Why C?

All the code in this book is written in C. It should recompile and run on almost any ANSI compiler. While many people prefer higher-level languages such as C++ and Java, hardware engineers need VHDL and similar languages to create ASICs. The C language is in between both extremes. This should allow anyone who wants to go further in abstraction an easy route and those who need hardware a method of verification.

The largest problem with high-level languages is the lack of access to processor resources. The finite field mathematics can be easily programmed in assembler, and this will make any software implementation run much faster. I will definitely be pointing this out in several chapters.

If you are building smart cards, you are going to be implementing this code in hardware. This is far more physically secure than a software program. If you try to write this code in Java, you have almost no control over the security precautions where your code runs. Different applications will have different uses for the same code. I have tried to make each subroutine self-contained so that the basic structure is clear. In many cases, there are several subroutines that expose the same external interface, but they use different underlying mathematics. This gives you many options, and it may take some testing to see which particular group of routines is best suited for any particular application.

In the first half of the book, each chapter consists of a description of a particular mathematical discipline followed by subroutines that implement the math. In most cases, the subroutines are written for readability, and I have tried to make the math obvious. These routines cannot be the most efficient for every application. By changing the most important routines for your particular situation to increase speed or decrease memory use, you should be able to get any application to be more efficient than just a straight copy. With a good compiler, a straight copy will still be reasonable for performance. The point is: Play with it! The math is fun to learn, and if you find ways to improve the code let the rest of the world know about it.

I have tried to make the book self-consistent. Every subroutine is presented in the text and is used in later chapters. Because elliptic curve crypto schemes use so many different types of math, I have given example routines for each. Where possible, I have copied code from others and included it with their permission.

The code described here has been developed over several years, and the style is not completely consistent. In some places, I use pointers; in others, I use subscripts. I am loath to change anything, because the code works. Hopefully, this will give you good ideas on how to improve the code and make it more useful in your own applications.

1.6 Comments on style

The writing style isn't copied from most academic or engineering texts. I'm writing as if I'm sitting next to you and trying to explain things as best I know how. Since I'm not very good at telling jokes, please don't throw anything at me. It takes a great deal of discipline to dig through all this math; I don't see any point in making it boring.

All the code in this book was written before any of the text. So the order of presentation has nothing to do with how the original code was created. The original order was normal basis math, elliptic curve math, polynomial math, and then the large integer math. The various protocols using combinations of all these routines were then written and tested. The text is there to explain the math and the thought process behind the code.

There are several statements in this book that indicate my attitude toward programming. There may be people who will object to these personal comments. I like knowing what voltage is on each wire in something I build. I want absolute control of everything. Comments on how to program should be ignored if you don't like the comment. But now you know where the attitude comes from.

The mathematics is really fun to learn, and it is even more fun to watch it work on a computer. I hope you will find putting the code to work as enjoyable a task as I had in creating it. And when you find a better way to do things, please let me know by sending e-mail to `cryptech@mcs.com`.

Now let's dig into some math.

1.7 References

1 B. Schneier, *Applied Cryptography*, 2d ed. (New York: John Wiley & Sons, 1996).

2 N. Koblitz, "Elliptic Curve Cryptosystems," *Mathematics of Computation* (1987): 203–209.

3 V. S. Miller, "Use of Elliptic Curves in Cryptography," in *CRYPTO '85* (New York: Springer-Verlag, 1986), 417–426.

4 N. Koblitz, *A Course in Number Theory and Cryptography* (New York: Springer-Verlag, 1987).

C H A P T E R   2

Basics of number theory

2.1 Large integer math header   14

2.2 Large integer math routines   19

2.3 Large integer code example   27

2.4 Back to number theory   29

2.5 Greatest common factor   30

2.6 Modular arithmetic   37

2.7 Fermat's Theorem   39

2.8 Finite fields   40

2.9 Generators   43

2.10 References   44

The simplest numerical operations become very complicated when the size of the numbers gets really big. As with everything else, we can break down numbers into subcomponents just as we break down chemicals into atoms. We're going to revisit addition, multiplication, and division so that we have the basic tools needed to deal with large numbers. With those tools, we can look at other simple operations such as modular mathematics and common factors between numbers.

As shown in figure 2.1, this chapter contains two parts. The first part is sample code for the basic math we all learn in grade school—addition, multiplication, and division. This really does come from the theory of numbers. As with everything else in this book, the mathematical theory is old and very deep. The second part discusses some of the old theories (e.g., Euclid's greatest common divisor algorithm), as well as the basics of number fields.

Since this is a book about code, I've decided to start with some basic large integer math routines. You can find better routines elsewhere, but they won't teach you much about the math. For those who want a deeper understanding, I strongly advise reading [1] or [2] to fully appreciate just how complex this can get. Advanced math packages can be found at various Web sites. Examples are the math packages such as freelip (free large integer package—URL: `ftp://ftp.ox.ac.uk/pub/math/free-lip/freelip_1.0.tar.gz`), LiDIA (URL: `ftp://ftp.informatik.th-darmstadt.de/pub/TI/systems/LiDIA/LC-1.4.x`), and another factoring program called MIRACL, which works on Windows machines and can be found at `ftp.com-papp.dcu.ie` in directory `/pub/crypto`.

2.1 Large integer math header

A major problem when attempting to write a large integer math package is not having access to the carry bit of the processor. For a good discussion of this topic, see [3]. I'm going to use the basic ideas from [3] to create a very simple large integer math package, which we can use later in the book to implement elliptic curve crypto protocols. For learning the concepts this code is fine, but if you want efficiency, look at the sources suggested above or at commercial math packages such as Macsyma, Maple, or Mathematica.

The large integer code that follows has both header files and subroutine files. The header files define many useful parameters and structures. I'll ignore some of them for now, because they will be described in later chapters. I'll describe all the subroutines eventually, but we have to discuss lots of math in between.

Let's go through the header files a few lines at a time. I'll list the whole thing again later. The first important line in the `field2n.h` file is:

```
#define WORDSIZE        (sizeof(int)*8)
```

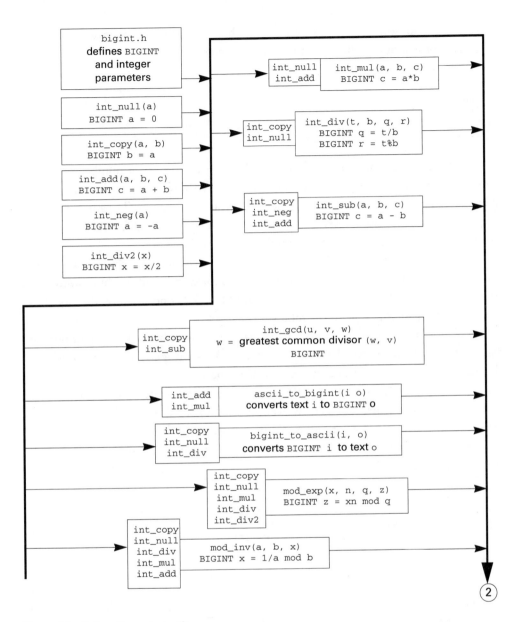

Figure 2.1 Subroutine schematic

By using the machine size, we can ignore big-endian and little-endian problems. Everything is a whole word—how it is stored in RAM does not matter. This parameter WORDSIZE is determined by the computer you run the code on. Since many things are derived from this parameter, it is worthwhile checking that this #define is correct. The above line did not work on one 64-bit platform, because `int`'s were defined as 32 bits. If things are not working at all, this is the first parameter to check.

The next set of parameters is:

```
#define NUMBITS        158
#define NUMWORD        (NUMBITS/WORDSIZE)
#define UPRSHIFT       (NUMBITS%WORDSIZE)
#define MAXLONG        (NUMWORD+1)
```

NUMBITS is used more in the following chapters; it is the total number of bits we expect to be working with. The exact value can be anything you like; the value shown above just happens to be what I was working on when I wrote this. The more advanced large integer packages do not fix this length. For modular math and for the mathematics described in chapters 3 and 4, a fixed number of bits will work fine.

NUMWORD is the maximum index into an array of machine words we need to represent NUMBITS. MAXLONG is useful in `for` loops; it is the number of machine words used in an array that holds NUMBITS. The parameter UPRSHIFT is not used by the large integer package; I'll describe that in the following chapter.

Specific parameters for the large integer package deal with the hardship of not having access to the carry bit. This implementation uses unsigned machine words and divides them in half to fake a carry. For example, a 32-bit machine will use 16 bits of an unsigned long in each array entry to store the bits; then, when two 32-bit machine words are added together, the 17th bit can be used to see if a carry occurred. This is really crude, but it should work on just about any processor that has a C compiler.

Here are the parameters specific to this large integer implementation, which are in the `bigint.h` file:

```
#define        HALFSIZE       (WORDSIZE/2)
#define        HIMASK         (-1L<<HALFSIZE)
#define        LOMASK         (~HIMASK)
#define        CARRY          (1L<<HALFSIZE)
#define        MSB_HW         (CARRY>>1)
#define        INTMAX         (4*MAXLONG-1)
#define        MAXSTRING      (MAXLONG*WORDSIZE/3)
```

The term HALFSIZE is obvious—it is just half the bits in a machine word. The HIMASK and LOMASK terms are used to mask off the upper or lower half of a machine word. The parameter CARRY is our faked carry bit, which is the last bit in the upper half of a machine word. The most significant bit in a half word is set by MSB_HW.

The term INTMAX is used as the largest index into a large integer array. This is set up as four times larger than our bit field to account for both multiplication and the wasted space of half a machine word. Again, this is inefficient, but it simplifies the overall code.

The parameter MAXSTRING is used to define the largest possible string needed to convert a large integer from binary to decimal. To be reasonable, we'll assume that only MAXLONG*WORDSIZE bits will be the largest integer we need to output. The number of digits we need can be found by solving the equation:

$$2^{\text{MAXLONG*WORDSIZE}} = 10^y \tag{2.1}$$

for the number of decimal digits y:

$$y = (\log 2)\text{MAXLONG*WORDSIZE}. \tag{2.2}$$

Unfortunately, $\log(2) = 0.30103 \ldots$ is not an exact number, so I've replaced it with $1/3$. This should leave more than enough space for reasonable numbers.

The structure used here to store a large integer is defined with the following code:

```
typedef unsigned long ELEMENT;

typedef struct {
        ELEMENT         hw[4*MAXLONG];
}  BIGINT;
```

The term ELEMENT is used as a machine-independent parameter. The purpose of the definition is to create an unsigned WORDSIZE block of bits. On 8- or 16-bit machines this definition may not work, because unsigned long may be several machine words. Since all structures are derived from this definition, it is important to make sure it is correct. Note that WORDSIZE and ELEMENT must be consistently defined for each machine architecture. All the code in this book was tested on 32-bit processors. Make certain WORDSIZE and ELEMENT are correct for your target machine!

A BIGINT is then an array of ELEMENTs and "hw" means "half word." Each entry in the array is part of the large integer. This code is written in big-endian fashion: The largest index into the array holds the least significant bits of the number. This is the way westerners (like me) write numbers, with the most significant digit to the left. Since a hex dump of RAM is usually done in increasing address order, the most significant bits get dumped first. It's arbitrary, but that is as good a reason as any for making a choice.

To understand the basics of what all this means, let's look at some math. A binary representation of a number can be written as:

$$x = a_n 2^n + a_{n-1} 2^{n-1} + \ldots + a_0. \tag{2.3}$$

The value for n is anything less than NUMBITS for our math package to work. The code that follows looks into RAM storage just as equation (2.3) writes it; the last bit, a_0, is in the half word location x.hw[INTMAX]. Let's look at a block of bits in the middle of a BIGINT array that represents the number x. We can factor out a common power of 2 to get:

$$x.hw[i] = 2^{(\text{INTMAX} - i) \cdot \text{HALFSIZE}}(b_{\text{HALFSIZE} - 1}2^{\text{HALFSIZE} - 1} + \ldots + b_0). \qquad (2.4)$$

Let's look at the example HALFSIZE = 16. There will be 16 bits labeled b_{15} through b_0, which give us a number in the range 0 through 65535. This is true of every half word block in the array. But each block is multiplied by a different power of 2, which is only represented by the position of the half word in the array.

Since we have to step through many structures, which are reasonably short, I have also defined the following parameter (in the field2n.h file):

```
typedef        short int INDEX;
```

The name was chosen to reflect the task—most counters are just an index into an array. I chose it to be an int to make it easy to test for negative when decrementing past 0.

There is only one item in the bigint.h header file that I've neglected. The following definition eliminates some, but not all for loops. It's a style definition that helped me develop the code.

```
#define        INTLOOP(i)      for(i=INTMAX;i>=0;i--)
```

This for loop proceeds from least significant half word block up to the most significant. The reason for going in this direction will be seen in the first subroutine when we add two large integers.

Here is the complete listing of the bigint.h header file. The prototypes may not be necessary for most compilers, or you may wish to declare things external if you use more than one file. Do what works!

```
/*** bigint.h ***/

#include "field2n.h"

/*  The following are used by the multiprecision integer package.
        This really is very crude.  See J. W. Crenshaw "Programmers
        Toolbox", Embedded Systems Programming Dec. 1996 for why you
        want to do this in assembler.
*/

#define        HALFSIZE        (WORDSIZE/2)
#define        HIMASK          (-1L<<HALFSIZE)
#define        LOMASK          (~HIMASK)
#define        CARRY           (1L<<HALFSIZE)
#define        MSB_HW          (CARRY>>1)
#define        INTMAX          (4*MAXLONG-1)
```

```
#define        MAXSTRING        (MAXLONG*WORDSIZE/3)
#define        INTLOOP(i)       for(i=INTMAX;i>=0;i--)

typedef struct {
        ELEMENT            hw[4*MAXLONG];
}  BIGINT;

void int_null();
void int_copy();
void field_to_int();
void int_to_field();
void int_neg();
void int_add();
void int_sub();
void int_mul();
void int_div();
void ascii_to_bigint();
void bigint_to_ascii();
void int_gcd();
void mod_exp();
void mod_inv();
void int_div2();
```

2.2 Large integer math routines

First, let's do some simple housekeeping. Zeroing out all array elements and copying one array to another are pretty basic things. Here are two examples that do just that for this particular large integer math representation.

```
/*  clear all bits in a large integer storage block.  */

void int_null( a)
BIGINT *a;
{
        INDEX i;

        INTLOOP (i) a->hw[i] = 0;
}

/*  copy one BIGINT block to another  */

void int_copy( a, b)
BIGINT *a, *b;
{
        INDEX i;

        INTLOOP (i) b->hw[i] = a->hw[i];
}
```

These are pretty obvious. I'll stick to using subscripts into the BIGINT variable array, because it is easier to follow the code that way. For speed you'll want to use auto-decrementing pointers.

The first "real" routine will be to add two large integers. Here's the code that adds two numbers, *a* and *b*, to get *c*:

```
/*  add two BIGINTS to get a third.  c = a + b
        Unlike the polynomial or ONB math, c can be one of a or b
*/

void int_add( a, b, c)
BIGINT *a, *b, *c;
{
        INDEX i;

        ELEMENT ec;


        ec = 0;
        INTLOOP (i)
        {
        /* add previous carry bit to each term  */
                ec = a->hw[i] + b->hw[i] + (ec >> HALFSIZE);
                c->hw[i] = ec & LOMASK;
        }
}
```

The internal variable, ec, is twice as big as the represented half word that gets copied into it. Since each half word is multiplied by the same power of 2, we only need to add similarly indexed half words. But this is where our carry problem occurs. The first time into the loop, ec is reset to 0 to clear the carry. We can then perform the addition of the two half words from inputs a and b plus the carry. To get the next carry bit the previous value of ec is shifted down. Finally, the answer is the lower half of what is contained in the ec variable, and this is stored in the final destination. The nice part of this is that we can add a number in place and overwrite the original variable. Not all code in this book is so nice.

Subtraction is simple, just negate the second number and then add. So let's look at the negation subroutine.

```
/*  Negate a BIGINT in place.  Each half word is complemented, then we add 1
*/

void int_neg( a)
BIGINT *a;
{
        register INDEX i;

        INTLOOP(i) a->hw[i] = ~a->hw[i] & LOMASK;
```

```
            INTLOOP(i)
            {
                    a->hw[i]++;
                    if (a->hw[i] & LOMASK) break;
                    a->hw[i] &= LOMASK;
            }
    }
```

To negate a two's complement number we just have to complement all the bits and then add 1. Since our binary representation is spread out over many words, the complement must also mask off the upper bits. The first line of code complements and masks. The loop adds 1 to the first word and then checks to see if that sum is not 0 in the bottom half word. If it isn't 0, the loop is finished. If it is 0, we have to mask off the whole word and increment the next one. This loop propagates the carry across our entire number if necessary and quits when there is none. Usually there isn't a carry, so we break out of the loop early.

Our subtraction routine is now trivial and looks like this:

```
/*  subtract two BIGINTS, c = a - b == a + (-b).
        as in addition, c can point to a or b and still works
*/

void int_sub( a, b, c)
BIGINT *a, *b, *c;
{
        BIGINT negb;

        int_copy( b, &negb);
        int_neg( &negb);
        int_add( a, &negb, c);
}
```

The intermediate variable, negb, protects us from future bugs. But the math is really simple; we take advantage of the computer's ability to add. Obviously, this is all rather inefficient—in assembler you have access to the carry bit!

2.2.1 Multiplication

Here is another good reason to use the half word representation. In assembler you have access to multiple word results from a pair of single machine word multiplies. In a high-level language we don't have that access. In unsigned format, two half words multiplied by each other will fit in a full word. All we have to do then is add the upper and lower halves to the correct position in the array.

The simplest process of multiplication is what we learned in grade school. The steps are to multiply one digit at a time and sum the results. Let's look at an example so that the following code will make some sense. When we multiply 345 * 26 by hand, we proceed with:

$$
\begin{array}{r}
345 \\
\times \quad 26 \\
\hline
\end{array}
$$

30	6×5
24	6×4
18	6×3
(2070	$6 \times 345)$
10	2×5
08	2×4
06	2×3
(0690	$2 \times 345)$

$$= \quad 8970$$

For the large integer package we use base 2^{HALFSIZE} instead of base 10, but the idea is the same. From equation (2.4) we can get the correct destination of the multiply of two arbitrary half words. This multiply routine runs by brute force; feel free to improve it.

```
/*  multiply two BIGINTs to get a third.
        Do NOT attempt to do 2 multiplies in a row without a division in
        between.
        You may get an overflow and there is no provision in this code to
        return
        an error condition for that.  See more advanced packages for correct
        way
        to do this.  c can *not* be one of a or b, it must be a separate
        storage location.
*/
void int_mul( a, b, c)
BIGINT *a, *b, *c;
{
        ELEMENT         ea, eb, mul;
        INDEX           i, j, k;
        BIGINT          sum;

        int_null(c);

        for ( i = INTMAX; i > INTMAX/2; i--)
        {
                ea = a->hw[i];
                int_null( &sum);
                for ( j = INTMAX; j > INTMAX/2; j--)
                {
                        eb = b->hw[j];
                        k = i + j - INTMAX;
                        mul = ea * eb + sum.hw[k];
```

```
                sum.hw[k] = mul & LOMASK;
                sum.hw[k-1] = mul >> HALFSIZE;
            }
            int_add( &sum, c, c);
        }
    }
}
```

The result of a multiply of two numbers is a number that has twice as many bits (or the sum of the number of bits in each source number). So this routine *assumes* that the input numbers only fill half the largest possible result of a multiply. Clearly this is simplistic and dangerous code. For our purposes that assumption is met, but be careful not to call the multiply routine twice in a row. It may not show up as a bug for a long time, but there is a reason the freelip and MIRACL packages are written differently.

The outer loop scans over the first number and picks up a half word digit and puts it in a local full word variable, ea. The inner loop scans over the second number, putting each half word into the local variable, eb. The large integer, sum holds the result of the multiplication of ea times the second number. This sum, is accumulated into the final result.

The calculation of the sum proceeds by multiplying the two source half words, adding in any previous digit result, and storing the resulting half words back into RAM. This process makes carry propagation easier. Note that the loops only go over half of each large integer. The index calculation for the variable k requires this. If i or j gets below the value of INTMAX/2, then k becomes negative. All this is because I chose a fixed-size storage for each number. This makes the code simple and should help you understand the better packages.

The biggest problem with this routine is that it only operates on positive numbers. Since the goal here is to deal with modular math, we'll always be able to work with positive numbers. If you need to work with signed numbers, the fix is easy. Check the most significant bit of each input number and exclusive-or them to determine the sign of the result. If an input number is negative, negate it. You will then have two positive numbers, which can pass through the multiply routine. At the end, you can check the result sign. If it is supposed to be negative, just change the sign of the result before returning.

For the purposes of this book, only positive numbers are needed. We'll get into exactly why that is later in the book. For now, let's look at the last "simple" math operation.

2.2.2 Division

Binary division is actually much easier than hand long division. In long division base 10 you guess the next value (when doing it by hand) and multiply by that digit to figure out what to subtract from the remaining digits. With binary division, either we can subtract or we can't; it's really easy to check.

Binary division also has some simple rules. If the most significant bit set in the numerator (top) is l, and the most significant bit set in the denominator (bottom) is m, the most significant bit that can be set in the quotient is $l - m$. Similarly, the most significant bit that could be set in the remainder is m.

Here's an example: In binary, divide 5 into 23:

```
              1
101 / 10111
          101
            0
```

As with long division, only one bit at a time instead of one digit at a time. The first time we subtract, there is no remainder, so we bring down more bits. For this example there are no more bits that can be subtracted, and the example looks like this:

```
            100
101 / 10111
          101
          011
```

The answer is 4 remainder 3. Notice that we shifted the bottom left two bit positions before the subtraction. This is what we'll do in the code as well. When the number of bits in the remainder is less than the number of bits in the denominator, we are finished.

This is not exactly the most efficient division algorithm, but here is some code that implements the basic unsigned binary division described above. The first thing we do is copy the top and bottom numbers to safe storage. Then we look for the most significant bit in the top and bottom numbers. I start with the maximum possible value and subtract HALFSIZE until a nonzero ELEMENT is found, and then subtract 1 until I find the most significant bit.

```
/*  unsigned divide.  Input full sized numerator (top),
        half sized denominator (bottom).
        Output half sized quotient and half sized remainder.
        Exceptionally crude but works ok for basics, error
        conditions return zero results.
*/

void int_div( top, bottom, quotient, remainder)
BIGINT *top, *bottom, *quotient, *remainder;
{
        BIGINT d, e;
        ELEMENT mask;
        INDEX  l, m, n, i, j;
```

```
/*  first step, initialize counters to most significant
        bit position in top and bottom.
*/
        int_copy( top, &d);
        int_copy( bottom, &e);
        l = (INTMAX + 1) * HALFSIZE;
        for( i=0; i<=INTMAX; i++)
        {
                if (!d.hw[i]) l -= HALFSIZE;
                else break;
        }
        mask = MSB_HW;
        for ( j=0; j<HALFSIZE; j++)
        {
                if ( !(d.hw[i] & mask))
                {
                        l--;
                        mask >>= 1;
                }
                else break;
        }

/*  same thing for bottom, compute msb position  */

        m = (INTMAX + 1) * HALFSIZE;
        for( i=0; i<=INTMAX; i++)
        {
                if (!e.hw[i]) m -= HALFSIZE;
                else break;
        }
        mask = MSB_HW;
        for ( j=0; j<HALFSIZE; j++)
        {
                if ( !(e.hw[i] & mask))
                {
                        m--;
                        mask >>= 1;
                }
                else break;
        }
```

The next thing I check for is error inputs. A good robust routine would check for 0 first, but then you have to tell the operator. This has the same result when dividing by 0 as dividing by 1, because m will be 0 in either case. The code returns the top as the quotient and clears the remainder. You won't see a divide by 0 error, but you may see some very strange results!

```
/*  check for error inputs, does not check for zero, so is
        actually incorrect.
*/
        if (!m)                    /*  x/1 = x */
```

```
                {
                        int_copy( top, quotient);
                        int_null( remainder);
                        return;
                }
```

If the bottom is larger than the top, or if the top is 1 (or 0), then return 0 for the quotient and the remainder is set equal to the bottom.

```
        if (!1 | (1<m))             /*  1/x = 0 */
        {
                int_null( quotient);
                int_copy( top, remainder);
                return;
        }
```

Next, we have to shift the bottom over by 1 - m bits so that it lines up for the first possible subtraction. First we move blocks of bits, and then single shift the entire array by less than HALFSIZE bits. The end result is that the bottom variable, e, is aligned with its most significant bit in the same position as the top variable's most significant bit.

```
/*   next step, shift bottom over to align msb with top msb   */

        n = 1 - m;
        i = n;
        while ( i > HALFSIZE )
        {
                for (j=0; j<INTMAX; j++) e.hw[j] = e.hw[j+1];
                i -= HALFSIZE;
                e.hw[INTMAX] = 0;
        }
        mask = 0;
        while ( i > 0 )
        {
                INTLOOP (j)
                {
                        e.hw[j] = (e.hw[j] << 1) | mask;
                        mask = e.hw[j] & CARRY ? 1 : 0;
                        e.hw[j] &= LOMASK;
                }
                i--;
        }
```

The variable n holds the maximum number of bits in the quotient. At each point in the subtraction loop, we check to see if we can subtract the bottom from the top. If we can, set bit n in the quotient and do the subtraction. In any case, shift the bottom right one position. The variable i is an index into the top and bottom BIGINT arrays that holds the most significant bit being operated on. The variable j is an index into the quotient's BIGINT array that holds bit n.

The check to see if a subtraction can be performed requires scanning across equal bit patterns of top and bottom. Until there is a difference, we can't do a comparison. And if we get an exact result, we do want to perform the subtraction and leave no remainder. After subtracting, the correct bit in the quotient gets set.

```
int_null( quotient);
while ( n>=0)
{
        i = INTMAX - 1/HALFSIZE;
        j = INTMAX - n/HALFSIZE;
        while ( (d.hw[i] == e.hw[i]) && ( i<INTMAX) ) i++;
        if ( d.hw[i] >= e.hw[i] )
        {
                int_sub( &d, &e, &d);
                mask = 1L << ( n%HALFSIZE );
                quotient->hw[j] |= mask;
        }
```

Shifting the bottom right one bit position is simple. After that, the bit counters for the most significant bit in top, bottom, and quotient are decremented.

```
        INTLOOP(j)
        {
                if (j) mask = ( e.hw[j-1] & 1) ? CARRY : 0;
                else mask = 0;
                e.hw[j] = (e.hw[j] | mask) >> 1;
        }
        n--;
        1--;
}
int_copy ( &d, remainder);
}
```

And the last operation of the division routine is to copy the bits left in the top over to the designated remainder storage location. Pretty easy, isn't it?

2.3 Large integer code example

Here are two simple routines that show how to use the above math subroutines. Since many papers publish large numbers in base 10, we need to convert them to a binary representation. The first routine converts from ASCII to large integer half words.

The string conversion assumes the last 4 bits of every byte are useful. This isn't really an ASCII string conversion, it's just an example of how to use the large integer math routines. The routine zeros out the result outhex and creates the constant 10. The basic loop multiplies the result by 10 and adds in the new digit. If any digit is not in the range 0 ... 9, it is ignored.

```
/*  Convert ascii string of decimal digits into BIGINT binary.
        Ignores out of range characters.  This is very crude, 'a' = '1',
        so watch out for input errors!
*/

void ascii_to_bigint( instring, outhex)
char *instring;
BIGINT *outhex;
{
        ELEMENT         ch;
        BIGINT          ten, digit, temp;
        INDEX           i=0;

        int_null( &ten);        /* create decimal multiplier */
        ten.hw[INTMAX] = 0xA;
        int_null( &digit);
        int_null( outhex);

        while (ch = *instring++)
        {
                digit.hw[INTMAX] = ch & 0xF;
                int_mul( outhex, &ten, &temp);
                if (digit.hw[INTMAX] > 9) continue;
                int_add( &temp, &digit, outhex);
        }
}
```

The second routine converts from a binary number to an ASCII string. In this case we're not cheating—the output really is ASCII. This routine works backwards by finding the remainder of a division by 10 as the next digit and then using the quotient to hold the remaining digits. When the quotient goes to zero, the routine exits.

```
/*  Convert binary BIGINT to ascii string.  Assumes destination has
        enough characters to hold result.  This is 4*HALFSIZE*MAXLONG bits
        = Log(2)*4*HALFSIZE*MAXLONG = 1.20412*HALFSIZE*MAXLONG characters
        or about 5/4*HALFSIZE*MAXLONG chars.  Works backwards and blank
        fills destination string.
*/

void bigint_to_ascii( inhex, outstring)
BIGINT *inhex;
char *outstring;
{
        BIGINT          top, ten, quotient, remainder;
        ELEMENT         check;
        INDEX           i;

        int_copy( inhex, &top);
        int_null( &ten);        /*  create constant 10 */
        ten.hw[INTMAX] = 0xA;
 /*  blank fill and null string */
        for (i=0; i<MAXSTRING; i++) *outstring++ = ' ';
        *outstring-- = 0;
```

```
check = 1;
while (check)
{
        int_div( &top, &ten, &quotient, &remainder);
        *outstring-- = remainder.hw[INTMAX] | '0';
        check = 0;
        INTLOOP(i) check |= quotient.hw[i];
        int_copy( &quotient, &top);
}
}
```

2.4 Back to number theory

We learn number theory at a relatively young age. We just don't call it that. We never think about numbers as symbols; we associate numbers with things. When counting time on a clock, the 24- or 12-hour limit (depending on where you live) is subconscious. One purpose of this chapter is to connect the obvious with abstract mathematics. After prime numbers and clocks we'll go into comparing numbers; finding things such as the greatest common factor; and learning how to combine primes, clocks, and multiplication to create cryptographic code.

Let's start with modular arithmetic. As previously mentioned, we compute time using modular arithmetic without thinking about it. Eleven o'clock plus two hours is one o'clock. Mathematically this is written as:

$$11 + 2 \equiv 1 \bmod 12 \,. \tag{2.5}$$

For regular-size integers, the C programming language has a modulo operation: the % operator. For example, the above clock addition becomes:

$$\text{time} = (11 + 2) \% 12 \,. \tag{2.6}$$

We can do all math operations such as multiplication, division, and exponentiation using modular math. This is the basis of most crypto systems used today, and it is also used by elliptic curve algorithms. You need to understand the rules of modular math to see how these crypto systems work. It really is as easy as it looks—it is the combination of details that can seem confusing.

Negative numbers modulo something can always be converted to positive numbers. A clock example is one o'clock minus two hours is minus one o'clock = eleven o'clock. Mathematically this is written as:

$$1 - 2 \equiv 11 \bmod 12 \,. \tag{2.7}$$

We can work with positive and negative modulo numbers. Modulo n will always have a remainder x in the range $-n < x < n$. Conversion to positive numbers is simple, just add n.

Yet another basic subject is prime numbers. Primes are atomic integers. They cannot be divided by any number (other than 1 and themselves). Every integer can be written as a multiple of its prime factors. Although simple in appearance, mathematicians have written many shelves of books about prime numbers. See [2] and references therein for more information than you thought possible on primes.

Sometimes you'll see references to "odd-primes." This is just another way of saying "all prime numbers except 2." Two is a rather magical prime and seems trivially obvious, but the complexity of computers is possible because 2 is prime. (The math joke is that 2 is the oddest prime of all.)

Number theory can also be thought of as counting. All we need to do is add 1 to get another number. If a number is not prime, it must be composed of several primes multiplied together. If you take any number and list its prime factors, you have what is called the "prime factorization" of that number. While simple in concept, several very secure crypto algorithms are based on the difficulty of actually finding the prime factorization of very large numbers. (See [4] and references therein for lots more details; we are going to build better cryptographic codes in this book.)

A similar idea is "relatively prime." Two numbers are relatively prime if they have no common factors. For example, 15 and 16 are relatively prime because $15 = 3 * 5$ and $16 = 2^4$. The prime factorization of two numbers tells us if they are relatively prime. There are other ways to do this without having to find the actual prime factors. We'll discuss how to do that next.

Finding prime numbers, and proving that a number is prime or composite (has factors), is beyond the scope of this book. A very good reference is [2]. Suffice it to say, there are useful tools for finding the various factors of numbers, especially very large ones. See the math packages mentioned at the beginning of the chapter for publicly available tools.

2.5 Greatest common factor

Euclid devised a scheme to find out if two numbers have any common factors. Euclid's algorithm finds the greatest common divisor between two numbers. Knuth [1] describes several methods to find the greatest common divisor, including Euclid's original algorithm and a more modern approach for binary computers that is extensible to any bit-length integer.

Euclid's algorithm for finding the greatest common divisor (gcd) is described in many places. For a nice history lesson see [1, 317]. Other expositions may be found in [2, 238] and [4, 245]. There is a good reason this algorithm has been around for two thousand years. If you aren't already familiar with it, now is a good time to learn it.

Euclid's Algorithm:

input: two positive integers u and v.

output: greatest common divisor $w = \gcd(u,v)$

Step 1: if $v = 0$, return $w = u$.

Step 2: $r = u \bmod v$

$u = v$

$v = r$

go to step 1.

This algorithm is important because it has applications far beyond integers (in other words, you should understand this or the next chapter won't make sense either). Let's take some time to discuss this, because it really will be very useful later on.

For a real example, take $\gcd(90155, 79716)$: $u = 90155$, $v = 79716$, v is not 0 so we go to step 2.

$$
\begin{aligned}
r &= 90155 \bmod 79716 = 10439 + 1 \bullet 79716 \\
u &= 79716 \\
v &= 10439 \neq 0
\end{aligned}
\tag{2.8}
$$

$$
\begin{aligned}
r &= 79716 \bmod 10439 = 6643 + 7 \bullet 10439 \\
u &= 10439 \\
v &= 6643 \neq 0
\end{aligned}
\tag{2.9}
$$

$$
\begin{aligned}
r &= 10439 \bmod 6643 = 3796 + 1 \bullet 6643 \\
u &= 6643 \\
v &= 3796 \neq 0
\end{aligned}
\tag{2.10}
$$

$$
\begin{aligned}
r &= 6643 \bmod 3796 = 2847 + 1 \bullet 3796 \\
u &= 3796 \\
v &= 2847 \neq 0
\end{aligned}
\tag{2.11}
$$

$$
\begin{aligned}
r &= 3796 \bmod 2847 = 949 + 1 \bullet 2847 \\
u &= 2847 \\
v &= 949 \neq 0
\end{aligned}
\tag{2.12}
$$

$$r = 2847 \bmod 949 = 0 + 3 \bullet 949$$
$$u = 949 = w \tag{2.13}$$
$$v = 0 \quad \text{done!}$$

Doing this example by hand gives some appreciation for what computers do for us. At each step we find the quotient and remainder. In practice the quotient isn't used for modulo operations and is never stored.

Another way to see the above example is to look at the prime factorization of each number: $90155 = 5 \times 13 \times 19 \times 73$, and $79716 = 2^2 \times 3 \times 7 \times 13 \times 73$. The common factors are $13 \times 73 = 949$.

What will be more useful than the original Euclid algorithm is what is known as the extended Euclid algorithm. It is more useful, because it can be used to find an inverse. More on that later.

Knuth gives the name "Algorithm X" to the extended Euclid algorithm [1, 325]. Given inputs u and v, the idea is to keep the equation:

$$ut_1 + vt_2 = t_3 = \gcd(u,v) \tag{2.14}$$

constant during all operations. There are two other similar equations that are also kept constant:

$$uu_1 + vu_2 = u_3$$
$$uv_1 + vv_2 = v_3. \tag{2.15}$$

The algorithm starts by setting:

$$u_1 = 1$$
$$u_2 = 0 \tag{2.16}$$
$$u_3 = u$$

and

$$v_1 = 0$$
$$v_2 = 1 \tag{2.17}$$
$$v_3 = v$$

and then proceeds with the following steps:

Step 1: is $v_3 = 0$? If yes, return u_1, u_2, and u_3.
Step 2: $q = u_3 / v_3$

for $i = 1, 2, 3$
$t_i = u_i - qv_i$
copy v_i to u_i
copy t_i to v_i
go to step 1.

In step 1 the value of u_3 is the greatest common divisor. In step 2 the division is an integer operation. The value of u_1 will also be useful later when we do modular inversion, but actual implementations will ignore u_2. Let's look at an example: Take $u = 18915$ and $v = 12727$. The initial variables are:

$$u_1 = 1 \qquad v_1 = 0$$
$$u_2 = 0 \qquad v_2 = 1 \tag{2.18}$$
$$u_3 = 18915 \qquad v_3 = 12727.$$

The algorithm proceeds as follows (eliminating t_i, which is just a storage value):

$$q = 1 \tag{2.19}$$

$$u_1 = 0 \qquad v_1 = 1$$
$$u_2 = 1 \qquad v_2 = -1 \tag{2.20}$$
$$u_3 = 12727 \qquad v_3 = 6188$$

$$q = 2 \tag{2.21}$$

$$u_1 = 1 \qquad v_1 = -2$$
$$u_2 = -1 \qquad v_2 = 3 \tag{2.22}$$
$$u_3 = 6188 \qquad v_3 = 351$$

$$q = 17 \tag{2.23}$$

$$u_1 = -2 \qquad v_1 = 35$$
$$u_2 = 3 \qquad v_2 = -52 \tag{2.24}$$
$$u_3 = 351 \qquad v_3 = 221$$

$$q = 1 \tag{2.25}$$

$$u_1 = 35 \qquad v_1 = -37$$
$$u_2 = -52 \qquad v_2 = 55 \qquad\qquad (2.26)$$
$$u_3 = 221 \qquad v_3 = 13$$

$$q = 17 \qquad\qquad\qquad\qquad (2.27)$$

$$u_1 = -37 \qquad v_1 = 664$$
$$u_2 = 55 \qquad v_2 = -987 \qquad\qquad (2.28)$$
$$u_3 = 13 \qquad v_3 = 0.$$

And the algorithm is done. The original numbers factor into $18915 = 3 \cdot 5 \cdot 13 \cdot 97$ and $12727 = 11 \cdot 13 \cdot 89$, so the greatest common factor is indeed 13. We'll see that -37 is the inverse of 18915 modulo 12727 later. But I'll stick to prime number moduli for reasons that have yet to be explained.

To just find the greatest common divisor without all the extraneous u's and v's, let's look at the binary gcd algorithm described by Knuth [1]. This is faster for determining if two numbers are relatively prime than either of the above methods.

Before getting into a real code example, here is a simple subroutine that divides a large integer by 2. We'll need it a few times in the int_gcd() routine.

```
/*   divide a large integer by 2.   A simple shift right operation.   */

void int_div2( x)
BIGINT *x;
{
        INDEX j;
        ELEMENT mask;

        INTLOOP(j)
        {
                if (j) mask = ( x->hw[j-1] & 1) ? CARRY : 0;
                else mask = 0;
                x->hw[j] = (x->hw[j] | mask) >> 1;
        }
}
```

Now, let's look at Knuth's Algorithm B [1, 321]. A more modern approach for binary computers, this method is extensible to any length integer. The binary gcd algorithm first eliminates common factors of 2 and saves the power of 2 in the variable k. This leaves at least one of the numbers odd.

The inputs are large integers u and v; the output is w: their greatest common divisor. This function can be found in any math package, but let's work through the code and see how these packages work. The first thing we do is save a local copy of the input integers, so we won't destroy them.

```
/* compute greatest common divisor using binary method.
        See [1, pg 321] Algorithm B for theoretical details.

        Enter with large integers u, v.
        Returns gcd(u, v) as large integer in w.
*/

void int_gcd(u, v, w)
BIGINT *u, *v, *w;
{
        INDEX  k, i, flag;
        ELEMENT check, carry_bit;
        BIGINT t, U, V;

        int_copy( u, &U);
        int_copy( v, &V);
```

The next step is to eliminate common factors of 2. This is where the division by 2 subroutine is handy. When the routine is finished, we can shift the result by the number of factors of 2 found at this point. Eliminating the common factors of 2 is the easiest thing for a binary computer, so that's the best place to start.

```
/*  find common powers of 2 and eliminate them */

        k = 0;

/*  check that both u and v are even */

        while ( !(U.hw[INTMAX] & 1 || V.hw[INTMAX] & 1))
        {
/*  increment power of 2 and divide both u and v by 2 */

                k++;
                int_div2( &U);
                int_div2( &V);
        }
```

In Knuth's algorithm, he flags which value is larger by the sign of the variable t. I'd rather just keep a flag that does the same thing and keep the absolute value of t. This is in line with the use of positive numbers for the multiply and divide routines. (A "set" flag is −1 and a "clear" flag is +1.)

```
/* Now both u and v have been divided by 2^k.
        If u is odd, set t = v and flag, otherwise t = u and clear flag   */

        if (U.hw[INTMAX] & 1)
```

```
        {
                int_copy( &V, &t);
                flag = -1;
        }
        else
        {
                int_copy( &U, &t);
                flag = 1;
        }
```

The process of reducing both numbers in size works by several not so obvious relationships. Eliminating the common factors of 2 is simple. Once one number is odd, the remaining factors of 2 are not common anymore. The following lines of code remove these "uncommon" factors of 2.

```
        check = 0;
        INTLOOP (i) check |= t.hw[i];
        while (check)
        {
/* while t is even, divide by 2  */
                while ( !(t.hw[INTMAX] & 1)) int_div2( &t);
```

The core reduction step is to subtract the two numbers. To check the sign of the result I use the defined value of MSB_HW to see if the most significant bit of t is set. If it is, the result was negative and we need to change the sign of t. If the result was positive, we set the flag to be positive.

```
/* reset u or v to t depending on sign of flag  */

                if (flag > 0) int_copy( &t, &U);
                else int_copy( &t, &V);
/*              t = u - v;     core reduction step, gcd remains unchanged  */
                int_sub( &U, &V, &t);
                if (t.hw[0] & MSB_HW)
                {
                        flag = -1;
                        int_neg( &t);
                }
                else flag = 1;
                check = 0;
                INTLOOP (i) check |= t.hw[i];
        }
```

Once t goes to 0, the algorithm is finished. We now have to reapply the original factors of 2 that were removed at the beginning. This is the same thing we did in the divide routine when shifting the bottom over to the left.

```
        /*   reapply common powers of 2. First do words, then do bits.*/

        int_copy( &U, w);
```

```
while ( k > HALFSIZE )
{
        for (i=0; i<INTMAX; i++) w->hw[i] = w->hw[i+1];
        k -= HALFSIZE;
        w->hw[INTMAX] = 0;
}
carry_bit = 0;
while ( k > 0 )
{
        INTLOOP (i)
        {
                w->hw[i] = (w->hw[i] << 1) | carry_bit;
                carry_bit = w->hw[i] & CARRY ? 1 : 0;
                w->hw[i] &= LOMASK;
        }
        k--;
}
}
```

Let's see how the core reduction step mentioned in the code works using a bit of math. Since we know there is some common factor between u and v, we can write them both as:

$$u = c \cdot r$$
$$v = c \cdot s. \tag{2.29}$$

The step $u - v$ can be written:

$$u - v = c \cdot (r - s). \tag{2.30}$$

Now, let's look at what happens in the greatest common divisor routine:

$$\gcd(u - v, v) = \gcd(c \cdot (r - s), c \cdot s) = c. \tag{2.31}$$

The subtraction step works because it leaves the answer unchanged. Notice also that any "uncommon" factors of 2 can be eliminated any time they are found. It still leaves the answer (or equation 2.31) unchanged.

2.6 Modular arithmetic

The large integer packages mentioned at the beginning of this chapter perform modular multiplication using efficient algorithms. Because the packages are available in a number of both free and commercial formats, the interested reader can find code elsewhere. Using the large integer math routines shown above, we'll implement modular arithmetic with division. The remainder is what we'll be interested in—not the quotient.

Let's start with $g^x \bmod n$. A simple routine to compute this can be written by modifying the binary method for exponentiation in [1, 442]. The idea of this algorithm is to square and multiply by g until we've reached g^x. By using modular arithmetic at each step we end up with $g^x \bmod n$. Here is code that directly implements Knuth's algorithm using the subroutines described previously.

```
/*  Binary method for modular exponentiation.  Taken from [1,pg 442]
        Algorithm A.
        Computes z = x^n mod q for x, n and q large integers.
*/

void mod_exp(x, n, q, z)
BIGINT *x, *n, *q, *z;
{
        BIGINT  N, Y, Z, temp, dummy;
        ELEMENT check;
        INDEX   i;

/*  initialize variables  */
        int_copy (n, &N);
        int_null( &Y);
        Y.hw[INTMAX] = 1;
        int_copy (x, &Z);

/*  Main loop divides N by 2 each step.  Repeat until N = 0, and return Y
        as result.  */

        check = 0;
        INTLOOP (i) check |= N.hw[i];
        while (check)
        {

/*  if N is odd, multiply by extra factor of Y */

                if (N.hw[INTMAX] & 1)
                {
                        /*  Y = (Y * Z) % q;  */
                        int_mul (&Y, &Z, &temp);
                        int_div (&temp, q, &dummy, &Y);
                }
                int_div2( &N);                          /* divide N by 2 */
        /*          Z = (Z * Z) % q;  square Z  */
                int_mul (&Z, &Z, &temp);
                int_div( &temp, q, &dummy, &Z);
                check = 0;
                INTLOOP (i) check |= N.hw[i];
        }
        int_copy (&Y, z);
}
```

This algorithm is simple and powerful. The variable z always holds the value of x^{2j}, where j is the number of times we've been through the loop. But this is modulo the value q, so we are constantly ensuring that our numbers never exceed storage capacity.

If the value of N is odd when we enter the loop, then we multiply the result by the present value of z. We initialize Y to 1 and z to x, so on the first entry if N is odd, Y = z mod q. All we are doing is multiplying in powers of x^{2j}, if they are needed, and then computing the next $j + 1$ power of x squared. N is divided by 2 each time through the loop, so it eventually goes to 0. At that point, we copy the result, Y, to the destination variable, z.

2.7 Fermat's Theorem

The next basic tool we need from number theory is Fermat's Little Theorem. Take any number a and any prime number p such that gcd$(a,p) = 1$ (i.e., a does not have p as a factor). We can write Fermat's Theorem as:

$$a^p = a \bmod p. \tag{2.32}$$

It is also written as:

$$a^{p-1} = 1 \bmod p \tag{2.33}$$

by taking out an extra factor of a. In many books the "mod p" is assumed, and you may see equations such as the following:

$$a^p = a. \tag{2.34}$$

The assumption is that all the math is modular; it is "obvious" what is being done. If you see situations such as this, then modular math is what you should be using.

Using the mod_exp routine you can verify that these expressions are true. It is quite amazing and very useful for manipulating numbers. Modifications of this basic rule are used to prove that numbers are prime.

For our purposes, it is really the modulo prime part that holds the most interest. Algorithms for finding out if a large number is prime and what its factors are can be found in [2]. Again, there are many software packages out there that will do this; see the URLs listed previously.

What makes Fermat's Theorem so useful to us will become more apparent later. Another way of stating it is to note that:

$$\frac{a^{p-1} - 1}{p} = \text{an integer}.\qquad(2.35)$$

In several chapters we'll set $a = 2$ and find out interesting things about computer arithmetic.

2.8 Finite fields

The last major concept we need to deal with in this chapter is what mathematicians call a "field." Many books have been written on finite fields and the theory surrounding the math (see [5], [6], and [7] as starting points). If you are not a mathematician, statements such as "Every finite integral domain is a field" won't mean very much.

Because the idea is actually easy to understand, I'm going to let the mathematicians get angry with me for not being precise. The reader should be careful attempting to extrapolate ideas from the following descriptions. If you really want to know more, go to the library and look up "finite fields." After 200+ years, there have been many books written on the subject.

A field has several properties.

1 The rules of addition apply, and the field contains an additive identity element.

2 The rules of multiplication apply, and the field contains a multiplicative identity element.

3 Every element in a field has an inverse.

The set of integers is not a field, because integers don't include fractions and so do not have multiplicative inverses. The main purpose of this book is to describe the code that implements finite field mathematics. Because there are many ways to represent the same math in a computer, we'll see several implementations of finite fields in the following chapters.

The simplest finite field is modulo prime arithmetic. Addition and multiplication both work:

$$a + b = c \bmod p$$
$$a \times b = c \bmod p.\qquad(2.36)$$

The identity element of addition is 0, and the additive inverse is a negation. The identity element of multiplication is 1. But what about the inverse?

Let's try $a \times x = 1 \bmod b$. x must be the inverse of a. For a moment, let's just look at integer math and write:

$$a \times x - b \times k = 1 \qquad (2.37)$$

Subtracting any multiple of the modulus does not change the equation. Notice the similarity of this equation to the extended Euclid algorithm described previously in equation (2.14). It turns out it is also similar to a continued fraction expansion. This is how the u_2, v_2, and t_2 variables are removed from the general description given before.

All that math can be found in [2, appendix 5]. The basic idea is to reduce a and increase k while keeping track of b in equation (2.37). The process involves approximating b/a as a continued fraction, and both the quotient and remainder are used. The interested reader is strongly urged to read the references. To understand the code a bit, let's take a quick look at the algorithm described in [2, 309].

Given inputs a and b, find x such that $a \cdot x$ mod $b = 1$:

Initialize:
$$sw = 1$$
$$m = b$$
$$n = a$$
$$p_0 = 1$$
$$p_1 = m/n$$
$$r = m \bmod n$$
$$q = p_1$$

Iterate until $r = 0$:
$$sw = -sw$$
$$m = n$$
$$n = r$$
$$q = m/n$$
$$r = m \bmod n$$
$$p_2 = q \cdot p_1 + p_0$$
$$p_0 = p_1$$
$$p_1 = p_2$$

Output:
$$x = sw * p_0$$

In this algorithm, sw is a switch that keeps track of the number of subtractions performed. Note that the addition and multiplication used to calculate p_2 are performed using mod b arithmetic. By using the sw variable the algorithm avoids negative numbers. Using the int_div routine we get the quotient q and remainder r in one step.

```
/*  Inversion of numbers in a prime field is similar to solving
        the linear congruence ax = c mod b.
        Replace c with 1 and x is the inverse of a mod b.  Taken from [2,
        pg. 309].
```

```
            Inputs are large integer a and modulus b.
            Output is x, inverse of a mod b   (ax = 1 mod b).
*/


void mod_inv(a, b, x)
BIGINT *a, *b, *x;
{
        BIGINT  m, n, p0, p1, p2, q, r, temp, dummy;
        ELEMENT check;
        INDEX   sw, i;

/*  initialize loop variables

        sw = 1;
        m = b;
        n = a;
        p0 = 1;
        p1 = m/n;
        q = p1;
        r = m % n;
*/
        sw = 1;
        int_copy( b, &m);
        int_copy( a, &n);
        int_null ( &p0);
        p0.hw[INTMAX] = 1;
        int_div ( &m, &n, &p1, &r);
        int_copy ( &p1, &q);


/*  main loop, compute continued fraction  intermediates   */

        check = 0;
        INTLOOP (i) check |= r.hw[i];
        while (check)
        {
                sw = -sw;
                int_copy( &n, &m);
                int_copy( &r, &n);
                int_div( &m, &n, &q, &r);
/*              p2 = (q * p1 + p0) % b;    core operation of routine   */
                int_mul( &q, &p1, &temp);
                int_add( &temp, &p0, &temp);
                int_div( &temp, b, &dummy, &p2);
                int_copy( &p1, &p0);
                int_copy( &p2, &p1);
                check = 0;
                INTLOOP (i) check |= r.hw[i];
        }

/*  sw keeps track of sign.  If sw < 0, add modulus to result */

        if (sw < 0) int_sub( b, &p0, x);
        else int_copy( &p0, x);
}
```

Every time we go through the loop, the variable sw changes sign. This keeps track of the sign of our result. If it was supposed to be negative, we need to subtract the result from the modulus (b) to return the correct positive answer for x.

Note that the routine does an addition after a multiply before reducing the size with a division. The assumption is that the terms to be added are only half the size of the multiplied result. The modular division will find the correct answer, and the remainder will be the same as if we did a modular reduction after the multiply and after the add. It saves a lot of processor time to do the division only once.

While there are many heavy-duty tricks to make the math implementations faster, the fundamental operation is the same. Modular arithmetic and integer operations are the basis of modern cryptography. With the inverse, we now have a complete set of tools to compute over finite fields of prime numbers.

There is yet another math term I need to define. This is the "characteristic" of a field. The mathematicians [6, 31] define it as the number of times the multiplicative identity can be added to itself before you get to 0. I prefer to think of it as the number of elements in the base field. In any case, a field of characteristic p is written as F_p. I use the term "base field," because I'll describe fields written as F_{p^n} in the next chapter. In that case, too, p is the characteristic of the field. These types of fields are also known as Galois Fields in honor of the mathematician who first described them.

2.9 Generators

The very last item we need to cover here is the concept of a generator. All fields have an element, which, raised to a power, gives rise to another element in the field.

More precisely, for prime number fields:

$$a = g^j \bmod p. \tag{2.38}$$

For every j between 0 and $p - 1$ we will get a different element in the field.

Not every element in a field is a generator. Another term is the "order" of an element. The order of an element is the smallest exponent that gets you the identity element. When:

$$a^j = 1 \quad \bmod p \tag{2.39}$$

for some $j < p$, then we say that the "order of a is j."

A generator has the maximum possible order of $p - 1$ elements. In a prime number field, all integers between 1 and $p - 1$ will be cycled through equation (2.38). Elements that skip terms are not generators.

Table 2.1 shows an example. Take $p = 11$ and compute a^j for all $0 < a < 11$ and $0 \le j < 11$.

Table 2.1 a^j mod 11

a \ j	0	1	2	3	4	5	6	7	8	9	10
1	1	1	1	1	1	1	1	1	1	1	1
2	1	2	4	8	5	10	9	7	3	6	1
3	1	3	9	5	4	1	3	9	5	4	1
4	1	4	5	9	3	1	4	5	9	3	1
5	1	5	3	4	9	1	5	3	4	9	1
6	1	6	3	7	9	10	5	8	4	2	1
7	1	7	5	2	3	10	4	6	9	8	1
8	1	8	9	6	4	10	3	2	5	7	1
9	1	9	4	3	5	1	9	4	3	5	1
10	1	10	1	10	1	10	1	10	1	10	1

We see that the order of 2^j mod 11 is 10, which makes 2 a generator. The order of 10^j mod 11 is 2, and the order of 3^j mod 11 is 5. Clearly 6, 7, and 8 are also generators. Fermat's Theorem is also obvious in the last column. Another term to describe a particular generator for a prime field is "primitive root." In chapter 4, we'll be looking for prime fields in which 2 is primitive.

All the math with prime numbers is pretty simple, and you've probably seen it all before. Hold on to your hat—we're about to take these simple ideas a few steps further.

2.10 References

1 D. E. Knuth, *Seminumerical Algorithms* (Reading, MA: Addison-Weasley, 1981).

2 H. Riesel, *Prime Numbers and Computer Methods for Factorization*, 2d ed. (Boston: Birkhauser, 1987).

3 J. W. Crenshaw, "Programmers Tool Box," *Embedded Systems Programming* (December 1996–September 1997).

4 B. Schneier, *Applied Cryptography*, 2d ed. (New York: John Wiley & Sons, 1996).

5 E. Bach and J. Shallit, *Algorithmic Number Theory* (Cambridge, MA: MIT Press, 1996).

6 N. Koblitz, *A Course in Number Theory and Cryptography* (New York: Springer-Verlag, 1987).

7 R. Lidl and H. Niederreiter, *Introduction to Finite Fields and Their Applications* (Cambridge, England: Cambridge University Press, 1994).

C H A P T E R   3

Polynomial math over finite fields

3.1 Introduction to polynomials   48

3.2 All structures are polynomials   52

3.3 Modular polynomial arithmetic   64

3.4 Inversion over prime polynomials   66

3.5 Polynomial greatest common divisor   67

3.6 Prime polynomials   68

3.7 Summary   72

3.8 References   72

3.1 Introduction to polynomials

In high school algebra we learned about the concept of variables. A variable is a symbol that has not yet been assigned a specific value. The classic symbol usually used is x, and we're going to use it too.

A polynomial is a sum of different powers of a variable. For example:

$$x^4 + 3x^2 + 4 \qquad (3.1)$$

is a polynomial in x. Because we have not set the polynomial equal to any particular constant, we don't know what x is. Further, we have assumed that the coefficients of the polynomial are real and that x is real or possibly complex.

For computer arithmetic (as opposed to numerical analysis) the assumption that the coefficients are real is no longer valid. To connect with the previous chapter, let's pick coefficients modulo 10. Suppose we add another polynomial in x to the above example:

$$x^3 + 7x^2 + 5x + 8 . \qquad (3.2)$$

Since we don't know what x is, the best we can do is add similar powers of x. Because the coefficients are modulo 10, we have:

$$
\begin{array}{ccccccc}
x^4 & + & & 3x^2 & & + & 4 \\
+ & & x^3 & + 7x^2 & + & 5x & + & 8 \\
\hline
x^4 & + & x^3 & + & & 5x & + & 2
\end{array}
\qquad \text{example 1}
$$

This type of arithmetic is called a "polynomial basis." It works because powers of the variable x are linearly independent. (If you don't know what that means, just remember that it works!)

Now, suppose we chose a prime number for the modulus of the coefficients. We then have a polynomial basis over a finite field. This is a very important concept for codes, error correction, and cryptography. There are many books covering the subject, most far beyond anything we need to discuss. Those who want to dig deeper should read [1] or [2].

For our application to computers and cryptography, we'll take the prime number 2 as our modulus. That means our coefficients can only take on the values of 0 or 1. Our polynomials can be stored as continuous bits in the computer with each bit position representing the coefficient of a power of x. For example, the polynomial:

$$x^7 + x^5 + x^4 + x + 1 \qquad (3.3)$$

would be stored in a byte on a computer as:

$$1\ 0\ 1\ 1\ 0\ 0\ 1\ 1 \quad \text{coefficients of polynomial}$$
$$7\ 6\ 5\ 4\ 3\ 2\ 1\ 0 \quad \text{offset in storage}$$

Note that the bit's offset in storage matches the power of x to which its coefficient corresponds. This is an arbitrary choice, which I find comfortable.

Addition modulo 2 is just exclusive-or. $1 + 1 = 0 \bmod 2$, $0 + 1 = 1$, and $0 + 0 = 0$. We can rapidly add two polynomials in a computer using the XOR instruction. Since there is no carry to propagate, this is very fast, even in high-level languages.

But, as we saw in chapter 2, a finite field has to obey the rules of multiplication and have an inverse for every element. Multiplication of polynomials is easy; we just multiply every term in one polynomial by every term in the other one. Let's pick another base 2 polynomial and show an example:

$$(x^3 \ + \ x \ + \ 1) \ * \ (x^7 \ + \ x^5 \ + \ x^4 \ + \ x \ + \ 1) \qquad\qquad \text{example 2}$$

$$
\begin{array}{l}
x^3 * (x^7 + x^5 + x^4 + x + 1) = x^{10} + x^8 + x^7 + \qquad\quad x^4 + x^3 \\
x \ * (x^7 + x^5 + x^4 + x + 1) = \qquad\quad x^8 + \quad x^6 + x^5 \quad + \quad x^2 + x \\
1 \ * (x^7 + x^5 + x^4 + x + 1) = \qquad\qquad x^7 + \quad x^5 + x^4 + \qquad\quad x + 1 \\
\hline
\qquad\qquad\qquad\qquad\qquad\quad x^{10} + \qquad\quad x^6 + \qquad\quad x^3 + x^2 + \quad 1
\end{array}
$$

On a computer, this is easy. The first term of $x^3 *()$ is just the first polynomial shifted left three places, or 3 bits in our memory representation. The second term is shifted 1 bit, and the last term is not shifted at all. The final result is the sum (exclusive-or) of all three terms.

Multiplication is simply a shift and exclusive-or. However, we're not quite done yet. Note that the highest exponent keeps increasing in the polynomial. This highest exponent is called the "degree" of the polynomial. We want the degree of our polynomials to never overflow our storage capacity. What is the right mathematical way of doing that?

Modular math, of course! But instead of doing modulo a prime we're going to use modulo an irreducible polynomial. An irreducible polynomial is a long name for prime polynomial. Just like prime numbers, an irreducible polynomial has no polynomial factors—it's not reducible. The terms "prime polynomial" and "irreducible polynomial" are identical; I'll try to stick with the former in most of this discussion.

Taking a polynomial modulo a prime polynomial leaves a remainder. The degree of the remainder polynomial is always less than the degree of the modulus polynomial. Using the previous two polynomials, here's an example:

$x^7 + x^5 + x^4 + x + 1 \bmod x^3 + x + 1$ example 3

$$
\begin{array}{r}
x^4 \\
\hline
x^3 + x + 1 \;\big/\; x^7 + x^5 + x^4 + x + 1 \\
x^7 + x^5 + x^4 \\
\hline
x + 1
\end{array}
$$

The division process is the same as long division. Since we are dealing with base 2 coefficients, it's really simple to figure out what the power is for the quotient. In this case, the quotient of x^4 times the divisor (modulus) wipes out all the higher-order terms. The remainder is $x + 1$, whose degree (1) is less than the degree of the modulus polynomial (3).

An interesting aspect of all this is that addition and subtraction are the same. This is only true for mod 2 coefficients. It is sort of obvious that $1 - 1 = 0$, and, since $1 + 1 = 0$ mod 2, $+ = -$. I know this seems kind of strange, but general math formulas will simplify a great deal when we recognize that addition and subtraction mean the same thing in modular binary math.

So far so good: Our polynomial field supports addition and multiplication. What about inversion? Just as with modular arithmetic using prime numbers, we can use the extended Euclid algorithm to compute an inverse.

To describe the algorithm, we'll follow [3]. Given a polynomial, $r(x)$, and a modulus polynomial, $M(x)$ (which needs to be irreducible), we need to find $p(x)$, which is the inverse of $r(x)$:

$$r(x)\ p(x) = 1 \bmod M(x) \tag{3.4}$$

The algorithm begins by initializing variables r_{k-2}, r_{k-1}, p_{k-2}, p_{k-1}, q_{k-2}, and q_{k-1}. Then we compute r_k, p_k, and q_k. We repeat these iterations until $r_k = 0$. The formulas for initialization are:

$$
\begin{aligned}
r_{k-2} &= M(x) \\
r_{k-1} &= r(x) \\
p_{k-2} &= 0
\end{aligned}
\tag{3.5}
$$

$$
\begin{aligned}
p_{k-1} &= 1 \\
q_{k-2} &= 1 \\
q_{k-1} &= 0.
\end{aligned}
\tag{3.6}
$$

Then the loop begins with these formulas:

$$r_k = r_{k-2} \bmod r_{k-1}$$
$$q_k = r_{k-2} \div r_{k-1} \qquad\qquad (3.7)$$
$$p_k = q_k \cdot p_{k-1} + p_{k-2}$$

Note that the modulus step is easily computed as the remainder from the division. If the remainder is not 0, the variables are exchanged to save memory:

$$r_{k-2} = r_{k-1} \qquad r_{k-1} = r_k$$
$$q_{k-2} = q_{k-1} \qquad q_{k-1} = q_k \qquad\qquad (3.8)$$
$$p_{k-2} = p_{k-1} \qquad p_{k-1} = p_k.$$

This is really the same algorithm from the previous chapter. It has just been rewritten using polynomials.

There are two basic formulas that make the algorithm work. The first is the division step, which generates q_k and r_k. The second is the last relationship in equation (3.7). The division step is computing a partial solution of the continued fraction. The last formula in equation (3.7), which uses q_k, combines the partial solutions to form the final solution. When the remainder from a division step goes to 0, the previous p_k is the answer we are looking for.

Figure 3.1 shows the subroutine schematic for this chapter. After defining some simple routines, we'll get into the mathematical ones.

Before getting into the multiply, divide, and modulus routines, let's first create two header files to define storage elements. The reason for two files is that the first one is common for both polynomial basis and optimal normal basis representations (to be described in the next chapter). The first header file will be the common parameters. The second will be used only for polynomial basis routines.

Here is the first header file, which I've called `field2n.h`, because it helps to define Galois Fields for our C code.

```
/*** field2n.h ***/

#define WORDSIZE        (sizeof(int)*8)
#define NUMBITS         93

#define NUMWORD         (NUMBITS/WORDSIZE)
#define UPRSHIFT        (NUMBITS%WORDSIZE)

#define MAXLONG         (NUMWORD+1)

#define MAXBITS         (MAXLONG*WORDSIZE)
#define MAXSHIFT        (WORDSIZE-1)
#define MSB             (1L<<MAXSHIFT)
```

```
#define UPRBIT        (1L<<(UPRSHIFT-1))
#define UPRMASK       (~(-1L<<UPRSHIFT))
#define SUMLOOP(i) for(i=0; i<MAXLONG; i++)

typedef short int INDEX;

typedef unsigned long ELEMENT;

typedef struct {
        ELEMENT         e[MAXLONG];
} FIELD2N;
```

3.2 All structures are polynomials

The first five parameters are described in chapter 2, but let's go over them again. WORD-SIZE is the number of bits in a machine word (see warnings in previous chapter about making sure this is correct for your target processor). NUMBITS is the number of bits the polynomial math will be expected to work on. The prime polynomial should have this power of x set as the most significant bit (mathematically: NUMBITS is the degree of our irreducible polynomial). NUMWORD is the maximum index of machine words into a polynomial array. UPRSHIFT is the number of left shifts needed to get to the most significant bit in the zero offset of the polynomial coefficient list. MAXLONG is the number of machine words needed to hold a polynomial.

The term MAXBITS is used in a few places; it is the maximum number of bits we can store in MAXLONG machine words.

The term MAXSHIFT is the largest number of shifts we need to move the most significant bit to the least in a single bit block. Since we're doing a lot of shifting, this will be useful later. MSB is a mask for the most significant bit in a WORDSIZE block of bits.

The term UPRSHIFT is used to compute the most significant bit position, UPRBIT, and a mask for the high-order ELEMENT UPRMASK. We will use UPRBIT for rotations and UPRMASK to clear bits after rotations and shifts. The macro SUMLOOP will be described later.

The next two items were also previously described. An INDEX is used for bookkeeping. We need to keep track of where we are in various algorithms, so let's call it what it is: an index. I call an unsigned long an ELEMENT, because it is the simplest thing I can work with. An ELEMENT is one machine word in size. Again, see the warnings in the previous chapter about ensuring this definition is correct for your application.

Finally, I define the field storage structure FIELD2N. This comes from the mathematician's symbol, F_{2^n}, which means a field of characteristic 2 and vector length n. Since we're going to reference each field element in the array a lot, I chose a single letter, "e," for ELEMENT. This structure is simple. But, as we shall see, it gives us a lot of power to

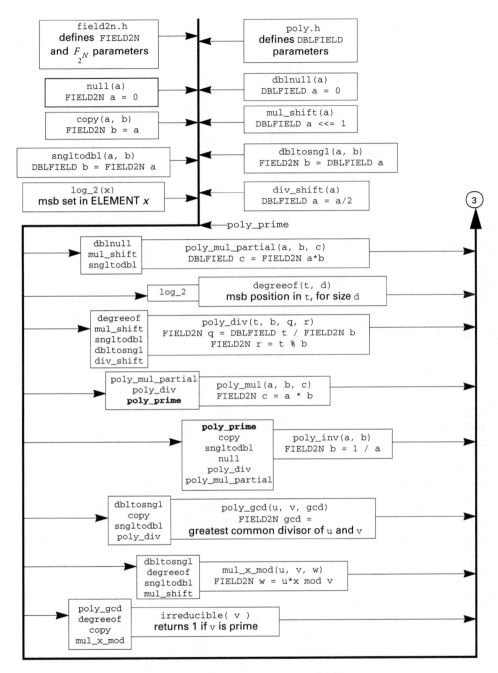

Figure 3.1   Subroutine schematic (all structures are polynomials)

manipulate mathematics easily. The coefficients are in big-endian order, for the same reasons as mentioned in the previous chapter. Again, this is an arbitrary choice, so if you change the order make sure you change it everywhere.

Here is the second header file, called `poly.h`:

```
/*  poly.h  */

/*  This header is required for the polynomial math section.
       The purpose is to define intermediate structure sizes
       for use with the multiply and divide routines.
       Place include header after field2n.h
*/

#define DBLBITS          2*NUMBITS
#define DBLWORD          (DBLBITS/WORDSIZE)
#define DBLSHIFT         (DBLBITS%WORDSIZE)
#define MAXDBL           (DBLWORD+1)

#define DERIVMASK        0x55555555

#define DBLLOOP(i)   for(i=0; i<MAXDBL; i++)

typedef struct {
        ELEMENT          e[MAXDBL];
} DBLFIELD;
```

`DBLBITS` is used to hold the result of a polynomial multiply. It is twice as long (in bits) as the field size we actually deal with. `DBLWORD`, `DBLSHIFT`, and `MAXDBL` are the same thing as `NUMWORD`, `UPRSHIFT`, and `MAXLONG` but for twice as many bits. Working with bits makes sure the definitions give us as many machine words of storage as we actually need.

The term `DERIVMASK` is used to check prime polynomials. We'll get into the mathematics of that later. `DBLLOOP` is similar to `SUMLOOP` but again for twice as many bits. And, finally, the double-size field `DBLFIELD` is used to define the array of machine words that holds the result of a multiply.

3.2.1 Polynomial addition

The first thing we need to implement is addition. As we said before, this is just the exclusive-or of two sets of coefficients. For example:

```
FIELD2N    a, b, c;
INDEX      i;

for( i=0; i<MAXLONG; i++) c.e[i] = a.e[i] ^ b.e[i];
```

This code performs $c = a + b$, where a, b, and c are polynomials with coefficients taken modulo 2. All we are doing is the exclusive-or of every coefficient in a with every coefficient in b, and we are doing WORDSIZE coefficients at a time.

Since the number of bits in our field might be anything, let's look at a few more items in that header file. We will be doing a lot of addition over variable-length fields. Choosing the number of bits depends on many parameters, including level of security and the particular application. Once you've read a few other books, that choice won't seem so arbitrary. For now, we'll pick a reasonable size field and derive all our other parameters from NUMBITS.

For all summations I will use the expansion SUMLOOP to mean a loop over some variable that goes from 0 to NUMWORD in steps of one. DBLLOOP is used to cover 0 to DBL-WORD. With these definitions our previous example becomes:

```
FIELD2N      a, b, c;
INDEX        i;

SUMLOOP(i)  c.e[i] = a.e[i] ^ b.e[i];
```

In addition to making our code more readable, it brings out mathematics. Instead of reading this as an XOR b, we should think of this as a plus b. (Note to C++ coders: Yes, you can define operator overrides for +, *, /, and %; the following code will be the core you need to do that.)

Stare at the above SUMLOOP for a second and compare this to the addition performed in example 1. We have done modulo 2 addition instead of modulo 10, but it's the same thing. Each power of x^i has a coefficient at bit position i. It is either a 0 or a 1. This really advanced polynomial math isn't so hard to do, is it? Now, let's try multiplication.

3.2.2 Polynomial multiplication

In example 2, I showed how to multiply two polynomials. The process is shifting, and, if a bit is set, adding to the result. This creates field elements that are twice as long as our inputs. To work with FIELD2N, we'll need to reduce this result via the modulus operator, but let's just do the multiply code first.

The first routine we need is a shift. Since we end up with twice as many bits, we need a shift routine that operates on DBLFIELD structures. The routine takes a pointer to the structure and operates on it in place.

```
/*  Shift left one bit used by multiply routine.  Make inline for speed.  */

void mul_shift(a)
DBLFIELD *a;
{
```

```
        ELEMENT  *eptr, temp, bit; /* eptr points to one ELEMENT at a time */
        INDEX    i;

        eptr = &a->e[DBLWORD];  /* point to end, note: bigendian processing */
        bit = 0;                        /*  initial carry bit is clear */
        DBLLOOP (i)
        {
                temp = (*eptr << 1) | bit;   /* compute result as temporary */
                bit = (*eptr & MSB) ? 1L : 0L; /* get carry bit from shift */
                *eptr-- = temp;                 /* save new result   */
        }
}
```

The variable, bit, is used as the carry bit from one ELEMENT to the next as we shift. eptr is used to point to each element. This is done in big-endian sequence, but, since we are working with machine-size words, it shouldn't matter what the actual storage mechanism is of the processor this is implemented on.

The least significant bit is initialized to 0. A temporary variable holds the combination of the least significant bit and the ELEMENT pointed to by eptr. The variable, bit, is then reset according to the most significant bit (MSB) of the eptr ELEMENT. The temporary word then gets stored on top of the original data.

Note that the loop INDEX variable, i, goes over twice as many elements. That's because when we multiply two polynomials, the maximum power of x will be the sum of the two highest exponents. Another way to improve efficiency of the mul_shift() routine would be to include the actual number of ELEMENTS required to be shifted.

The next five really basic routines will be used a lot. They can probably be turned into macros and compiled inline to increase speed. The first routine clears all the bits in a FIELD2N variable, and the second clears all the bits in a DBLFIELD variable. The third routine copies all the bits from one FIELD2N variable to another.

```
/*  null out a FIELD2N variable.  Make inline for speed.   */

void null(a)
FIELD2N *a;
{
        INDEX i;

        SUMLOOP(i) a->e[i] = 0L;
}

void dblnull(a)
DBLFIELD *a;
{
        INDEX i;

        DBLLOOP(i) a->e[i] = 0L;
}
```

```
/*  copy one FIELD2N variable to another.  Make inline for speed.  */

void copy(from, to)
FIELD2N *from, *to;
{
        INDEX  i;

        SUMLOOP(i) to->e[i] = from->e[i];
}
```

The next two routines convert from `FIELD2N` to `DBLFIELD` and back. These are used inside the multiply and divide routines. Once we get into modular polynomial math, we won't see much of the `DBLFIELD` size variables.

```
/*  copy a FIELD2N variable into a DBLFIELD variable */

void sngltodbl(from, to)
FIELD2N *from;
DBLFIELD *to;
{
        INDEX i;

        dblnull (to);
        SUMLOOP(i) to->e[DBLWORD - NUMWORD + i] = from->e[i];
}

/*  copy the bottom portion of DBLFIELD to FIELD2N variable  */

void dbltosngl(from, to)
FIELD2N *to;
DBLFIELD *from;
{
        INDEX i;

        SUMLOOP(i) to->e[i] = from->e[DBLWORD - NUMWORD + i];
}
```

Now we are ready for the partial multiply routine. Our inputs will be two `FIELD2N` structures (a and b), and our output will be a double-length `DBLFIELD` structure, which represents $c = a \cdot b$. The use of pointers to `WORDSIZE ELEMENTS` makes code more efficient. As in example 2, all we're doing is shifting and exclusive-or(ing).

```
/*  Simple polynomial multiply.
        Enter with 2 single FIELD2N variables to multiply.
        Result is double length DBLFIELD variable.
        user supplys all storage space, only pointers used here.
*/

void poly_mul_partial(a, b, c)
FIELD2N *a, *b;
DBLFIELD *c;
{
```

```
            INDEX i, bit_count, word;
            ELEMENT mask;
            DBLFIELD B;

/*  clear all bits in result  */

            dblnull(c);

/*  initialize local copy of b so we can shift it  */

            sngltodbl(b, &B);

/*  for every bit in 'a' that is set, add present B to result  */

            mask = 1;
            for (bit_count=0; bit_count<NUMBITS; bit_count++)
            {
                    word = NUMWORD - bit_count/WORDSIZE;
                    if (mask & a->e[word])
                    {
                            DBLLOOP(i) c->e[i] ^= B.e[i];
                    }
                    mul_shift( &B);       /* multiply copy of b by x  */
                    mask <<= 1;           /* shift mask bit up  */
                    if (!mask) mask = 1; /* when it goes to zero, reset to 1  */
            }
}
```

After copying input b to a double-size variable, B, and clearing the result (c), the routine sets ELEMENT mask to 1. This is our bit testing flag. It steps through every bit of a. To keep track of which ELEMENT of a we are in, the INDEX variable, word, is computed at the beginning of each bit_count loop. For speed, change the variable word only when mask goes to 0, instead of computing it every time in the bit_count loop.

If the a bit in question is clear, b is shifted once (i.e., we multiply the polynomial by x), and the mask is shifted as well. If the mask goes to 0, it is reset to 1. An assembler rotation would be more appropriate here.

If the a bit in question is set, then the double-length b and c arrays are exclusive-or(ed) with each other. This is the same as adding all matching coefficients of similar powers. As we step through the bit_count loop, the power of x increases. That is, we are multiplying b by $x^{\text{bit\_count}}$, and, if the coefficient of a for the term $x^{\text{bit\_count}}$ is set, then this value of $b \cdot x^{\text{bit\_count}}$ is added to the result. It's really simple: Shift and XOR, do for every bit.

3.2.3 Polynomial division

The next item to implement is division with remainder. We need these routines to compute an inverse, as well as to ensure we are operating in a true field, F_{2^n}. The following code is definitely not optimal. The point here is understanding. The reader interested in maximum speed should read [3], [4], and [5] for ideas on improved implementations. For a complete description of polynomial division see [6].

Let's look at the division operation in example 3. First, we noted the difference between the maximum powers of the polynomials in the top and bottom terms. If the degree of the top term was less than the degree of the bottom, there would be no division. So that has to be our first check: What are the degrees of the input terms?

The second thing we did was to multiply the bottom by the difference in degrees. This amounts to a shift of the bottom term so that it aligns with the top. The quotient is just a 1 shifted by the same amount. In math it's written quotient = $x^{top-bottom}$.

The last thing we did was to add (subtraction = addition mod 2 remember!) terms to cancel out coefficients. In general, we'll just be wiping out the most significant bit. At each step of this long division process we check to see whether the most significant bit of the shifted bottom is aligned with a set bit of the top. If it is, we set a bit in the quotient and compute top = top + bottom. This does a subtraction. If that bit is not set, we skip that step.

In both cases we shift the bottom right one bit. This amounts to dividing by x. The whole process repeats for the next bit.

Since the top is a double-size DBLFIELD structure, the shifted bottom is too. Here is a routine to shift a double-wide variable right one bit. This should be optimized in assembler to take advantage of a carry bit (or, better, a barrel shifter).

```
/*  Shift right routine for polynomial divide.  Convert to inline for speed.
        Enter with pointer to DBLFIELD variable.
        shifts whole thing right one bit;
*/

void div_shift(a)
DBLFIELD *a;
{
        ELEMENT         *eptr, temp, bit;
        INDEX           i;

        eptr = (ELEMENT*) &a->e[0];
        bit = 0;
        DBLLOOP (i)
        {
                temp = (*eptr>>1) | bit;  /* same as shift left but  */
                bit = (*eptr & 1) ? MSB : 0L;
                                    /* carry bit goes off other end  */
                *eptr++ = temp;
        }
}
```

As explained previously, the first thing we do before polynomial division is to compare the degree of the top and bottom. To compute the degree I use the following subroutines. The first routine computes the most significant bit in a single ELEMENT, and the second routine computes the full degree. The reason I split it up is because the first will be useful in the next chapter as well. (The name of the routine means logarithm base 2.)

```
/*  binary search for most significant bit within word */

INDEX log_2 (x)
ELEMENT x;
{
        ELEMENT ebit, bitsave, bitmask;
        INDEX   k, lg2;

        lg2 = 0;
        bitsave = x;                  /* grab bits we're interested in.  */
        k = WORDSIZE/2;               /* first see if msb is in top half */
        bitmask = -1L<<k;             /* of all bits   */
        while (k)
        {
                ebit = bitsave & bitmask;/* did we hit a bit?  */
                if (ebit)                     /* yes */
                {
                        lg2 += k;
                        /* increment degree by minimum possible offset */
                        bitsave = ebit;/* and zero out non useful bits   */
                }
/*  The following two lines are slick and tricky.  We are binary
        searching, so k is divided by 2.  It's also the base amount
        we can add at any given search point.  The mask continuously
        searches for upper blocks being set.
        Once found, the remaining lower blocks are zeroed, to make
        sure we don't use bits which aren't the most significant.
*/
                k /= 2;
                bitmask ^= (bitmask >> k);
        }
        return( lg2);
}
```

The first subroutine performs a binary search for the most significant bit of the input ELEMENT. The best thing to do to understand what this code does is to watch it on a debugger. It "combs" over the bits in an ELEMENT and adds up the maximum possible bit position.

The second routine is called degreeof. There are two input arguments, and it returns an INDEX value. The inputs are a pointer to a FIELD2N and the number of ELEMENTS over which to compute the degree. For top polynomials, dim = DBLWORD; for bottom, dim = NUMWORD.

The degreeof routine begins with a scan for the first nonzero ELEMENT. The degree count is initialized to a maximum, and for each zero ELEMENT the degree is decremented by WORDSIZE. If the entire array is 0, it returns −1. This is used by the inversion routine to determine when it's finished. The leading term is then fed to the log_2 routine, and the result is summed to form the full value of the polynomials' degree.

```
/*  find most significant bit in multiple ELEMENT array.
        Enter with pointer to array (t) and number of elements (dim).
        Returns degree of polynomial == position count of most signicant bit
        set */

INDEX degreeof(t, dim)
ELEMENT *t;
INDEX   dim;
{
        INDEX   degree, k;
        ELEMENT ebit, bitsave, bitmask;

/*  This is generic routine for arbitrary length arrays. use ELEMENT
        pointer to find first non-zero ELEMENT.  We will add degree from
        some base, so initial base is at least one WORDSIZE smaller than
        maximum possible.
*/

        degree = dim * WORDSIZE;
        for (k=0; k<dim; k++)            /* search for a non-zero ELEMENT  */
        {
                if (*t) break;
                degree -= WORDSIZE;
                t++;
        }

/* for inversion routine, need to know when all bits zero.  */

        if (!*t) return(-1);

        degree += log_2( *t);
        return(degree);
}
```

With the above routines we can begin to construct the polynomial division code. The basic steps have already been outlined: First find the degree of the polynomials, shift and subtract the divisor from the dividend, and repeat until the remainder is less than the divisor.

While not optimal, the following poly_div routine will be very useful to us. For modulo polynomial arithmetic we can use poly_div after poly_mul_partial to get our remainder. It divides a double-length FIELD2N polynomial top by a single-length FIELD2N polynomial bottom. The output consists of two single-length FIELD2N polynomials: quotient and remainder.

Here is the start of the routine; let's see what the variables are.

```
/*  division of two polynomials.  Major use is reduction modulo
        irreducible polynomials.
        Enter with pointers to top, bottom, quotient and remainder.
          Assumes top is DBLFIELD and all other arrays are
          FIELD2N variables.
        Returns with top destroyed, and the following satisfied:
          top = quotient * bottom + remainder.
*/

void poly_div(top, bottom, quotient, remainder)
DBLFIELD *top;
FIELD2N  *bottom, *quotient, *remainder;
{
        INDEX           deg_top;
        INDEX           deg_bot;
        INDEX           deg_quot;
        INDEX           bit_count;
        INDEX           i;
        INDEX           equot;
        ELEMENT         topbit, *tptr;
        DBLFIELD        shift;
```

The variables deg_* are used to hold the maximum degree of the top, bottom, and quotient. The variable bit_count is used to count over all bits, i is used as a SUMLOOP variable, and equot is an ELEMENT index into the quotient. The variable topbit is a mask used to test if a bit is set in top, and tptr is an ELEMENT pointer, which scans over top. Finally, the variable shift is a DBLFIELD storage location used to align the bottom with the top.

```
/*  Step 1: find degree of top and bottom polynomials.  */

        deg_top = degreeof( top, DBLWORD);
        deg_bot = degreeof( bottom, NUMWORD);

/*  prepare for null return and check for null quotient */

        null (quotient);
        if (deg_top < deg_bot)
        {
                dbltosngl(top, remainder);
                return;
        }
```

As in the hand calculation, the first step is to find the degree of top and bottom polynomials. If the degree of top is less than the degree of bottom, there is no need to do anything; the quotient is nulled and top is copied to remainder. Nulling the quotient first clears all the bits for the eventual correct answer.

```
/*  Step 2: shift bottom to align with top.  Note that there
                are much more efficient ways to do this. */
```

```
deg_quot = deg_top - deg_bot;
bit_count = deg_quot + 1;
sngltodbl(bottom, &shift);
for (i = 0; i<deg_quot; i++)
        mul_shift(&shift);
```

The second step is to figure out how many bits will be in the quotient. That determines the number of shifts we need to do on bottom to make it line up with the top. The call to mul_shift is nonoptimal; a barrel shift routine would be much faster.

```
/* Step 3: create bit mask to check if msb of top is set   */

        topbit = 1L << (deg_top % WORDSIZE);
        tptr = (ELEMENT*) top + DBLWORD - deg_top/WORDSIZE;
```

The third step is to create a bit mask that scans along the top to see if we need to do a subtraction at any given step. It is initialized to the bit position that equals the degree of the top polynomial; we know that subtraction must be performed. The topbit mask is a single bit located in the most significant ELEMENT. The pointer tptr is set to point at the first nonzero value found for top.

```
/*  for each possible quotient bit, see if bottom can be subtracted
        (added, it's modulo 2!) from top. If it can, set that bit in
        quotient. If it can't, clear that bit in quotient.  Shift bottom
        right once and keep going for total bit_count.
*/

        while (bit_count)
        {
/*  Step 4: determine one bit of the quotient.   */

                if (*tptr & topbit)    /* is bit set in top?  */
                {
                        DBLLOOP (i)    /* yes, subtract shift from top  */
                                top->e[i] ^= shift.e[i];

                /* find word and bit in quotient to be set   */

                        equot = NUMWORD - deg_quot/WORDSIZE;
                        quotient->e[equot] |= 1L << (deg_quot % WORDSIZE);
                }
```

The meat of the code is performed in the while (bit_count) loop. If the topbit mask hits a bit (which it should, the first time into the loop!), then the shifted bottom (variable shift) is added to the top to eliminate the bit (i.e., to perform a subtraction step). Then, the correct quotient bit is set to reflect the fact that we did a multiply by that power of x and subtracted it from the top. This is brute-force long division, with single bits instead of numbers.

```
/*  Step 5: advance to the next quotient bit and perform the necessary
                        shifts.  */

                bit_count--;            /*  number of bits is one more  */
                deg_quot--;             /*  than polynomial degree  */
                div_shift(&shift);      /*  divide by 2  */
                topbit >>= 1;           /*  move mask over one bit also  */
                if (!topbit)
                {
                        topbit = MSB;   /*  reset mask bit to next word  */
                        tptr++;         /*  when it goes to zero  */
                }
        }
```

Whether or not a subtraction is performed, step 5 decrements the loop counter, bit_count, and the degree of the quotient. The bottom is shifted right one bit position to align it with the next possible top bit that may need to be eliminated. The topbit mask is shifted over, and, if it goes to 0, it is set to MSB. In assembler one would simply use a single rotate instruction and bypass that whole mess. The top ELEMENT pointer, tptr, is also bumped to point at the next word.

```
/*  Step 6: return the remainder in FIELD2N size  */

        dbltosngl (top, remainder);
}
```

Steps 4 and 5 are iterated by counting down the total number of bits that have to be checked. At each point the bottom is checked to see if it can be subtracted from what is left in the top, and a quotient bit is set if necessary. When that is done, the final step (step 6) moves what is left over in top to the remainder.

In the next section, we'll see that the bottom can be one bit larger than any other field size we normally deal with. The above code was written with that in mind. An example would be a 64-bit field size on a 32-bit machine. Note that we'll set up MAXLONG to be 3 for this case, because x^{64} will be set in our prime polynomial.

3.3 Modular polynomial arithmetic

OK now, let's see where we are. As we said before, a field has to obey the rules of multiplication and addition, and every element in a field must have an inverse. Both prime number fields and prime polynomial fields are cyclical—after some number of operations you get back to where you started. For every degree (or NUMBITS) we choose to work with we can find a prime polynomial. Figuring out how to choose the optimal polynomial for a given field size and application will not be described here. See [5] and references therein for comments on this.

To complete our multiply routine over a field, we need a prime polynomial p. With inputs a and b we compute $prtl = a * b$ and then return $c = prtl\%p$ using the remainder of the above division routine. The whole routine is just this:

```
/*  Polynomial multiplication modulo poly_prime.   */

void poly_mul(a, b, c)
FIELD2N *a, *b, *c;
{
        DBLFIELD temp;
        FIELD2N  dummy;

        poly_mul_partial(a, b, &temp);
        poly_div(&temp, &poly_prime, &dummy, c);
}
```

For the `poly_mul` routine to work we need a prime polynomial. I will give a routine for checking prime polynomials after the inversion routine. It turns out [7, 134] that the number of prime polynomials less than x^d is approximately $2^d/d$, so picking them at random will find one reasonably quickly.

Hardware implementations should not need a division routine. By storing the values of x^j modulo the prime polynomial, you only need to perform a look up for each bit, j, set in `temp` and exclusive-or it with the result. There will be a maximum of NUMBITS terms. The construction of tables such as this will be described later in the chapter.

Here are a few values of `poly_prime` that I have found useful for testing all these routines. They come from [8, 376]. There are much better ways to write code to make it more flexible. I leave it to the programmer to conjure up those better methods. Some of my worst problems were changing `poly_prime` to some large value from a small one and forgetting to change NUMBITS in the header file accordingly. This won't be a problem for an application using fixed sizes. In the following listing, I was working with NUMBITS = 93, which is the same as the value given in the `field2n.h` file shown previously.

```
/*  Define irreducible polynomial for field here.  Use table, or evaluate your
        own, but the math won't work if it' isn't really a prime polynomial.
        NOTE: the value you pick must be consistent with NUMBITS.
*/

/*FIELD2N  poly_prime =
        {0x08000000,0x00000000,0x00000000,0x00000000,0x000000B1}; */ /*155*/
/*FIELD2N poly_prime =
        {0x00000001,0x00000000,0x00000000,0x00000000,0x00000087};*/  /*128*/
FIELD2N  poly_prime = {0x20000000,0x00000000,0x00000005};        /*93*/
/*FIELD2N poly_prime = {0x0000800,0x00000000,0x0000004b};*/       /*75*/
/*FIELD2N poly_prime = {0x0000020,0x00000000,0x00000065};*/       /*69*/
/*FIELD2N poly_prime = {0x00000002,0x00000000,0x0000001b};*/      /*65*/
/*FIELD2N poly_prime = {0x00000001,0x00000000,0x0000001b};*/      /*64*/
```

```
/*FIELD2N poly_prime = {0x80000000,0x00000003};*/      /*63*/
/*FIELD2N poly_prime = {0x00000002,0x00002001};*/      /*33*/
/*FIELD2N poly_prime = {0x00000001,0x000000c5};*/      /*32*/
/*FIELD2N poly_prime = {0x80000009};*/ /*31*/
/*FIELD2N poly_prime = {0x800021};*/      /* 23*/
/*FIELD2N poly_prime = {0x100009};*/      /* 20*/
/*FIELD2N poly_prime = {0x20021};*/      /* 17*/
/*FIELD2N poly_prime = {0x1002B};*/      /* 16*/
/*FIELD2N poly_prime = {0x8003}; */      /* 15*/
/*FIELD2N poly_prime = {0x89};*/      /* 7*/
/*FIELD2N poly_prime = {0x43};*/      /*6*/
/*FIELD2N poly_prime = {0x25};*/      /*5*/
/*FIELD2N poly_prime = {0x13};*/      /*4*/
```

3.4 Inversion over prime polynomials

Just as with prime number arithmetic we can use Euclid's greatest common divisor routine to compute inverses over prime polynomials. We showed the algorithm before, now let's look at some code.

```
/*  Polynomial inversion routine.  Computes inverse of polynomial
        field element assuming irreducible polynomial "poly_prime"
        defines the field.
*/

void poly_inv(a, inverse)
FIELD2N *a, *inverse;
{
        FIELD2N pk, pk1, pk2;
        FIELD2N rk, rk1;
        FIELD2N qk, qk1, qk2;
        INDEX   i;
        DBLFIELD rk2;

/*  initialize remainder, quotient and product terms   */

        sngltodbl (&poly_prime, &rk2);

        copy( a, &rk1);
        null( &pk2);
        null( &pk1);
        pk1.e[NUMWORD] = 1L;
        null( &qk2);
        null( &qk1);
        qk1.e[NUMWORD] = 1L;

/*  compute quotient and remainder for Euclid's algorithm.
    when degree of remainder is < 0, there is no remainder, and we're done.
    At that point, pk is the answer.
*/
        null( &pk);
```

```
                pk.e[NUMWORD] = 1L;
                poly_div(&rk2, &rk1, &qk, &rk);
                while (degreeof(&rk, NUMWORD) >= 0)
                {
                        poly_mul_partial( &qk, &pk1, &rk2);
                        SUMLOOP(i) pk.e[i] = rk2.e[i+DBLWORD-NUMWORD] ^ pk2.e[i];

/*  set up variables for next loop */

                        sngltodbl(&rk1, &rk2);
                        copy( &rk, &rk1);
                        copy( &qk1, &qk2);
                        copy( &qk, &qk1);
                        copy( &pk1, &pk2);
                        copy( &pk, &pk1);
                        poly_div( &rk2, &rk1, &qk, &rk);
                }
                copy( &pk, inverse);            /* copy answer to output  */
}
```

The routine is a straightforward copy of the algorithm presented at the beginning of the chapter. Instead of subscripts, I use different variable names. The variables are all initialized as single field elements except for rk2. This is defined as a DBLFIELD array, so we can use the multiply and divide routines. See [3, 36] for ways to avoid this.

The loop terminates when rk goes to 0. Since the degreeof subroutine will return −1 if all bits are 0, this is used to terminate the loop.

If the input happens to be poly_prime, then the output is 1. If the mathematics is right, this situation should never occur. That is because the degree of remainders produced after reduction with poly_prime is less than the degree of poly_prime. It is good procedure to write reasonably robust code, just in case garbage gets fed into a routine, to be able to give an answer. It will be garbage, but it will be mathematically correct garbage!

3.5 Polynomial greatest common divisor

With a division routine it is easy to implement Euclid's algorithm to compute the greatest common divisor of two polynomials. The only tricks we have to play have to do with the input to the division routine being a DBLFIELD size variable. The math is identical to Euclid's 2,000-year-old algorithm, but instead of using integers we use polynomials.

Here is a very simple routine that uses the code described in the previous sections. The inputs are two FIELD2N polynomials, and the output is filled with the answer. If the two polynomials are relatively prime, the answer will be 1. If there is a common factor, the answer will be found in location gcd. This routine also uses degreeof to find the end point. When the remainder is 0, degreeof returns −1, and the loop terminates.

```
/*   polynomial greatest common divisor routine.
        Same as Euclid's algorithm.   */

void poly_gcd( u, v, gcd)
FIELD2N *u, *v, *gcd;
{
        DBLFIELD        top;
        FIELD2N         r, dummy, temp;

        sngltodbl( u, &top);
        copy( v, &r);

        while( degreeof( &r, NUMWORD) >= 0)
        {
                poly_div( &top, &r, &dummy, &temp);
                sngltodbl( &r, &top);
                copy( &temp, &r);
        }
        dbltosngl( &top, gcd);
}
```

3.6 Prime polynomials

Mathematicians consider the concept of prime polynomials so trivial that they don't talk about them much other than to state a one-sentence definition: A prime polynomial has no factors. It turns out it is relatively easy to prove that a polynomial is prime.

Knuth [6, 429] describes a way to factor polynomials over F_2. Since we only need to determine if a polynomial has factors, and not what they are, I use a simpler algorithm provided by Richard Pinch. We first determine if there are any square factors, and we then institute a brute-force search for any others.

The first step is to compute the greatest common divisor between the polynomial and its "derivative." I put the word derivative in quotes, because the mathematics is defined to operate the same way as a continuous variable, but it's not really a calculus derivative.

Suppose we have a polynomial of the form:

$$u(x) = u_n x^n + u_{n-1} x^{n-1} + \ldots + u_0 .$$

(3.9)

Its "derivative" is defined to be (see [6]):

$$u'(x) = n u_n x^{n-1} + (n-1) u_{n-1} x^{n-2} + \ldots + u_1 .$$

(3.10)

This is fine for arbitrary fields, but we are working over F_2. That means all our coefficients are taken modulo 2. If n is even, then that term is 0 no matter what the coefficient was. In fact, all the even coefficients go to 0. But we have performed a shift right as well, since all the powers of x have been reduced by 1. So the work required to compute the derivative is really simple: We just shift right and mask off every other bit. This is where the DERIVMASK comes from in the poly.h header file.

The second step relies on the amazing fact that:

$$\Omega_r(x) = x^{p^r} - x \qquad (3.11)$$

contains all prime polynomials of degree r (see [2] or [1, 35]). There aren't enough atoms in the universe to store a polynomial for $p = 2$ and $r = 256$. So we have to do all our math modulo the polynomial being tested.

The brute-force search checks to see if $u(x)$ has any common factors with $\Omega_r(x)$ for every r less than half the degree of $u(x)$. If there is a common factor, the routine poly_gcd will not return 1 as a result. We only have to cover half the degree of $u(x)$ because if there are any factors, at least one of them will be in that range. So let's see how to generate $\Omega_r(x)$.

The first routine needed is a simple multiply by x modulo and an arbitrary polynomial (v). To multiply by x is just a left shift. If the degree of the result is the same as the degree of v, the result is summed with v. This reduces the result modulo v. Not efficient for all cases, but this routine will be useful later.

```
/*  multiply a polynomial u by x modulo polynomial v.  Useful in
        several places.  Enter with u and v, returns polynomial w.
        w can equal to u, so this will work in place.
*/

void mul_x_mod( u, v, w)
FIELD2N *u, *v, *w;
{
        DBLFIELD mulx;
        INDEX    i, deg_v;

        deg_v = degreeof(v, NUMWORD);
        sngltodbl( u, &mulx);
        mul_shift( &mulx);  /*  multiply u by x  */
        dbltosngl( &mulx, w);
        if (w->e[ (NUMWORD - (deg_v/WORDSIZE)] & ( 1L << (deg_v % WORDSIZE)))
                SUMLOOP (i) w->e[i] ^= v->e[i];
}
```

To build the value of $\Omega_r(x)$ modulo $v(x)$ takes two components. The first part is to notice that:

$$u^2(x) = u(x^2). \qquad (3.12)$$

What this means is that to square a polynomial, we only need to shift each coefficient from position j to position $2j$. The second part is that this has to be reduced modulo v. So the simplest method is to build a lookup table of $x^{2j} \bmod v(x)$ for all j less than the degree of v.

Now, to compute $x^{2^r} \bmod v(x)$ let's start with $r = 0$: 2^0 is 1 and we have $x^{2^0} = x$. Starting with this we only need to square $x^{2^{r-1}}$ to find x^{2^r}. Using the tabulated values of $x^{2j} \bmod v(x)$ the squaring operation is just a sum of at most the degree of $v(x)$ values.

That's the theory; let's take a look at some code to see what this means in practice.

```
/*  check to see if input polynomial is irreducible.
        Returns 1 if irreducible, 0 if not.

        This method explained by Richard Pinch.  The idea is to use
        gcd algorithm to test if x^2^r - x has input v as a factor
        for all r <= degree(v)/2.  If there is any common factor,
        then v is not irreducible.  This works because x^2^r - x
        contains all possible irreducible factors of degree r, and
        because we only need to find the smallest degree such factor
        if one exists.
*/

INDEX irreducible( v)
FIELD2N *v;
{
        FIELD2N         vprm, gcd, x2r, x2rx, temp;
        FIELD2N         sqr_x[NUMBITS+1];
        INDEX           i, r, deg_v, k;

/*  check that gcd(v, v') = 1.  If not, then v not irreducible.  */

        SUMLOOP(i) vprm.e[i] = (v->e[i] >> 1) & DERIVMASK;
        poly_gcd( v, &vprm, &gcd);
        if (gcd.e[NUMWORD] > 1) return(0);
        for (i=0; i<NUMWORD; i++)  if (gcd.e[i]) return(0);
```

The first test computes the derivative of the input polynomial as described previously. If there is any common factor between the input polynomial and its derivative, then we already know the input cannot be irreducible. The first check looks at the least significant ELEMENT to see if it is greater than 1. If so, we can report a negative result. The remaining ELEMENTs had better be 0, or we can also return a negative answer.

Once past that step, we'll need the degree of the input polynomial, so that is saved in the following code:

```
/*  find maximum power we have to deal with  */

        deg_v = degreeof(v, NUMWORD);
```

Next, I build up an array containing powers of x^{2j} modulo $v(x)$ in the variable `sqr_x`. This starts with $j = 0$ and then multiplies each successive entry in the array by x^2 using the `mul_x_mod` routine.

```
/*  create a vector table of powers of x^2k mod v.
       this will be used to compute square of x^2^r
*/

       null (&sqr_x[0]);
       sqr_x[0].e[NUMWORD] = 1;
       for (i=1; i<= deg_v; i++)
       {
              mul_x_mod( &sqr_x[i-1], v, &temp);
              mul_x_mod( &temp, v, &sqr_x[i]);
       }
```

The brute-force test then starts with $r = 0$. Since $x - x = 0$ is pointless to check, the test starts by computing the square of $x^{2^{r-1}}$. This is saved in variable `x2r`. For any bit j set in $x^{2^{r-1}}$ we only need add in the entry `sqr_x[j]` to find the next power of r. The last step in computing $\Omega_r(x)$ is to add in x; the result of that operation is saved in variable `x2rx`.

```
/*  check that gcd( x^2^r - x, v) == 1 for all r <= degreeof(v)/2.
       set x^2^r = x for r = 0 to initialize.
*/
       null( &x2r);
       x2r.e[NUMWORD] = 2;
       for ( r=1; r <= deg_v/2; r++)
       {
/*  square x^2^r mod v.  We do this by seeing that s^2(x) = s(x^2).
       for each bit j set in x^2^(r-1) add in x^2j mod v to find x^2^r.
*/
              null( &x2rx);
              for (i=0; i <= deg_v; i++)
              {
                     if ( x2r.e[NUMWORD - (i/WORDSIZE)] & ( 1L << (i%WORDSIZE) ))
                            SUMLOOP(k) x2rx.e[k] ^= sqr_x[i].e[k];
              }

/*  save new value of x^2^r mod v and compute x^2^r - x mod v */

              copy( &x2rx, &x2r);
              x2rx.e[NUMWORD] ^= 2;
```

The last step is to see if there are any common factors between the input polynomial v and $\Omega_r(x)$. This is the same process used with the derivative check. A big thanks to Dave Dahm for pointing this out to me.

```
/*  is gcd( x^2^r - x, v) == 1?  if not, exit with negative result  */
```

```
            poly_gcd( &x2rx, v, &gcd);
            if (gcd.e[NUMWORD] > 1) return (0);
            for (i=0; i<NUMWORD; i++) if ( gcd.e[i]) return (0);
      }

/* passed all tests, provably irreducible */

      return (1);
}
```

If no common factors are found, the polynomial *v(x)* is proved to be prime. This algorithm uses two major tricks: The first is doing all multiplications modulo the input, and the second is recognizing that all possible factors have been tested.

There is one other term you may run across in the literature. This is "primitive polynomials." A primitive polynomial is irreducible, and its roots are generators of a field. Another way to look at it is that the order of a primitive polynomial is $2^n - 1$. If we take *x* to every possible power (modulo a primitive polynomial), we'll get every field element. This maps the integers to polynomials and can be useful for bookkeeping.

3.7 Summary

In this chapter we've learned about polynomial mathematics as it applies to base 2 computer arithmetic. It's really simple, because addition is just exclusive-or and multiplication is shifting and adding. Division is also simple; it too is shifting and adding, but we come out with a quotient and a remainder. The remainder is very useful for modular mathematics. So we now have tools for computing modular math over polynomials—this gives us a field. And it can be made into a very large field by using lots of machine words connected together.

Unlike integer math, polynomial math is very fast. In fact, there are a great many ways to speed up the arithmetic presented in this chapter. Even as I write this, mathematicians and academics are writing papers that advance the state of the art and introduce new tricks of the trade. These are just refinements to what you've seen here. By understanding the basics of the mathematics presented here and seeing how the code works, you can incorporate the state-of-the-art tricks quite easily.

3.8 References

1 N. Koblitz, *A Course in Number Theory and Cryptography* (New York: Springer-Verlag, 1987).

2 R. Lidl and H. Niederreiter, *Introduction to Finite Fields and Their Applications* (Cambridge, England: Cambridge University Press, 1994).

3 E. R. Berlekamp, *Algebraic Coding Theory* (New York: McGraw-Hill, 1968).

4 R. Schroeppel, H. Orman, and S. O'Mally, "Fast Key Exchange with Elliptic Curve Systems," TR-95-03 (Tucson, AZ: University of Arizona, Computer Sciences Department, 1995). (Also appears in *CRYPTO '95* [Berlin and New York: Springer-Verlag, 1995].)

5 E. De Win, A. Bosselaers, S. Vandenberghe, P. De Gersem, and J. Vandewalle, "A Fast Software Implementation for Arithmentic Operations in GF (2^n)," *ASIACRYPT '96* (Berlin: Springer-Verlag, 1996), 65–76.

6 D. E. Knuth, *Seminumerical Algorithms* (Reading, MA: Addison-Wesley, 1981).

7 E. Bach and J. Shallit, *Algorithmic Number Theory* (Cambridge, MA: MIT Press, 1996).

8 B. Schneier, *Applied Cryptography,* 2d ed. (New York: John Wiley & Sons, 1996).

C H A P T E R   4

Normal basis mathematics

4.1 What is a normal basis?   76

4.2 Squaring normal basis numbers   78

4.3 Multiplication in theory   78

4.4 Type I optimal normal basis   80

4.5 Type II optimal normal basis   85

4.6 Multiplication in practice   92

4.7 Inversion over optimal normal basis   97

4.8 References   102

4.1 What is a normal basis?

The mathematics introduced in this chapter are probably unfamiliar to most readers. When elliptic curve crypto systems were first proposed, "optimal normal bases" were considered the fastest implementation method. At the present time there are a few hardware devices that take advantage of this. Over the past few years polynomial basis math has been faster in software. It has recently been shown [1] that a combination of both normal basis and polynomial basis can take advantage of the strength of each for maximum efficiency.

The mathematical symbols of normal basis may seem overly complex, but the implementation in computer hardware or software is very easy. Only AND, XOR, and, ROTATE operations are needed. The fact that these are the fastest operations possible on any microprocessor is what makes optimal normal basis (ONB) so attractive.

I'll first go through the theory of normal basis mathematics and then delve into the subroutines. The subroutine schematic is shown in figure 4.1. There are two types of normal basis that are useful for elliptic curve cryptography, and both need different initialization routines. The rest of the chapter will discuss the theory behind normal basis multiplication and inversion.

To explain what a normal basis is, I'll start with algebraic polynomials. As shown in the previous chapter, we can describe elements in a field using a polynomial over an arbitrary variable (x in most books). If we take some element β in the field F_{p^m}, the polynomial representation is:

$$\beta = a_n x^n + \dots + a_1 x + a_0 \tag{4.1}$$

where $n < m$.

A normal basis can be formed using the set:

$$\{\beta^{p^{m-1}}, \dots, \beta^{p^2}, \beta^p, \beta\}. \tag{4.2}$$

A normal basis can be found for any finite field. For computers, we use $p = 2$. For the purposes of this book that's all we need to know. The interested reader should see advanced math texts for the general case [2].

Any element in a field F_{2^m} can be represented in a normal basis format. Since all representations are "isomorphic" (meaning "the same structure"), we can do the same math but with different operations. An element, e, can be written in a normal basis as:

$$e = e_{m-1}\beta^{2^{m-1}} + \dots + e_2\beta^{2^2} + e_1\beta^2 + e_0\beta \tag{4.3}$$

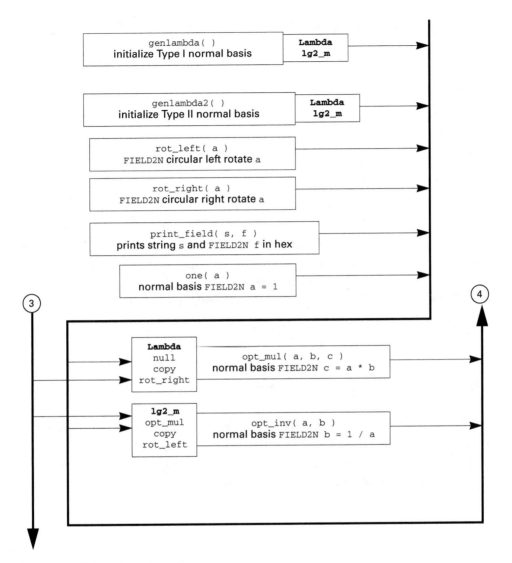

Figure 4.1 Subroutine schematic

or, more succinctly, as:

$$e = \sum_{i=0}^{m-1} e_i \beta^{2^i}.$$

(4.4)

Note that the index is over an exponent of an exponent. This is going to seem pretty bizarre, but hang in there. The magic reduces to amazing simplicity after a little digging.

4.2 Squaring normal basis numbers

The nicest aspect of this representation is that squaring a number amounts to a rotation. There are two reasons for this:

$$\mathbf{1} \left(\beta^{2^i}\right)^2 = \beta^{2^{i+1}} \tag{4.5}$$

$$\mathbf{2} \ \beta^{2^m} = \beta. \tag{4.6}$$

The first statement is obvious: $\left(\beta^{2^i}\right)^2 = \beta^{2(2^i)} = \beta^{2^{i+1}}$. The second statement comes from the rules of finite fields and is similar to Fermat's Theorem. So squaring e amounts to shifting each coefficient up to the next term and rotating the last coefficient down to 0 position. Squaring is very fast in a normal basis.

Addition is the same as polynomial basis. In base 2, all the coefficients can only be 0 or 1, and addition is simply an exclusive-or operation. For $m = 8$, 16, 32, or 64 we would have perfect word-size alignment for any processor. Unfortunately, these are too small for cryptographic purposes and not mathematically optimal.

4.3 Multiplication in theory

Multiplication over a normal basis gets a touch complicated. The basics are the same in any mathematical system, just multiply coefficients and sum over all those that have the same power of x. What makes normal bases slick is that most of those terms are 0.

To show how multiply works, take two elements in F_{2^m}:

$$A = \sum a_i \beta^{2^i} \tag{4.7}$$

and

$$B = \sum b_j \beta^{2^j}. \tag{4.8}$$

The formal multiplication is:

$$C = A \bullet B = \sum_{i=0}^{m-1} \sum_{j=0}^{m-1} a_i b_j \beta^{2^i} \beta^{2^j} \tag{4.9}$$

but

     CHAPTER 4 NORMAL BASIS MATHEMATICS

$$C = \sum_{k=0}^{m-1} c_k \beta^{2^k} \qquad\qquad (4.10)$$

by definition of an element in a normal basis, so the double sum in the first equation (4.9) has to match the single sum in the second equation (4.10). In fact, we must have each cross-product term map to a sum over the basis terms:

$$\beta^{2^i} \beta^{2^j} = \sum_{k=0}^{m-1} \lambda_{ijk} \beta^{2^k} \quad . \qquad\qquad (4.11)$$

The λ_{ijk} coefficient is called "the lambda matrix" or "multiplication table." If we substitute the multiplication table formula (4.11) into the $C = A \bullet B$ formula (4.9), we get a mess.

From that mess we can find the solution to each c_k coefficient of β^{2^k} in equation (4.10), which is "only" a double sum:

$$c_k = \sum_{i=0}^{m-1} \sum_{j=0}^{m-1} a_i b_j \lambda_{ijk} \quad . \qquad\qquad (4.12)$$

The mathematicians can prove to you that equation (4.12) can be transmogrified into a form that requires only λ_{ij0} (see [3] for proof). That reduces the amount of work required to construct the λ matrix (multiplication table). See [4] for hints and [3] for a derivation of the following:

$$k = \sum_{i=0}^{m-1} \sum_{j=0}^{m-1} a_{i+k} b_{j+k} \lambda_{ij0} \quad . \qquad\qquad (4.13)$$

What makes equation (4.13) so awesome is that all we need to do is shift the inputs by the correct amount and all coefficients can be computed in parallel. Because there is no carry, even high-level languages can reasonably implement normal basis math using very little memory. Of course, assembler and hardware will always be faster.

An "optimal" normal basis has the minimum number of nonzero λ_{ij} terms. This number is called the "complexity" of the multiplication table. For fields F_{2^m} the optimal (minimum) complexity is $2m - 1$. See [5] for proof of this.

There are two types of optimal normal basis over F_{2^m}. They are called Type I and Type II. The only real difference between them is the way we find which bits in the λ matrix are set. For Type I ONB we only need to store one vector; for Type II ONB we'll need to store two vectors. For the code I'm presenting here, I'll make them both look the same so that the multiply routine will work in either case. A Type I ONB multiply could be made quicker with a few math tricks.

4.4 Type I optimal normal basis

The rules for creating Type I ONB over the field F_{2^m} are:

1 $m + 1$ must be prime.

2 2 must be primitive in Z_{m+1}.

Rule 2 means that 2 raised to any power in the range $0 \ldots m - 1$ modulo $m + 1$ must result in a unique integer in the range $1 \ldots m$. (Z is used to mean the set of integers by mathematicians, but they use a different font.)

We need to find the cross-product terms of $\beta^{2^i} \cdot \beta^{2^j}$ in equation (4.11) to make the multiplication work. Because we can transform the λ matrix to $k = 0$ for all cross-terms, we really only need to solve the equation:

$$\beta^{2^i} \beta^{2^j} = \beta. \qquad (4.14)$$

There is also the special case:

$$\beta^{2^i} \beta^{2^j} = 1 \qquad (4.15)$$

when $2^i + 2^j$ is congruent to 0 modulo $m + 1$.

To proceed, we need to know some math rules. For all the above to work optimally we must have β be an element of order $m + 1$ in F_{2^m}. Since 2 is primitive in Z_{m+1}, 2^i mod $m + 1$ will run through all the integers between 1 and m as i runs through all values $0, 1, \ldots, m - 1$. The combination β^{2^i} is just another way of counting through all powers of β, which is what generates our basis. The order is scrambled compared to β^j, but all powers of the generator are accounted for.

The easy way to solve equations (4.14) and (4.15) is to rewrite them as modulo $m + 1$ and to "step into the exponent." We only need to solve:

$$2^i + 2^j = 1 \mod m + 1 \qquad (4.16)$$

and

$$2^i + 2^j = 0 \mod m + 1. \qquad (4.17)$$

Let's start with $i = 0$. $2^0 = 1$ and $2^m = 1$, since $m + 1$ is prime. This last point comes from Fermat's Theorem. The first equation (4.16) cannot have a solution for $i = 0$. Only the second equation (4.17) can. If we take the square root of $2^m = 1$, we find:

$$2^{m/2} = \pm 1 \mod m + 1 . \tag{4.18}$$

But we already know that $2^0 = +1$, and, since 2 generates all the numbers mod $m + 1$, equation (4.18) has only one choice:

$$2^{m/2} = -1 \mod m + 1. \tag{4.19}$$

Equation (4.17) thus has a solution for $i = 0$, which is:

$$2^0 + 2^{m/2} = 0 \mod m + 1. \tag{4.20}$$

I said previously that the Type I ONB only needs a single vector to keep track of all the cross-product terms. The first entry in the table is at offset 0 (we're programming in C) and has value $m/2$.

We don't need to store any more of the values to solutions of equation (4.17), because we can multiply equation (4.20) by 2 and still have 0 on the right-hand side. For every i, the nonzero λ_{ij} element from equation (4.17) will always be:

$$j = m/2 + i \mod m . \tag{4.21}$$

We do have to tabulate the values from equation (4.16) once and then use those to look up the correct shift amounts. The first value for $i = 1$ is easy, since:

$$2 + 2^j = 1$$
$$2^j = -1 \tag{4.22}$$

so $j = m/2$ from equation (4.19).

After that we need to use antilog and log tables so we can find $2^i \mod m + 1$ easily and j from $1 - 2^i \mod m + 1$ just as easily. Let's look at a set of simple tables for $m = 4$. The antilog table (table 4.1) is really simple; just multiply i by 2 modulo 5 for each entry.

Table 4.1 Antilog Table for 2^i for $m = 4$

i	0	1	2	3	4
2^i	1	2	4	3	1

The log table (table 4.2) takes each value of 2^i as the index and places i as the entry. The zero offset isn't used in this case, but we'll find a use for that storage location later. The log table is sometimes called the Zech logarithm and has uses in other places such as spread-spectrum communications.

Table 4.2 Log Table for 2^i for $m = 4$

2^i	1	2	3	4
i	0	1	3	2

The code for generating the single vector we need is given below. It does two things. The first is a construction of log tables for 2^i mod $m + 1$. I have called the prime number $m + 1$ "`field_prime`" in the code. This must be set in a header file. The best thing to do is a simple addition to the `field2n.h` file with the following line:

```
#define field_prime (NUMBITS+1)
```

The second step is to create a lambda vector, which stores all the values of j for each value of i that satisfies equation (4.16). The lambda vector is a global and is defined using these lines:

```
INDEX   Lambda[2][field_prime];
INDEX   lg2_m;
```

A two-dimensional vector is not needed for the Type I ONB, but it is required for the Type II ONB. To make both types work with one multiply routine, equation (4.21) is copied into the `Lambda[0]` array. The `Lambda[1]` array holds the lambda vector solution to equation (4.16). The second global will be used in the inversion algorithm. It is the number of bits used to construct m—that is, $\log_2 m$.

Here's the code that creates the log table.

```
/* create Lambda [i,j] table. indexed by j, each entry contains the
value of i which satisfies 2^i + 2^j = 1 || 0 mod field_prime.  There are
two 16 bit entries per index j except for zero.  See references for
details.  Since 2^0 = 1 and 2^2n = 1, 2^n = -1 and the first entry would
be 2^0 + 2^n = 0.  Multiplying both sides by 2, it stays congruent to
zero.  So Half the table is unnecessary since multiplying exponents by
2 is the same as squaring is the same as rotation once.  Lambda[0][0] stores
n = (field_prime - 1)/2.  The terms congruent to one must be found via
lookup in the log table.  Since every entry for (i,j) also generates an
entry for (j,i), the whole 1D table can be built quickly.
*/

void genlambda()
```

```
{
        INDEX i, logof, n, index;
        INDEX log2[field_prime], twoexp;

        for (i=0; i<field_prime; i++) log2[i] = -1;

/*  build antilog table first  */

        twoexp = 1;
        for (i=0; i<field_prime; i++)
        {
                log2[twoexp] = i;
                twoexp = (twoexp << 1) % field_prime;
        }
```

Because the lambda matrix is symmetric, we only need to do half of it. The variable n in the code is used more than once, so it is convenient to define it as:

$$n = \frac{\text{field\_prime} - 1}{2} .$$ (4.23)

```
/*  compute n for easy reference */

        n = (field_prime - 1)/2;
```

Creating the log table takes four lines of code, only two of which are inside the loop. Each multiple of two is stored in the variable twoexp. The first line of code initializes twoexp to 1, since $2^0 = 1$. Log base 2 of 1 is 0, so the first entry in the loop sets offset 1 to the value 0.

The next line of code shifts twoexp left once, which is the same as multiplying by 2. That value is reduced modulo field_prime. The value of i is incremented at the bottom of the loop, and the next entry in the log table is log base 2 of twoexp, which equals i. All values of i will be stored somewhere in the log table and never overlap as long as the fundamental rule that 2 is a generator modulo field_prime $(m + 1)$ is not broken. It is awesome to watch the vector get filled using a debugger, a very controlled chaos.

```
/*  fill in first vector with indicies shifted by half table size  */
        Lambda[0][0] = n;
        for (i=1; i<field_prime; i++)
                Lambda[0][i] = (Lambda[0][i-1] + 1) % NUMBITS;
```

The above code fills in the Lambda[0] table. Starting with $i = 0$ in equation (4.21), each succeeding value is just 1 plus the previous value modulo NUMBITS. For memory-constrained systems using only Type I ONB math, only one vector is needed.

Here is the code that generates the single important lambda vector.

```
/*  initialize second vector with known values  */
```

```
        Lambda[1][0]= -1;                          /*  never used  */
        Lambda[1][1] = n;
        Lambda[1][n] = 1;

/*  loop over result space.  Since we want 2^i + 2^j = 1 mod field_prime
        it's a ton easier to loop on 2^i and look up i then solve the silly
        equations.  Think about it, make a table, and it'll be obvious.  */

        for (i=2; i<=n; i++) {
                index = log2[i];
                logof = log2[field_prime - i + 1];
                Lambda[1][index] = logof;
                Lambda[1][logof] = index;
        }
/*  last term, it's the only one which equals itself.  See references.  */
        Lambda[1][log2[n+1]] = log2[n+1];
```

Let's see how this works. The first thing to recognize is that equation (4.16) is symmetric. If entry $\lambda_{ij} = 1$, then $\lambda_{ji} = 1$ too. The counter i is taken as the value of 2^i in equation (4.16). Because we'll hit every value only once, the counter steps through every possible value of 2^i (mod $m + 1$). The variable index is log base 2 of i, so that tells us where to store the value of j in the Lambda vector.

Since $1 - 2^i$ modulo field_prime does not change if we add field_prime, we can write equation (4.16) as:

$$2^j = \text{field\_prime} + 1 - 2^i. \tag{4.24}$$

Take log base 2 of both sides, and we have the second line of code in the loop. This eliminates negative lookups, which would give the code some major headaches.

The last two lines in the loop simply set the entry point index to the value of j (called logof in the code) and entry point j to the value of index. The very last line in the above listing fills in the only nonsymmetric term.

```
/*  find most significant bit of NUMBITS.  This is int(log_2(NUMBITS)).
    Used in opt_inv to count number of bits.  */

    lg2_m = log_2((ELEMENT)(NUMBITS - 1));
}
```

Since genlambda() is only called once to set up the math parameters, the last chunk of code is a one of a kind initialization used by the inversion routine. We need to know the number of bits in m. This is the same routine used for degreeof in the previous chapter.

4.5 Type II optimal normal basis

For a Type II optimal normal basis we have the same number of terms. But both sets are scrambled, so we end up with two sets of vectors. As with a Type I ONB (discussed in section 4.4), let's start with the rules and work our way through the math. There are two possible Type II ONBs: I'll call them Type IIa and Type IIb.

A Type II optimal normal basis over F_{2^m} can be created if:

1 $2m + 1$ is prime

and either

2a 2 is primitive in $Z_{2m + 1}$

or

2b $2m + 1 \equiv 3 \mod 4$ and 2 generates the quadratic residues in $Z_{2m + 1}$

What does 2a mean? If we take $2^k \mod 2m + 1$ for $k = 0, 1, 2 \ldots, 2m - 1$ then we get every value in the range $[1 \ldots 2m]$ back. What does 2b mean? The first part is simple: The last two bits are set in the binary representation of the prime $2m + 1$. The second part means that even if $2^k \mod 2m + 1$ does not generate every element in the range $[0 \ldots 2m]$, we can at least take the square root mod $2m + 1$ of 2^k. To learn more about quadratic residues see [6, appendix 3].

For Type II ONB we need to modify the `field2n.h` header file again. To make life a bit simpler, I've added some conditional code. This allows all the modifications to work when needed. By simply changing `TYPE2` to `TYPE1` in one place the entire code package will compile correctly.

```
#define TYPE2

#ifdef TYPE2
#define field_prime          ((NUMBITS<<1)+1)
#else
#define field_prime          (NUMBITS+1)
#endif
```

To generate a Type II ONB we'll use two field elements from two different fields. First pick an element γ of order $2m + 1$ in $F_{2^{2m}}$. We'll use that to find β, which is in the field F_{2^m}. We won't actually have to find the γ element; we're just going to use it symbolically to help us create the λ matrix. Form the sum of $\gamma + \gamma^{-1}$. This element gives us the first element, β, of our normal basis. The interested reader should see [3] for proof.

The cross-product terms of $\beta^{2^i} \cdot \beta^{2^j}$ are:

$$\beta^{2^i} \cdot \beta^{2^j} = \left(\gamma^{2^i} + \gamma^{-2^i}\right)\left(\gamma^{2^j} + \gamma^{-2^j}\right) \tag{4.25}$$

which, multiplied out, gives:

$$= \left(\gamma^{2^i + 2^j} + \gamma^{-(2^i + 2^j)}\right) + \left(\gamma^{2^i - 2^j} + \gamma^{-(2^i - 2^j)}\right). \tag{4.26}$$

The next step is actually simple math, but it's close to magic without some background. The curious should see [7, 421] as well as [3] for proof that:

$$\gamma^{2^k} + \gamma^{-2^k} = (\gamma + \gamma^{-1})^{2^k}. \tag{4.27}$$

Accepting that bit of mathematical magic, we get:

$$\beta^{2^i} \cdot \beta^{2^j} = \beta^{2^k} + \beta^{2^{k'}} \qquad \text{if } 2^i \neq 2^j \mod 2m + 1 \tag{4.28}$$

$$= \beta^{2^k} \qquad \text{if } 2^i \equiv 2^j \mod 2m + 1. \tag{4.29}$$

In equations (4.28) and (4.29), k and k' are the two possible solutions to the multiplication of any two basis elements. That's what makes this normal basis optimal: It has the minimum number of possible terms. In the case of $2^i = 2^j$, the terms $\gamma^0 + \gamma^0$, in equation (4.26), cancel, because the exclusive-or of anything with itself is 0. In the case of $2^i \neq 2^j \mod 2m + 1$, at least one of these equations:

$$2^i + 2^j = 2^k \qquad \mod 2m + 1$$
$$2^i + 2^j = -2^k \qquad \mod 2m + 1 \tag{4.30}$$

will have a solution, and at least one of these equations:

$$2^i - 2^j = 2^{k'} \qquad \mod 2m + 1$$
$$2^i - 2^j = -2^{k'} \qquad \mod 2m + 1 \tag{4.31}$$

also has a solution.

In the case of $2^i = \pm 2^j \mod 2m + 1$, at least one of the following four equations has a solution:

$$2^i + 2^j \equiv 2^k \qquad \mod 2m + 1 \tag{4.32}$$

$$2^i - 2^j \equiv 2^k \qquad \mod 2m + 1 \tag{4.33}$$

$$2^i + 2^j \equiv -2^k \quad \mod 2m + 1 \tag{4.34}$$

$$2^i - 2^j \equiv -2^k \quad \mod 2m + 1 . \tag{4.35}$$

In the first set of equations, (4.30) and (4.31), there are two possible solutions, and in the second set of equations, (4.32) through (4.35), there is only one possible solution. It is easy to see that the equations are all similar, so instead of working with two different sets we can combine them and work with just one group of four equations. To build our λ matrix, we set $k = 0$ and find solutions to:

$$2^i + 2^j = 1 \tag{4.36}$$

$$2^i + 2^j = -1 \tag{4.37}$$

$$2^i - 2^j = 1 \tag{4.38}$$

$$2^i - 2^j = -1 . \tag{4.39}$$

As an example of Type IIa, take $2m + 1 = 19$. Then our field size $m = 9$. This will be the length of the λ matrix. The first thing we need to build are log and antilog tables.

Table 4.3   Powers of 2^i mod 19 (antilog)

i	0	1	2	3	4	5	6	7	8	9	10	11	12	13	14	15	16	17	18
2^i	1	2	4	8	16	13	7	14	9	18	17	15	11	3	6	12	5	10	1

The antilog table (table 4.3) takes an index, i, and returns $l = 2^i$ mod $2m + 1$. The log table (table 4.4) takes an index, l, and returns the value of i.

Table 4.4   Log base 2 of i modulo 19 (log table)

i	1	2	3	4	5	6	7	8	9	10	11	12	13	14	15	16	17	18
$\text{Log}_2(i)$	0	1	13	2	16	14	6	3	8	17	12	15	5	7	11	4	10	9

The code to compute the log table is as follows:

```
twoexp = 1;
for (i=0; i<field_prime; i++)
{
```

```
        log2[twoexp] = i;
        twoexp = (twoexp << 1) % field_prime;
    }
```

Note that the log table is built using 2^i modulo `field_prime` as the subscript, and the loop counter `i` is the value. This builds table 4.4 in the order of table 4.3. This is one of those things that can be really confusing, and I urge anyone who really wants to understand this to step through these few lines of code with a debugger.

To continue the example, let's start with $i = 1$ in equations (4.36) through (4.39). Writing down all four equations mod 19 and subtracting 2 from both sides gives us the following:

$$2^j = -1 = 18 \Rightarrow j = 9$$

$$2^j = -3 = 16 \Rightarrow j = 4$$

$$-2^j = -1 \quad \text{is} \quad 2^j = 1 \Rightarrow j = 0$$

$$-2^j = -3 \quad \text{is} \quad 2^j = 3 \Rightarrow j = 13$$

Since the λ matrix has only nine entries per column, the solutions for j must be in the range of 0 ... 8. Only two terms for j are less than 9. These are the two terms we need. So we have our first nonzero entries in the λ matrix: $\lambda_{1,0} = 1$ and $\lambda_{1,4} = 1$. All other entries, $\lambda_{1,j}$, must be 0.

Continuing in this manner we can find two values of j for each value of i, which give us nonzero entries in the λ matrix. We'll mark these with two vectors: Λ_0 and Λ_1. I'll call them `Lambda[0][]` and `Lambda[1][]` in the code. Each position in the Λ table corresponds to a value of i in cross-product term $\beta^{2^i} \cdot \beta^{2^j}$, and each entry is the matching value of j, which gives one of the terms in equation (4.28) that has k or $k' = 0$. The results are shown in table 4.5.

Table 4.5 Λ Vectors for $m = 9$

i	$\Lambda_0 = j_1$	$\Lambda_1 = j_2$
0	1	
1	4	0
2	4	7
3	6	8
4	2	1
5	6	5

Table 4.5 Λ Vectors for $m = 9$ (continued)

i	$\Lambda_0 = j_1$	$\Lambda_1 = j_2$
6	5	3
7	2	5
8	8	3

The choice of value in either column for any row does not really matter, since we are going to combine matching coefficients in the multiply routine eventually. Note that there are a total of $2m - 1$ terms. The zero entry will always be 1 for any Type II ONB. We'll fill in this spot just to make the code simple, but we'll take advantage of it when we do the actual multiply.

That's fairly straightforward. Now, let's look at a Type IIb ONB. When the field_prime is 23, for example, we have a Type II ONB, which is congruent to 3 mod 4 and in which 2 generates the quadratic residues of mod 23. Let's first look at the anti-log table (table 4.6) to see what this really means.

Table 4.6 Powers of 2^i mod 23 (antilog)

i	0	1	2	3	4	5	6	7	8	9	10	
2^i	1	2	4	8	16	9	18	13	3	6	12	

i	11	12	13	14	15	16	17	18	19	20	21	22
2^i	1	2	4	8	16	9	18	13	3	6	12	1

Note that only half the values of 1 … 22 appear in table 4.6. But if we take $23 - 2^i$ for all values greater than 11, we get the results shown in table 4.7.

Table 4.7 Powers of 2^i mod 23 (antilog)

i	0	1	2	3	4	5	6	7	8	9	10	
2^i	1	2	4	8	7	9	5	10	3	6	11	

	11	12	13	14	15	16	17	18	19	20	21	22
	1	2	4	8	7	9	5	10	3	6	11	1

Now, $23 - 2^i$ modulo 23 is just -2^i, which we use in equations (4.36) through (4.39). If, after building half the log table, we find that `twoexp` ($=2^i$) equals 1, then we know we will cycle through the same values of 2^i that we just finished. To solve this problem we can restart at $i = 1$ but do the subscript on negative values of 2^i. Since subscripts need to be positive (for us to fill in a useful table relative to the rest of the code anyway), we can start with `twoexp = field_prime - 1 = 2*NUMBITS`, which is congruent to -1.

The Type IIb routine proceeds as follows:

```
if (twoexp == 1)        /*  if so, then deal with quadradic residues */
{
        twoexp = 2*NUMBITS;
        for (i=0; i<NUMBITS; i++)
        {
                log2[twoexp] = i;
                twoexp = (twoexp << 1) % field_prime;
        }
}
```

This code fills in the rest of the log table. The final result for our example of modulo 23 is shown in table 4.8.

Table 4.8 Log base 2 of i modulo 23 (log)

i	1	2	3	4	5	6	7	8	9	10	11
$\text{Log}_2(i)$	0	1	8	2	6	9	4	3	5	7	10

i	12	13	14	15	16	17	18	19	20	21	22
$\text{Log}_2(i)$	10	7	5	3	4	9	6	2	8	1	0

Now, i and j are exponents of exponents. Don't be alarmed if you are confused—it seems pretty hairy at first sight. All we are doing is bookkeeping: tracking all the coefficients we need to add in order to compute the multiplication of two normal basis numbers. Since all we had to solve for was $k = 0$, instead of a complete matrix, we only need to store two vectors.

Once we have the log and antilog tables, creating the vectors is easy. Here is the code for generating the Λ vectors for a Type II ONB.

```
/*  Type II ONB initialization.  Fills 2D Lambda matrix.  */

void genlambda2()
{
        INDEX   i, logof[4], n, index,  k, j;
```

```
        INDEX   log2[field_prime], twoexp;

/*  build log table first.  For the case where 2 generates the quadradic
        residues instead of the field, duplicate all the entries to ensure
        positive and negative matches in the lookup table (that is, -k mod
        field_prime is congruent to entry field_prime + k).   */

        twoexp = 1;
        for (i=0; i<NUMBITS; i++)
        {
                log2[twoexp] = i;
                twoexp = (twoexp << 1) % field_prime;
        }
        if (twoexp == 1)          /*  if so, then deal with quadradic residues */
        {
                twoexp = 2*NUMBITS;
                for (i=0; i<NUMBITS; i++)
                {
                        log2[twoexp] = i;
                        twoexp = (twoexp << 1) % field_prime;
                }
        }
        else
        {
                for (i=NUMBITS; i<field_prime-1; i++)
                {
                        log2[twoexp] = i;
                        twoexp = (twoexp << 1) % field_prime;
                }
        }

/*  first element in vector 1 always = 1  */

        Lambda[0][0] = 1;
        Lambda[1][0] = -1;

/*  again compute n = (field_prime - 1)/2 but this time we use it to see if
        an equation applies   */

        n = (field_prime - 1)/2;

/*  as in genlambda for Type I we can loop over 2^index and look up index
        from the log table previously built.  But we have to work with 4
        equations instead of one and only two of those are useful.  Look up
        all four solutions and put them into an array.  Use two counters, one
        called j to step thru the 4 solutions and the other called k to track
        the two valid ones.

        For the case when 2 generates quadradic residues only 2 equations are
        really needed.  But the same math works due to the way we filled the
        log2 table.
*/

        twoexp = 1;
```

```
for (i=1; i<n; i++)
{
        twoexp = (twoexp<<1) % field_prime;
        logof[0] = log2[field_prime + 1 - twoexp];
        logof[1] = log2[field_prime - 1 - twoexp];
        logof[2] = log2[twoexp - 1];
        logof[3] = log2[twoexp + 1];
        k = 0;
        j = 0;
        while (k<2)
        {
                if (logof[j] < n)
                {
                        Lambda[k][i] = logof[j];
                        k++;
                }
                j++;
        }
}

/*  find most significant bit of NUMBITS.  This is int(log_2(NUMBITS)).
    Used in opt_inv to count number of bits.   */

    lg2_m = log_2((ELEMENT)(NUMBITS - 1));
}
```

The `genlambda2` routine is very similar to the previous `genlambda` routine. The main difference is that we now have to check four equations instead of one. The four equations are solved as a look up in the log table and saved in the `logof[]` array.

Since there are two solutions and four variables to check, we use two counters. The variable `j` counts over the `logof[]` array, and the variable `k` counts over the solutions. A solution is valid only if less than n. For Type IIb that's automatic, and only the first two equations will ever be used. But anything modulo `field_prime` will give us an index into the array in the range of 1 … 2*NUMBITS, and for Type IIa we have to check that we get the right two solutions.

Going from 2 to $m - 1$ and getting two solutions gives us $2m - 2$ terms. The first term is already known and is set at offset 0 in `Lambda[0][]`. So we have found all the terms that the mathematicians tell us must be there.

4.6 *Multiplication in practice*

The next question is: How do we multiply? The starting point is equation (4.13). Here it is again, so you don't have to flip back to find it:

$$c_k = \sum_{i=0}^{m-1} \sum_{j=0}^{m-1} a_{i+k} b_{j+k} \lambda_{ij0}. \tag{4.40}$$

From the previous efforts we know that there are only two values of j for each value of i (or vice versa, since multiplication is independent of order). Note that each subscript of a and b is shifted by the same value of k. This means we can shift all the a coefficients and all the b coefficients for any particular values of i and j to find one term for all the c coefficients.

An example will help. Let's take the $i = 2$ index of the Type II F_{2^9} example worked out before. From table 4.5 we have $\Lambda_{2,1} = 4$ and $\Lambda_{2,2} = 7$. Equation (4.13) has one explicit term, which looks like this:

$$c_k = \ldots + b_{2+k}(a_{4+k} + a_{7+k}) + \ldots. \tag{4.41}$$

Only one term is written down; the other (i, j) combinations are left out. For $k = 0$, the partial sum is $b_2(a_4 + a_7)$. For $k = 1$, the partial sum is $b_3(a_5 + a_8)$ and so on through $k = 9$. All of these bitwise manipulations can be done in parallel. What we have to do is shift the B vector right two places and multiply it with the sum of the A vector shifted right four and seven places. Graphically this appears as follows:

b_1	b_0	b_8	b_7	b_6	b_5	b_4	b_3	b_2
				$\bullet$				
$(a_3$	a_2	a_1	a_0	a_8	a_7	a_6	a_5	a_4
				$+$				
a_6	a_5	a_4	a_3	a_2	a_1	a_0	a_8	$a_7)$
$\downarrow$	$\downarrow$	$\downarrow$	$\downarrow$	$\downarrow$	$\downarrow$	$\downarrow$	$\downarrow$	$\downarrow$
c_8	c_7	c_6	c_5	c_4	c_3	c_2	c_1	c_0

The addition is performed by first using exclusive-or. The multiplication is performed using AND. Depending on machine size, we can do 8, 16, 32, or 64 coefficients simultaneously.

Since multiplication is commutative, we can choose either A or B to be summed. In the code, I shift B once for each term and use the count of that offset as the index into the lambda vector table to find each proper shift of A.

The first routine we need is a shift. This is similar to the previous `mul_shift` routines, but now we are actually rotating the bits. Going right, the least significant bit needs to be placed into the most significant bit. Going left we do the opposite. The two routines operate in place. Here are single bit rotation routines.

```
void rot_left(a)
FIELD2N *a;
{
        INDEX i;
        ELEMENT bit,temp;

        bit = (a->e[0] & UPRBIT) ? 1L : 0L;
        for (i=NUMWORD; i>=0; i--) {
           temp = (a->e[i] & MSB) ? 1L : 0L;
           a->e[i] = ( a->e[i] << 1) | bit;
           bit = temp;
        }
        a->e[0] &= UPRMASK;
}

void rot_right(a)
FIELD2N *a;
{
        INDEX i;
        ELEMENT bit,temp;

        bit = (a->e[NUMWORD] & 1) ? UPRBIT : 0L;
        SUMLOOP(i) {
           temp = ( a->e[i] >> 1)  | bit;
           bit = (a->e[i] & 1) ? MSB : 0L;
           a->e[i] = temp;
        }
        a->e[0] &= UPRMASK;
}
```

The first routine is actually a squaring operation, and the second is a square root operation in a normal basis. This is a great speed advantage over polynomial basis applications. The problem is that there are more things we have to do than just square and square root.

For every sum we need two shifts of A. So it is faster to compute all the shifts once and store them in a lookup table. This is the first `for()` loop in the `opt_mul` routine. This section of code would be much faster if implemented in assembler. It might even be possible to eliminate it for those processors that have barrel shifters.

```
/*  Generalized Optimal Normal Basis multiply.
        Assumes two dimensional Lambda vector already initialized.
        Will work for both type 1 and type 2 ONB.  Enter with pointers
        to FIELD2N a, b and result area c.  Returns with c = a*b over
        GF(2^NUMBITS).
*/

void opt_mul(a, b, c)
FIELD2N *a, *b, *c;
{
        INDEX           i, j;
        INDEX           k, zero_index, one_index;
```

```
ELEMENT          bit, temp;
FIELD2N          amatrix[NUMBITS], copyb;

/*  clear result and copy b to protect original  */

null(c);
copy(b, &copyb);
```

```
/*  To perform the multiply we need two rotations of the input a.
        Performing all the rotations once and then using the Lambda
        vector as an index into a table makes the multiply almost
        twice as fast.
*/

copy( a, &amatrix[0]);
for (i = 1;  i < NUMBITS;  i++)
{
        copy( &amatrix[i-1], &amatrix[i]);
        rot_right( &amatrix[i]);
}
```

The basic idea of the multiply is really simple: Look up the two terms we need from the shifted table, XOR them, then AND that with the present *B* vector. XOR this term with the *C* vector as a partial sum. Shift the *B* vector and repeat until all *n* partial terms have been summed with the result.

```
/*  Lambda[1][0] is non existent, deal with Lambda[0][0] as speical case.  */
        zero_index = Lambda[0][0];
        SUMLOOP (i) c->e[i] = copyb.e[i] & amatrix[zero_index].e[i];

/*  main loop has two lookups for every position.  */

        for (j = 1;  j<NUMBITS;  j++)
        {
                rot_right( &copyb);
                zero_index = Lambda[0][j];
                one_index = Lambda[1][j];
                SUMLOOP (i) c->e[i] ^= copyb.e[i] &
                        (amatrix[zero_index].e[i] ^ amatrix[one_index].e[i]);
        }
}
```

The code is very simple. Making it simple took a bit of math. And optimizing it for speed is obviously important but implementation dependent. For a Type I ONB, there is no need for two lookup vectors. In fact, we only need to perform the multiplication (AND) of *A* shifted half its length with *B* and take the "trace" of the result, which gets summed with the single lookup vector result [1] for a very high speed Type I ONB algorithm. (We'll get to the trace function in chapter 6; for ONB it is identical to a parity bit calculation.)

Following this code with a simple number as input will convince you that normal basis multiply scrambles bits really well. Here is a simple example. First we need a simple output routine, as follows:

```
void print_field( string, field)
char *string;
FIELD2N *field;
{
        INDEX i;

        printf("%s : ", string);
        SUMLOOP(i) printf("%8x ", field->e[i]);
        printf("\n");
}
```

The code example looks like this:

```
#define NUMBITS         131
#define TYPE2

main()
{
        FIELD2N         test1, test2, test3, test4;
        INDEX i;

#ifdef TYPE2
        genlambda2();
#else
        genlambda();
#endif
        null(&test1);
        null(&test2);
        test1.e[NUMWORD] = 0x1;
        SUMLOOP(i) test2.e[i] = 0x1;
        print_field("test1", &test1);
        print_field("test2", &test2);
        opt_mul (&test1, &test2, &test3);
        print_field("test3 = test1 * test2", &test3);
/* continued with inversion.... */
```

The output appears as follows:

```
test1 :        0        0        0        0        1
test2 :        1        1        1        1        1
test3 = test1 * test2 :        1   208008        0        1 12000022
```

But we are not done yet. To implement elliptic curves we need a complete field, and that requires an ability to compute an inverse over a normal basis.

4.7 Inversion over optimal normal basis

The history of inversion is a rather interesting one. When elliptic curves were first proposed, inversion was so slow a process that methods were suggested for avoiding inversion. These methods required ten or more multiplies, but this seemed (at the time) preferable to using an inversion process that took the time equivalent of 15 multiplies. See [4] under "projective coordinates."

In the late 1990s, several methods of computing inverses over polynomial basis and normal basis were published. The fastest inversion routines I have seen will perform as fast as, if not faster than, a single optimal normal basis multiply. In the future I expect we will see more algorithms that improve on higher-level math (at the elliptic curve level; see next chapter) and not worry too much about the lower-level processes other than to increase speed.

To begin with, let's look at a very straightforward method of inversion over a normal basis. The starting point is again mathematics.

The first weird thing to recognize is what 1 is in a normal basis:

$$1 = \sum_{i=0}^{m-1} \beta^{2^i} = \beta + \beta^2 + \beta^4 + \dots + \beta^{2^{m-1}}. \tag{4.42}$$

In other words, the fundamental constant, 1, is represented as *all bits set* in a normal basis. Here is a subroutine that will be useful later when we need 1 as a constant for any field size.

```
/*  One is not what it appears to be.  In any normal basis, "1" is the sum of
all powers of the generator.  So this routine puts ones to fill the number size
being used in the address of the FIELD2N supplied.  */

void one (place)

FIELD2N *place;

{
        INDEX i;

        SUMLOOP(i) place->e[i] = -1L;
        place->e[0] &= UPRMASK;
}
```

Adding 1 to any normal basis number is the same as exclusive-or against all bits set. This is simply the 1's complement of a number. So, adding 1 to a normal basis number amounts to flipping all the bits—not counting as we're used to.

With that under our belt, we now look for a way to compute an inverse. The rules are the same as normal math:

$$a \cdot a^{-1} = 1.$$

(4.43)

But "1" looks different. The first trick is to use Fermat's Theorem (see [4, 85]):

$$a^{-1} = a^{2^m - 2}.$$

(4.44)

At this point we could just exponentiate directly. But this would require m squarings and $m - 1$ multiplies. For m on the order of 200 this would be exceptionally slow. The following is a way around the problem.

Now, let's work up in the exponent, so we don't get too lost. Equation (4.44) can be transmogrified to:

$$-1 = 2^m - 2 \quad \mod m + 1.$$

(4.45)

This in turn can be factored as:

$$2^m - 2 = 2(2^{m-1} - 1).$$

(4.46)

Since this was factored in the exponent, we're really taking:

$$\left(a^{2^{m-1} - 1} \right)^2.$$

(4.47)

To continue, let's call $m - 1 = r_0$. Suppose r_0 is even. We can factor:

$$2^{r_0} - 1 = (2^{r_0/2} - 1)(2^{r_0/2} + 1).$$

(4.48)

Computing a to the power $2^{r_0/2} + 1$ is easy. This is just a rotation and a multiply. What if r_0 is odd? Then we take:

$$2^{r_0} - 1 = 2\left(2^{\frac{r_0 - 1}{2}} - 1 \right)\left(2^{\frac{r_0 - 1}{2}} + 1 \right) + 1.$$

(4.49)

Let's see what this means in the exponent again:

$$\left[\left(a^{2^{\frac{r_0 - 1}{2}} - 1} \right)^{2^{\frac{r_0 - 1}{2}} + 1} \right]^2 \cdot a.$$

(4.50)

OK, now DON'T PANIC! This isn't as bad as it looks. If r_0 is odd, we have an additional squaring operation (which is just a rotation for normal basis) and an extra multiply.

Let $r_1 = r_0/2$. This tosses the last bit. We can do the same expansion with r_1 as we did with r_0. This works us down a chain of multiplies and squarings until we get to r_l, where l is the number of bits in m. At that point, $r_l = 1$, and the innermost term is:

$$a^{2^1 - 1} = a.\tag{4.51}$$

The formula at each stage is easy to see if we look at the binary representation of m:

$$m = \sum_{k=0}^{l} m_k 2^k = m_l 2^l + m_{l-1} 2^{l-1} + \dots + m_0.\tag{4.52}$$

Just an integer that we're used to. But now let's look at each r_s in our expansion formula:

$$r_s = m_l 2^{l-s} + m_{l-1} 2^{l-1-s} + \dots + m_s\tag{4.53}$$

or, more formally:

$$r_s = \sum_{k=0}^{l-s} m_{k+s} 2^k.\tag{4.54}$$

Still not obvious? OK, let's pick an example: $m = 29 = 11101$ binary. Then:

$$
\begin{aligned}
m - 1 = 28 &= 11100 = r_0 \\
& 1110 = r_1 = 14 \\
& 111 = r_2 = 7 \\
& 11 = r_3 = 3 \\
& 1 = r_4 = 1
\end{aligned}
$$

All we are doing is sliding a window over the bit pattern from the first bit to the last. We can find $a^{2^{r_s} - 1}$ from the bit pattern of r_{s+1}. If the last bit of r_{s+1} is set, we need an extra squaring and multiply as in equation (4.50). If the last bit is clear, we only need to rotate the previous result by r_{s+1} and multiply.

A generic inversion routine won't be as fast as a specialized one. However, it is adaptable to any situation. The purpose of the following code is to show how to implement an inversion over an optimal normal basis. It will work for either Type I or Type II ONB.

```
/*  Generic ONB inversion routine.
        Input is pointer to ONB number.
        Output is inverse of input.
*/

void opt_inv(a, result)
FIELD2N *a, *result;
{
        FIELD2N  shift, temp;
        INDEX    m, s, r, rsft;

/*  initialize s to lg2_m computed in genlambda.  Since msb is always set,
        initialize result to input a and skip first math loop.
*/

        s = lg2_m - 1;
        copy( a, result);
        m = NUMBITS - 1;

/*  create window over m and walk up chain of terms  */

        while (s >= 0)
        {
                r = m >> s;
                copy( result, &shift);
                for (rsft = 0; rsft < (r>>1); rsft++) rot_left( &shift);
                opt_mul( result, &shift, &temp);
                if ( r&1 )              /* if window value odd  */
                {
                        rot_left( &temp);               /*  do extra square  */
                        opt_mul( &temp, a, result);    /*  and multiply  */
                }
                else copy( &temp, result);
                s--;
        }
        rot_left(result);                      /*  final squaring  */
}
```

There is a lot of room for optimization here. The basic idea is to convert powers of $2^x - 1$ to $2^{x/2} - 1$ until $x \to 0$, at which point we know how to do the multiply. The variable r holds the sliding window values of the binary representation of powers, as in equation (4.53). Because this is a normal basis, each of these powers is just a rotation. Instead of doing individual shifts, use a barrel shift operation and speed things up tremendously before the first opt_mul.

The mathematicians have shown that the total number of multiplies is $\{\log_2(m-1) + $ (the number of bits set in $m - 1) - 1\}$ [4, 86]. For the example of $m = 29$, that is $4 + 3 - 1 = 6$. As we go to more bits this grows slowly.

The inversion operation can be performed in about four multiplies using special polynomial bases. For this reason, one should look at polynomial basis if speed is the most important property. However, if RAM storage is more important than speed, optimal normal bases offer better resource utilization.

Continuing the multiply example from the previous section, let's see what the above routine does with an inverse. The code looks like this:

```
/*  ...... continued from multiply  */

    opt_inv( &test1, &test4);
    print_field("test4 = 1/test1", &test4);
    opt_mul( &test4, &test1, &test2);
    print_field("test1 * test4",&test2);
}
```

The initial value, its inverse, and the product for $m = 131$ for this example are as follows:

```
test1 :         0       0       0       0       1

test4 = 1/test1 :       3 74ab9127 9c16cbd4 7dfc5319 ac3b4203
test1 * test4 :         7 ffffffff ffffffff ffffffff ffffffff
```

It is clear that the inverse function is correct, because the product of an element and its inverse satisfies equation (4.42). This is an excellent way to test many low-level math routines. Every time you change a fundamental component, ensure that the simplest operations such as inversion and multiplication still work. I've found a great many bugs when the above simple code doesn't work.

There are specific values of NUMBITS for which an optimal normal basis exists. Table 4.9 shows a few values taken from an appendix of the IEEE P1363 draft dated November 1995. The first column is the field size, m, and the second column is the type. For cases that are both, I've left these as Type I.

Table 4.9 Optimal Normal Bases for F_{2^m}

m	T	m	T	m	T	m	T	m	T
82	I	148	I	226	I	306	II	393	II
83	II	155	II	230	II	309	II	398	II
86	II	158	II	231	II	316	I	410	II
89	II	162	I	233	II	323	II	411	II
90	II	172	I	239	II	326	II	413	II
95	II	173	II	243	II	329	II	414	II
98	II	174	II	245	II	330	II	418	I

Table 4.9   Optimal Normal Bases for F_{2^m} (continued)

m	T	m	T	m	T	m	T	m	T
99	II	178	I	251	II	338	II	419	II
100	I	179	II	254	II	346	I	420	I
105	II	180	I	261	II	348	I	426	II
106	I	183	II	268	I	350	II	429	I
113	II	186	II	270	II	354	II	431	II
119	II	189	II	273	II	359	II	438	II
130	I	191	II	278	II	371	II	441	II
131	II	194	II	281	II	372	I	442	I
134	II	196	I	292	I	375	II	443	II
135	II	209	II	293	II	378	I	453	II
138	I	210	I	299	II	386	II	460	I
146	II	221	II	303	II	388	I	466	I

Choosing between normal basis and polynomial basis depends on the application at hand. The fundamental properties are the same. Mathematically speaking the field representations are isomorphic and give the same security. In fact, by combining polynomial basis and optimal normal basis we can reduce the time of an inversion to the cost of a single multiply. That's a bit advanced for this stage of the game, so let's get into elliptic curves and see why having a fast inverse will be useful.

4.8 *References*

1 D. Dahm, personal communication and sci.crypt postings, September 1997.

2 R. Lidl and H. Niederreiter, *Introduction to Finite Fields and Their Applications* (Cambridge, England: Cambridge University Press, 1994).

3 R. C. Mullin, I. M. Onyszchuk, S. A. Vanstone, and R. M. Wilson, "Optimal Normal Bases in GF (p^n)," in *Discrete Applied Math*, vol. 22 (Amsterdam: Elsevier Science Publishers/North-Holland, 1988), 149–161.

4 A. J. Menezes, *Elliptic Curve Public Key Cryptosystems* (Boston: Kluwer Academic Publishers, 1993).

5 D. W. Ash, I. F. Blake, and S. A. Vanstone, "Low Complexity Normal Bases," in *Discrete Applied Math*, vol. 25 (Amsterdam: Elsevier Science Publishers/North-Holland, 1989), 191–210.

6 H. Reisel, *Prime Numbers and Computer Methods for Factorization*, 2d ed. (Boston: Birkhauser, 1987).

7 D. E. Knuth, *Seminumerical Algorithms* (Reading, MA: Addison-Wesley, 1981).

C H A P T E R   5

Elliptic curves

5.1 Mathematics of elliptic curves over real numbers   104

5.2 Mathematics of elliptic curves over prime fields   108

5.3 Mathematics of elliptic curves over Galois Fields   109

5.4 Polynomial basis elliptic curve subroutines   114

5.5 Optimal normal basis elliptic curve subroutines   118

5.6 Multiplication over elliptic curves   120

5.7 Balanced integer conversion code   122

5.8 Following the balanced representation   125

5.9 References   126

The mathematics associated with elliptic curves is old. Formerly "pure" with no practical applications, the math is very deep and fascinating. We will barely skim the surface in this book of what is a very beautiful and fruitful line of research, even today.

The use of elliptic curves for cryptography is not the same as their use for factoring or for solving Fermat's Theorem, as was announced a few years ago. We are going to use elliptic curves as an "algebra," or higher-level abstraction over all the math discussed previously. Chill out—it's not as scary as it sounds.

The magic of elliptic curves comes from the ability to take any two points on a specific curve, add them together, and get another point on the same curve. More importantly for cryptography is the difficulty of figuring out which two points were added together to get there. For the right choice of various parameters, that difficulty is exponential with key length. While the cryptanalyst must use very advanced mathematics to even begin attempting to crack a code, it does not take very many bits before the task is practically impossible. We will get into more details on that later.

5.1 Mathematics of elliptic curves over real numbers

First, let's start with what mathematicians call the "Weierstrass" form of an elliptic curve equation [1, chapter 3; 2, 15]:

$$y^2 + a_1 xy + a_3 y = x^3 + a_2 x^2 + a_4 x + a_6. \tag{5.1}$$

The variables x and y cover a plane. In fact, x and y can be complex, real, integers, polynomial basis, optimal normal basis, or any other kind of field element. That's part of what makes the math so deep.

Because we are only interested in a few special cases of equation (5.1), we'll stick to some really simple aspects of the math. The interested reader should seek out [1] or [3] to get a better background.

Let's start with something familiar: real numbers on the real plane. A simple form of equation (5.1), which will work for us, is:

$$y^2 = x^3 + a_4 x + a_6. \tag{5.2}$$

As an example, let's plot the curve for $a_4 = -7$, $a_6 = 5$ for x and y in the set of real numbers. To do this we only need to find:

$$y = \sqrt{x^3 - 7x + 5} \tag{5.3}$$

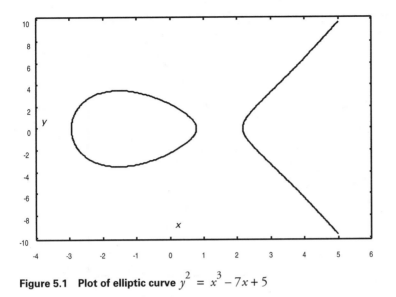

Figure 5.1 Plot of elliptic curve $y^2 = x^3 - 7x + 5$

and plot both negative and positive values of y for the same x. (See figure 5.1.)

This curve looks neat, but how do you create an algebra from something like that? The basic idea is to find a way to define "addition" of two points that lie on the curve such that the "sum" is another point on the curve. If we can do that, and invent an identity element, then we have an algebra—that is, a higher level of abstraction but following the same basic rules of math we're used to.

The identity element $\boldsymbol{O}_\infty$ is the point that, added to any point on the curve, gives the same point back:

$$P + \boldsymbol{O}_\infty = P. \tag{5.4}$$

It is also called "the point at infinity." Under normal conditions we'll never use this point in real code. The formulas to be presented later won't work if $\boldsymbol{O}_\infty$ is an input. However, we can still see if we are about to hit the identity element because:

$$-P = \boldsymbol{O}_\infty - (P). \tag{5.5}$$

To understand why mathematicians write down obvious equations like that, let's take a point $P = (x, y)$. The formula for finding $-P$, for the real valued equation (5.2), is:

$$-P = (x, -y). \tag{5.6}$$

Now, let's look at our previous example and see where the points P and $-P$ lie on our curve. (See figure 5.2.)

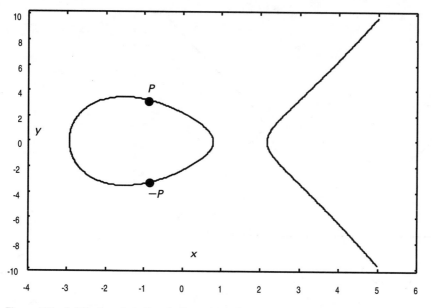

Figure 5.2 Arbitrary points *P* and *−P* on example curve

We see that the two points lie on top of each other. Now, let's do another obvious thing; we'll add:

$$P + (-P) = \mathbf{O}_\infty \ . \tag{5.7}$$

If we draw a line between P and $-P$, the next point on the curve it hits is "the point at infinity." In fact, we can define the addition of any two points on an elliptic curve by drawing a line between the two points and finding the point at which the line intersects the curve.

For the math to work, the negative of the intersection point is defined as the "elliptic sum." (See figure 5.3.) Mathematically we write:

$$R = P + Q. \tag{5.8}$$

There is a direct geometric relationship between every point on the curve. It is a good homework problem to derive the relationship, and it has been done elsewhere [3]. The rules are as follows:

Given:

$$P = (x_1, y_1) \tag{5.9}$$

$$Q = (x_2, y_2) \tag{5.10}$$

then:

CHAPTER 5   ELLIPTIC CURVES

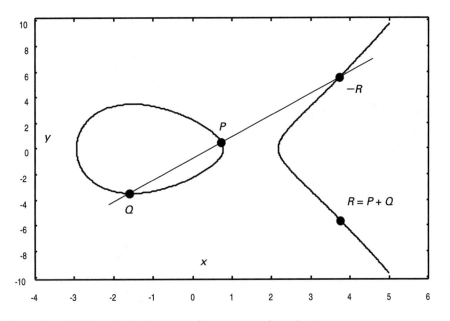

Figure 5.3 Addition of elliptic curve points over a real number curve

$$R = P + Q = (x_3, y_3) \tag{5.11}$$

where

$$x_3 = \theta^2 - x_1 - x_2 \tag{5.12}$$

$$y_3 = \theta(x_1 + x_3) - y_1 \tag{5.13}$$

$$\theta = \frac{y_2 - y_1}{x_2 - x_1} \qquad \text{if} \qquad P \neq Q \tag{5.14}$$

or

$$\theta = \frac{3x_1^2 + a_4}{2y_1} \qquad \text{if} \qquad P = Q. \tag{5.15}$$

Adding a point to itself is a special case; the line used is the tangent to the curve at
P. This is shown in figure 5.4. There is a lot of algebra required to derive the above equations from the figures. You can cheat and use relationships between the roots of cubic
equations, which are found in many reference books, and save most of the work (see [4,
17] and [5, chapter 6]).

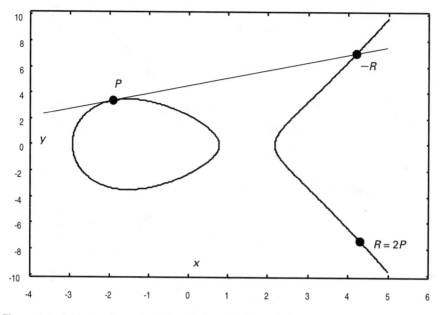

Figure 5.4 Addition of a point to itself, also called "doubling"

5.2 Mathematics of elliptic curves over prime fields

Section 5.1 is interesting, but what does it have to do with cryptography? It turns out that similar formulas work if we replace real numbers with finite fields. As a first attempt, let's look at finite fields generated using large primes (see [6] for more details).

The formulas stated previously don't change. But instead of using floating-point arithmetic we use a large number package and do all our calculations modulo a large prime. This method has been investigated by the academic community and is mentioned in the IEEE P1363 draft crypto standard. (See [6–8] for more details.)

The major advantage of choosing this for computing elliptic curves is that the number of points on the curve can be computed easily. We'll see why this is important later. For now, we'll define yet another new term: "the order of an elliptic curve." Since the math of a finite field only covers a finite set of points, the total number of points on an elliptic curve defined over a finite field is fixed. This number is sometimes called the "cardinality" of an elliptic curve.

The number of points on an elliptic curve over a finite field must satisfy Hasse's Theorem. Given a field, F_q, the order of the curve (N) will satisfy this equation [2, 5]:

$$|N - (q + 1)| \leq 2\sqrt{q}.$$ (5.16)

Another way to put it is:

$$q + 1 - 2\sqrt{q} \leq N \leq q + 1 + 2\sqrt{q}.$$ (5.17)

So the number of points on the curve is approximately the field size. For $q = 10^{40}$ this is a pretty big number, but there are other problems.

Both "order" and "cardinality" of a curve mean the total number of points that satisfy a specific equation. The order of a point is defined by the number of times we can add the point to itself until we get to the point at infinity. The order of any point on a curve will evenly divide the order of the curve. This amazing fact will be very useful later. (Math wizards will know that all Abelian groups have this property.) If the order of the curve is "smooth," meaning lots of small factors, it is easier to crack.

Koyama et al. [8] give a description of how to pick elliptic curves such that finding their order is trivial. The problem they encounter is in using these elliptic curves: The computational cost is much higher than for modular exponentiation (e.g., RSA). Furthermore, the crypto schemes they present rely on using two fields and computing the math using a public key created by multiplying two large primes. The net end result is that this method is vulnerable to factoring just as RSA is, and it is six times slower too.

There may be schemes proposed in the future that solve these problems. For now, we'll consider it an academic curiosity and move on to polynomial and normal basis mathematics over finite fields.

5.3 Mathematics of elliptic curves over Galois Fields

Let's look at elliptic curves over F_{2^n}. That means our constants are either polynomial or normal basis numbers. It also means we cannot use the simplified version of equation (5.1), which we used for real numbers, for our elliptic curve equations.

The mathematicians tell us [2, 22] that we need to use either this version:

$$y^2 + xy = x^3 + a_2 x^2 + a_6$$ (5.18)

or this version:

$$y^2 + y = x^3 + a_4 x + a_6.$$ (5.19)

Now, the mathematicians can prove to you (if you care to listen) that the second form above, equation (5.19), is called a "supersingular" curve. These forms have the advantage that they can be computed quickly. However, being a special class of curves, they have some very special properties. These properties make supersingular curves unsuitable for cryptography.

The curves of equation (5.18) are called "nonsupersingular." To date, no method of attack is known to be less than fully exponential in time. Curves of this form are excellent for cryptographic applications. One must be careful in choosing the coefficients to get maximum benefit of security. A poor choice can create a curve that is easier for the cryptanalyst to attack.

For equation (5.18) to be valid, a_6 must never be 0. However, a_2 can be 0. The rules are the same as before: Take any two points on the curve; draw a line between them; and the negative of the third point, which intersects both the curve and the line, is the "sum" of the first two points.

Unfortunately, this is very hard to picture. For example, the rule to negate a point $P = (x,y)$ is:

$$-P = (x, y + x). \tag{5.20}$$

Because x and y are now variables in the field F_{2^n}, the + operation is just an exclusive-or of all the bits of x with all the bits of y.

The rules for adding two points over F_{2^n} can be stated as follows [2, 87; 9]:
Given:

$$P = (x_1, y_1) \tag{5.21}$$

$$Q = (x_2, y_2) \tag{5.22}$$

then:

$$R = P + Q = (x_3, y_3) \tag{5.23}$$

if $P \neq Q$:

$$\theta = \frac{y_2 - y_1}{x_2 - x_1} \tag{5.24}$$

$$x_3 = \theta^2 + \theta + x_1 + x_2 + a_2 \tag{5.25}$$

$$y_3 = \theta(x_1 + x_3) - y_1 \tag{5.26}$$

if $P = Q$:

$$\theta = x + \frac{y}{x} \tag{5.27}$$

$$x_3 = \theta^2 + \theta + a_2 \tag{5.28}$$

$$y_3 = x^2 + (\theta + 1)x_3 . \tag{5.29}$$

In equations (5.27) through (5.29), I left off subscript $_1$ to the x and y terms because there is only one input point.

Note that the initial calculation of θ requires an inversion operation over the field F_{2^n}. Schroeppel et al. [9] showed how this could be done in very few operations for the right choice of polynomial basis. This inversion calculation is the most time consuming for any basis and has prevented elliptic curve cryptography from really moving into the main stream. Over the past two years there have been some great improvements in speeding up this calculation. At the end of this book, I'll present one of the more amazing solutions to this problem I've ever seen. It should make elliptic curve crypto one of the faster public key systems available.

Before getting to the code, let's do a little recap. The elliptic curve math we've talked about so far is a higher-level algebra that adds any two points on a curve and gets a third one. To keep things straight, we'll talk about "adding points" to indicate addition over an elliptic curve and we'll say "adding field elements" when discussing addition using F_{2^n} (exclusive-or). This is probably the most confusing part of discussions about elliptic curve math. Once you get it straight, it will seem pretty simple.

The subroutine schematic for this chapter is shown in figure 5.5. The polynomial basis is parallel to the normal basis in the sense that either can be used to implement the elliptic curve math. Once you pick which basis to use, the choice of subroutines is fixed. Simple routines from chapters 3 and 4 are included in both versions, and this is seen as a dependency in the schematic.

After describing the definitions for points and curves, I'll go into code that is common to both polynomial and normal basis math, including some simple output routines. Then I'll get into sums of points over curves: first with polynomials and then with normal basis representations. Then I'll get into the code that does multiplication.

For code, the first thing we need to define is a point and the second is a curve. Our elliptic math header file, `eliptic.h` looks like this:

```
/******   eliptic.h   *****/
/************************************************************
*                                                          *
*       These are structures used to create elliptic curve        *
*  points and parameters.  "form" is a just a fast way to check *
```

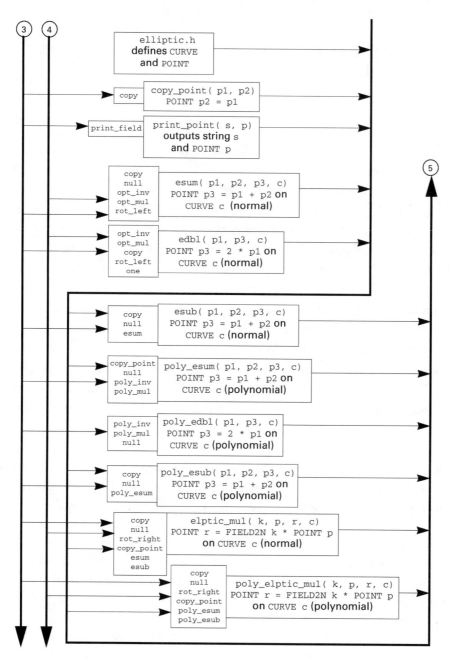

Figure 5.5 Subroutine schematic

```
*    if a2 == 0.                                                    *
*              form            equation                             *
*                                                                   *
*                0             y^2 + xy = x^3 + a_6                  *
```

```
*               1               y^2 + xy = x^3 + a_2*x^2 + a_6      *
*                                                                  *
***************************************************************/

typedef struct
{
        INDEX    form;
        FIELD2N  a2;
        FIELD2N  a6;
} CURVE;

/*  coordinates for a point  */

typedef struct
{
        FIELD2N  x;
        FIELD2N  y;
} POINT;
```

A point is defined as an (x,y) pair over the field F_{2^n}. From here on we'll use the math of chapters 3 or 4 to operate on these values and to find new ones.

A curve is defined from equation (5.18). If you've looked at equations (5.21) through (5.29) for summing and doubling, you'll notice that a_6 in equation (5.18), does not enter into them anywhere. The choice of a_2 and a_6 does have cryptographic implications, so we'll save that for the next chapter. The value of the INDEX variable form is 0 for a2 = 0. I originally thought it would be useful for other possible curve formulas, but the forms listed above turn out to be the best possible for cryptographic use.

Let's implement equation (5.20) first, the negative of an elliptic curve point.

```
void eneg (p)
FIELD2N  *p;
{
        register     INDEX    i;

        SUMLOOP (i)   p-> y.e[i]   ^= p->x.e[i];
}
```

This routine steps through every element in the stored array and XOR's the x component with the y component. This negates the point in place. Because this is so simple, we don't really need to use eneg, but you'll see it in the subtraction routine as a single line of code.

One common routine we need for both polynomial and normal basis is very simple: It just copies a point from one storage array to another.

```
/*  need to move points around, not just values.  Optimize later.  */

void copy_point (p1, p2)
POINT *p1, *p2;
```

```
{
        copy (&p1->x, &p2->x);
        copy (&p1->y, &p2->y);
}
```

Here are three simple routines that I have found useful for debugging code. The only purpose is to see data printed out in a quick-and-dirty format. The first routine prints out a hex dump of a FIELD2N variable, the second prints out a POINT, and the third prints out the data of a CURVE. Feel free to change these to whatever your taste desires.

```
void print_field( string, field)
char *string;
FIELD2N *field;
{
        INDEX i;

        printf("%s : ", string);
        SUMLOOP(i) printf("%8x ", field->e[i]);
        printf("\n");
}

void print_point( string, point)
char *string;
POINT *point;
{
        printf("%s\n", string);
        print_field( "x", &point->x);
        print_field( "y", &point->y);
        printf("\n");
}
void print_curve( string, curv)
char *string;
CURVE *curv;
{
        printf("%s\n", string);
        printf("form = %d\n", curv->form);
        if (curv->form) print_field( "a2", &curv->a2);
        print_field( "a6", &curv->a6);
        printf("\n");
}
```

Each routine expects a string pointer and a structure pointer for arguments. All outputs from test code in this book are printed with these simple subroutines.

5.4 Polynomial basis elliptic curve subroutines

Next, let's implement equations (5.24) through (5.26) using the polynomial subroutines of chapter 3. To prevent the math package from going berserk I've defined O_∞ to be

(0,0). Since (0,0) cannot be on any nonsupersingular curve, it can be used as the point at infinity. On entrance to the summation routine we first check to see if either point is O_∞. If it is, the answer is the other point.

Here is the summation routine for polynomial math.

```
/*****************************************************************************
 *                                                                           *
 *     Implement elliptic curve point addition for polynomial basis form.    *
 *     This follows R. Schroeppel, H. Orman, S. O'Mally, "Fast Key Exchange with*
 *     Elliptic Curve Systems", CRYPTO '95, TR-95-03, Univ. of Arizona, Comp. *
 *     Science Dept.                                                          *
 *****************************************************************************/

void poly_esum (p1, p2, p3, curv)
POINT    *p1, *p2, *p3;
CURVE    *curv;
{
    INDEX   i;
    FIELD2N x1, y1, theta, onex, theta2;
    ELEMENT check;

/*  check if p1 or p2 is point at infinity  */

        check = 0;
        SUMLOOP(i) check |= p1->x.e[i] | p1->y.e[i];
        if (!check)
        {
                copy_point( p2, p3);
                return;
        }
        check = 0;
        SUMLOOP(i) check |= p2->x.e[i] | p2->y.e[i];
        if (!check)
        {
                copy_point( p1, p3);
                return;
        }
```

The lines that compute $\theta = (y_1 + y_2)/(x_1 + x_2)$ also check to see if the sum $x_1 + x_2$ is 0. The error check only tells us if the input x field elements are identical. Since we are not doubling, this error check assumes we are adding P to $-P$. The result is the point at infinity. If we should be doubling, it is an error at a higher level.

```
/*  compute theta = (y_1 + y_2)/(x_1 + x_2)  */

    null(&x1);
    null(&y1);
    check = 0;
    SUMLOOP(i)
    {
            x1.e[i] = p1->x.e[i] ^ p2->x.e[i];
```

```
            y1.e[i] = p1->y.e[i] ^ p2->y.e[i];
            check |= x1.e[i];
    }
    if (!check)    /* return point at infinity  */
    {
        null(&p3->x);
        null(&p3->y);
        return;
    }
```

The error check does prevent us from attempting to invert 0. The θ value is computed first. The check for the value of `curv->form` is performed once, and the loop contains only the terms required to create the sum. The result is the value for x_3 in equation (5.25).

```
    poly_inv( &x1, &onex);
    poly_mul( &onex, &y1, &theta);   /*  compute y_1/x_1 = theta */
    poly_mul(&theta, &theta, &theta2);   /* then theta^2  */

/*  with theta and theta^2, compute x_3  */

    if (curv->form)
                SUMLOOP (i)
                p3->x.e[i] = theta.e[i] ^ theta2.e[i] ^ p1->x.e[i] ^ p2->x.e[i]
                       ^ curv->a2.e[i];
    else
                SUMLOOP (i)
                p3->x.e[i] = theta.e[i] ^ theta2.e[i] ^ p1->x.e[i]
                        ^ p2->x.e[i];

/*  next find y_3  */

    SUMLOOP (i) x1.e[i] = p1->x.e[i] ^ p3->x.e[i];
    poly_mul( &x1, &theta, &theta2);
    SUMLOOP (i) p3->y.e[i] = theta2.e[i] ^ p3->x.e[i] ^ p1->y.e[i];
}
```

The last three lines of code implement equation (5.26). All field elements are handled as members of the field modulo `poly_prime`, the irreducible polynomial. The (x,y) point value is returned in the designated location.

OK, now let's code up equations (5.27) through (5.29). This time there is one point of input, one curve input, and one point as output for $P_3 = 2P_1$.

```
/*  elliptic curve doubling routine for Schroeppel's algorithm over polymomial
       basis.  Enter with p1, p3 as source and destination as well as curv
       to operate on.  Returns p3 = 2*p1.
*/

void poly_edbl (p1, p3, curv)
POINT *p1, *p3;
CURVE *curv;
```

```
{
    FIELD2N  x1, y1, theta, theta2, t1;
    INDEX    i;
    ELEMENT  check;

    check = 0;
    SUMLOOP (i) check |= p1->x.e[i];
    if (!check)
    {
        null(&p3->x);
        null(&p3->y);
        return;
    }

/*  first compute theta = x + y/x   */

    poly_inv( &p1->x, &x1);
    poly_mul( &x1, &p1->y, &y1);
    SUMLOOP (i) theta.e[i] = p1->x.e[i] ^ y1.e[i];

/*  next compute x_3   */

    poly_mul( &theta, &theta, &theta2);
    if(curv->form)
        SUMLOOP (i) p3->x.e[i] = theta.e[i] ^ theta2.e[i] ^ curv->a2.e[i];
    else
        SUMLOOP (i) p3->x.e[i] = theta.e[i] ^ theta2.e[i];

/*  and lastly y_3   */

    theta.e[NUMWORD] ^= 1;                    /*  theta + 1 */
    poly_mul( &theta, &p3->x, &t1);
    poly_mul( &p1->x, &p1->x, &x1);
    SUMLOOP (i) p3->y.e[i] = x1.e[i] ^ t1.e[i];
}
```

This routine is a straightforward copy of the equations. Adding 1 to the `theta` value is simple; we just flip the last bit. Again, we check to see if the input attempts to double a zero x value. The routine returns the point at infinity if so. That this is the correct value is obvious from equation (5.18). The point $(0, \sqrt{a_6})$ is on the curve, and, since $-P = (x, y + x)$, we have a point that is its own negative. Doubling this point is the same as adding the negative of the same point, which gives us the point at infinity.

Finally, we need to be able to subtract two points. Just as we can negate and add with integers, this routine negates the second point, as in equation (5.20), and adds it to the first point. Here's the code.

```
/*  subtract two points on a curve.  just negates p2 and does a sum.
    Returns p3 = p1 - p2 over curv.
*/

void poly_esub (p1, p2, p3, curv)
```

```
POINT    *p1, *p2, *p3;
CURVE    *curv;
{
    POINT   negp;
    INDEX   i;

    copy ( &p2->x, &negp.x);
    null (&negp.y);
    SUMLOOP(i) negp.y.e[i] = p2->x.e[i] ^ p2->y.e[i];
    poly_esum (p1, &negp, p3, curv);
}
```

Now let's take a quick look at the same routines transformed to work with normal basis representations.

5.5 *Optimal normal basis elliptic curve subroutines*

Equations (5.24) through (5.29) can also be implemented using optimal normal basis field elements. Instead of calling the polynomial subroutines, we call the normal basis field element addition and multiplication routines.

Here is the code for adding two points.

```
void esum (p1, p2, p3, curv)
POINT    *p1, *p2, *p3;
CURVE    *curv;
{
    INDEX   i;
    FIELD2N x1, y1, theta, onex, theta2;

/*  compute theta = (y_1 + y_2)/(x_1 + x_2)   */

    null(&x1);
    null(&y1);
    SUMLOOP(i)
    {
            x1.e[i] = p1->x.e[i] ^ p2->x.e[i];
            y1.e[i] = p1->y.e[i] ^ p2->y.e[i];
    }
    opt_inv( &x1, &onex);
    opt_mul( &onex, &y1, &theta);
    copy( &theta, &theta2);
    rot_left(&theta2);

/*  with theta and theta^2, compute x_3   */

    if (curv->form)
            SUMLOOP (i)
            p3->x.e[i] = theta.e[i] ^ theta2.e[i] ^ p1->x.e[i] ^ p2->x.e[i]
```

```
                    ^ curv->a2.e[i];
    else
            SUMLOOP (i)
            p3->x.e[i] = theta.e[i] ^ theta2.e[i] ^ p1->x.e[i] ^ p2->x.e[i];
/*  next find y_3  */

    SUMLOOP (i) x1.e[i] = p1->x.e[i] ^ p3->x.e[i];
    opt_mul( &x1, &theta, &theta2);
    SUMLOOP (i) p3->y.e[i] = theta2.e[i] ^ p3->x.e[i] ^ p1->y.e[i];
}
```

The only real difference here is the squaring of theta. This is a simple rotation. The opt_inv routine given in chapter 4 is a bit slow, but the call to it won't change if we replace it with something faster. Other than the replacement calls to opt_* routines instead of poly_* routines, the code is almost the same as previously described.

Here is the code to double a point using optimal normal basis mathematics.

```
/*  elliptic curve doubling routine for Schroeppel's algorithm over normal
    basis.  Enter with p1, p3 as source and destination as well as curv
    to operate on.  Returns p3 = 2*p1.
*/

void edbl (p1, p3, curv)
POINT *p1, *p3;
CURVE *curv;
{
    FIELD2N  x1, y1, theta, theta2, t1;
    INDEX    i;

/*  first compute theta = x + y/x  */

    opt_inv( &p1->x, &x1);
    opt_mul( &x1, &p1->y, &y1);
    SUMLOOP (i) theta.e[i] = p1->x.e[i] ^ y1.e[i];

/*  next compute x_3  */

    copy( &theta, &theta2);
    rot_left(&theta2);
    if(curv->form)
            SUMLOOP (i) p3->x.e[i] = theta.e[i] ^ theta2.e[i] ^ curv-
>a2.e[i];
    else
            SUMLOOP (i) p3->x.e[i] = theta.e[i] ^ theta2.e[i];

/*  and lastly y_3  */

    one( &y1);
    SUMLOOP (i) y1.e[i] ^= theta.e[i];
    opt_mul( &y1, &p3->x, &t1);
    copy( &p1->x, &x1);
    rot_left( &x1);
```

```
    SUMLOOP (i) p3->y.e[i] = x1.e[i] ^ t1.e[i];
}
```

The major differences here are, again, that the squaring operation is only a rotation and the way we add 1. The subroutine one is called to create the constant first and then it is added to theta. This takes a few more steps, but the squaring operation makes up for it.

Finally, we subtract two points. This is the same as the polynomial math routine, but we have to call the optimal normal basis algorithms to get the right answers.

```
void esub (p1, p2, p3, curv)
POINT    *p1, *p2, *p3;
CURVE    *curv;
{
    POINT    negp;
    INDEX    i;

    copy ( &p2->x, &negp.x);
    null (&negp.y);
    SUMLOOP(i) negp.y.e[i] = p2->x.e[i] ^ p2->y.e[i];
    esum (p1, &negp, p3, curv);
}
```

5.6 *Multiplication over elliptic curves*

The next idea we need to look at is multiplication over an elliptic curve. If not *the* most confusing term, certainly the idea of multiplying points is a touch weird. In fact, the idea refers to computing:

$$Q = kP \tag{5.30}$$

where Q and P are points on an elliptic curve and k is an integer. What this really means is that we add P to itself k times.

Some people have a hard time with the term "multiplication" in this context. After all, we are mixing integers and points, so they can't really be multiplied. But this is where I think the mathematicians have named it correctly. When we multiply 3 times 5, we simply sum 5 plus 5 plus 5. That is multiplication by definition. When we add point P plus P plus P, we have added P three times, so why not call it 3 times P? Just as with multiplication of integers, there are more efficient ways to find the final answer than doing the straight sum.

Before getting into efficient methods of computing elliptic curve multiplication, let's review again what we have in terms of mathematics.

1 An elliptic curve is defined over some field, F_q, where q is a large prime or 2^n.

2 The math used to compute addition of points on a particular elliptic curve is performed using a field.

3 The elliptic curve itself—that is, the points on it—forms a cyclic group (a field) also.

The last item is important, because the integer k in equation (5.30) need not be larger than the "order" of the point P. In fact, we can use modular math and reduce k modulo the order of P before doing anything else and save a great deal of processing time.

Unfortunately, finding the order of a point is not so easy. There has been a great deal of research performed in the late 1990s to reduce the effort needed to compute the order of a point. The order of any particular point will be one of the factors that compose the cardinality of the curve. Mathematicians use the symbol E to denote equation (5.18) (or any elliptic curve) and the combination #E to denote the order of an elliptic curve.

Factoring is an important field for cryptographers. The mathematics of factoring will not be described here (see [10] and references therein to get into factoring). Elliptic curves with specific properties are needed for factoring large numbers. In turn, factoring algorithms are needed for finding the properties of elliptic curves!

If we do not know the order of a point P we can still compute equation (5.30), but we may not be as efficient as we could be. Be warned that you may find the order of a point by accident. If N is the order of a point, then $NP = \mathbf{O}_\infty$ over an elliptic curve. A good crypto system will avoid this case if N is initially unknown and save N for future reference. For large field sizes the probability is exceptionally small that you'll find this by accident, so it's not really worth the effort.

So much for a few preliminaries. Let's see how to perform an elliptic multiply. This algorithm comes from [11]. The first assumption we need to make is that the number k, which is an integer, will fit into the same number of bits as our FIELD2N. This is a valid assumption based on Hasse's Theorem, equation (5.16).

Let's first look at the math. Suppose we want to compute $15P$. We can expand this as:

$$15P = P + 2(P + 2(P + 2P)). \tag{5.31}$$

What we have done here is a binary expansion of 15. Since $15 = 1111_2$, starting the chain with 0, the most significant bit is set so we add P. Then we double the result (2*) and add P, repeating until all bits are done. This is exactly the same algorithm used with the mod_exp routine of chapter 2. We just replace multiplication with addition over an elliptic curve. This expansion requires three doubling operations and three sums, a total of six operations instead of 15.

Now for Koblitz's, trick [11]: $15 = 16 - 1$. $15P = (2P)2 * 2 * 2 - P$. There are now only five operations instead of six. On top of that a doubling operation is slightly faster than a summing operation. Koblitz calls this a "balanced" expansion. The algorithm converts a string of set bits to a string of zero bits followed by -1. To make this clear, I'll show another example:

$$10045 * P = 10011100111101_2 * P. \tag{5.32}$$

The last bit in the chain of set bits is replaced with -1, all the other bits are replaced with 0's, and the leading 0 is set. So the balanced representation becomes:

$$1\ 0\ 1\ 0\ 0\ -1\ 0\ 1\ 0\ 0\ 0\ -1\ 0\ 1 \tag{5.33}$$

and the operations are:

$$(((((2P * 2 + P)2 * 2 * 2 - P)2 * 2 + P)2 * 2 * 2 * 2 - P)2 * 2 + P. \tag{5.34}$$

To follow this example, start with 0. Find the first bit (always set to $+1$) and add P. Going to the next bit we multiply by 2. That bit is clear, so just multiply by 2 again. The next bit is $+1$, so add P. Then multiply the whole thing by 2. That bit is clear, as is the next one, so we just multiply by 2 again. The next position is -1, so subtract P from the total this time. And so on down the chain.

Since 0, 1, and -1 all need to be represented, we need to expand the integer k from single bits to multiple bits. There are many ways to do this. For our purposes we'll use an array of characters. Clearly there is room for optimization to reduce RAM usage for embedded systems.

5.7 Balanced integer conversion code

A very recent paper [12] describes a simple way to create the balanced representation. It is called "nonadjacent form" in the paper, but it means the same thing. The method is called "Algorithm 2" and is shown in figure 5.6 in a slightly modified form. The input is n; the balanced array output is S.

Creating the balanced version of the integer comprises the major chunk of code in the elliptic multiply routine. It is also common to both polynomial and optimal normal basis versions. Let's look at this segment of code first.

The inputs to the elliptic multiply routine are the integer k, the point P, and the curve we are working with. The output is the new point $R = kP$. Internal to the routine we need the balanced array, a temporary working point, and various INDEX counters.

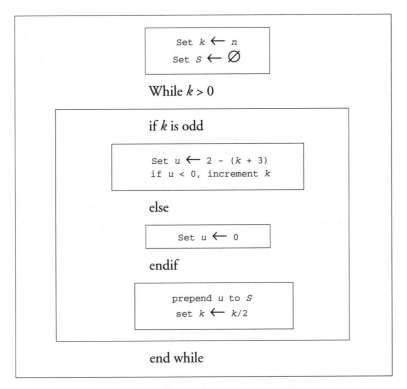

Figure 5.6 Algorithm 2 (slightly modified)

```
void  elptic_mul(k, p, r, curv)
FIELD2N        *k;
POINT          *p, *r;
CURVE          *curv;
{
       char           blncd[NUMBITS+1];
       INDEX          bit_count, i;
       ELEMENT        notzero;
       FIELD2N        number;
       POINT          temp;

/*  make sure input multiplier k is not zero.
       Return point at infinity if it is.
*/
       copy( k, &number);
       notzero = 0;
       SUMLOOP (i) notzero |= number.e[i];
       if (!notzero)
       {
              null (&r->x);
              null (&r->y);
              return;
       }
```

After saving a copy of the input, the first thing I do is check to see if an attempt is being made to multiply by 0. If so, the routine returns null for x and y values of the result point. Some people suggest that (0,0) be used to represent the point at infinity, so this may work out OK. It may be better to simply flag this as an error. Be careful to deal with these exceptions in a manner consistent with your application. I have used (0,0) with the polynomial package, but not the normal basis math. In normal basis this does not seem to be a problem (yet).

The next portion of code implements the above algorithm. I use the variable bit_count to keep track of which bit is being checked. The variable u is not required, because the compiler can do the ELEMENT to char conversion correctly for positive or negative 1. (Note for AIX users: This did not work, because the compiler assumed unsigned char, so check the output of your compiler compared with this code.)

```
/*  convert integer k (number) to balanced representation.
        Called non-adjacent form in "An Improved Algorithm for
        Arithmetic on a Family of Elliptic Curves", J. Solinas
        CRYPTO '97. This follows algorithm 2 in that paper.
*/
        bit_count = 0;
        while (notzero)
        {
/*  if number odd, create 1 or -1 from last 2 bits  */

                if ( number.e[NUMWORD] & 1 )
                {
                        blncd[bit_count] = 2 - (number.e[NUMWORD] & 3);

/*  if -1, then add 1 and propagate carry if needed  */

                        if ( blncd[bit_count] < 0 )
                        {
                                for (i=NUMWORD; i>=0; i--)
                                {
                                        number.e[i]++;
                                        if (number.e[i]) break;
                                }
                        }
                }
                else
                        blncd[bit_count] = 0;

/*  divide number by 2, increment bit counter, and see if done  */

                number.e[NUMWORD] &= ~0 << 1;
                rot_right( &number);
                bit_count++;
                notzero = 0;
                SUMLOOP (i) notzero |= number.e[i];
        }
```

The only minor problem we have here with the algorithm is the increment step. This zeros out a sequence of ones. If an ELEMENT goes to 0, then we have to propagate a carry. Since we are only adding 1, the only time we actually have to propagate the carry is if we add 1 to an ELEMENT that has all bits set.

The last bit of number is cleared before we call the rot_right function. This performs the division with a predefined function, which is in both the polynomial and normal basis listings. The variable bit_count is bumped, and then I create the check to see if the algorithm is finished.

The last step is to unwind the balanced representation to perform the multiply. This is the same for both polynomial and normal basis, but we call different routines.

5.8 Following the balanced representation

The bit_count variable has to be decremented, because the last time through the above loop it was incremented once too many. This points us to the first entry in the balanced representation, which must be set. So we only need to copy the input point to the result. From there on, we only need to double the result and step through the blncd array to add, subtract, or do nothing as appropriate.

```
/*  now follow balanced representation and compute kP  */

        bit_count--;
        copy_point(p,r);            /* first bit always set */
        while (bit_count > 0)
        {
          edbl(r, &temp, curv);
          bit_count--;
          switch (blncd[bit_count])
          {
            case 1: esum (p, &temp, r, curv);
                            break;
            case -1: esub (&temp, p, r, curv);
                             break;
            case 0: copy_point (&temp, r);
          }
        }
}
```

Creating the balanced representation does not take too long. The doubling and summing loop takes the most time. Improving the efficiency of these routines, and especially inversion, will help improve overall throughput. Each time the loop ends, the result is stored in the destination POINT r. At the end of the loop, we can exit the routine.

The polynomial version of the elliptic curve multiplication routine ends as follows:

```
/*  now follow balanced representation and compute kP  */

        bit_count--;
        copy_point(p,r);        /* first bit always set */
        while (bit_count > 0)
        {
          poly_edbl(r, &temp, curv);
          bit_count--;
          switch (blncd[bit_count])
          {
            case 1: poly_esum (p, &temp, r, curv);
                            break;
            case -1: poly_esub (&temp, p, r, curv);
                            break;
            case 0: copy_point (&temp, r);
          }
        }
}
```

This is exactly the same as the optimal normal basis routines, but we replace the sum, double, and subtract routines with their polynomial equivalents.

As far as the math goes, we now have the core routines we need to implement elliptic curve crypto systems. The first choice is our basis: either polynomial or normal. The tradeoff between these is a tradeoff between speed (polynomial) or space (normal). Polynomial basis gives more speed but takes twice as much RAM, because multiplication doubles the number of bits stored before being reduced modulo the basis function. Normal basis uses minimal RAM but takes longer to compute, because the inversion routine of chapter 4 is slower. A combination of both can work the best, but this makes things a bit more complicated.

The second choice is our curve. There are important cryptographic implications here, and these need to be discussed in detail in the next chapter. Choosing points on the curve is somewhat arbitrary, but we don't want to choose points of particularly low order. So on with the show!

5.9 *References*

1 J. H. Silverman, *The Arithmentic of Elliptic Curves* (New York: Springer-Verlag, 1985).

2 A. J. Menezes, *Elliptic Curve Public Key Cryptosystems* (Boston: Kluwer Academic Publishers, 1993).

3 N. Koblitz, *Introduction to Elliptic Curves and Modular Forms* (New York: Springer-Verlag, 1993).

4 S. Abramowitz, *Handbook of Mathematical Fuctions*, 9th ed. (New York: Dover, 1972), 17.

5 N. Koblitz, *A Course in Number Theory and Cryptography* (New York: Springer-Verlag, 1987).

6   F. Morain, "Building Cyclic Elliptic Curves Modulo Large Primes," in *EUROCRYPT '91* (Berlin: Springer-Verlag, 1991), 328–336).

7   T. Beth and F. Schaefer, "NonSuper Singular Elliptic Curves for Public Key Cryptosystems," in *EUROCRYPT '91* (Berlin: Springer-Verlag, 1991), 316–327.

8   K. Koyama, U. M. Maurer, T. Okamoto, and S. A. Vanstone, "New Public Key Schemes Based on Elliptic Curves over the Ring Z_n," in *EUROCRYPT '91* (Berlin: Springer-Verlag, 1991), 252–266.

9   R. Schroeppel, H. Orman, and S. O'Mally, "Fast Key Exchange with Elliptic Curve Systems," TR-95-03 (Tucson, AZ: University of Arizona, Computer Sciences Department, 1995). (Also appears in *CRYPTO '95* [New York: Springer-Verlag, 1995].)

10 H. Riesel, *Prime Numbers and Computer Methods for Factorization*, 2d ed. (Boston: Birkhauser, 1987).

11 N. Koblitz, "CM—Curves with Good Cryptographic Properties" in *CRYPTO '91*(New York: Springer-Verlag, 1992), 279.

12 J. A. Solinas, "An Improved Algorithm for Arithmetic on a Family of Elliptic Curves," in *CRYPTO '97* (New York: Springer-Verlag, 1997).

C H A P T E R   6

Cryptography

6.1 Fundamentals of elliptic curve cryptography   131

6.2 Choosing an elliptic curve   132

6.3 Nonsupersingular curves   133

6.4 Embedding data on a curve   136

6.5 Solving quadratic equations in binary fields   137

6.6 The Trace function   138

6.7 Solving quadratic equations in normal basis   141

6.8 Solving quadratic equations in polynomial basis   148

6.9 Quadratic polynomials: the code   149

6.10 Using the T matrix   158

6.11 Embedding data using polynomial basis   161

6.12 Summary of quadratic solving   162

6.13 References   163

Now that the basic math has been described, it's time to put it to work. In this chapter, I'll present methods for converting data into points on elliptic curves. The reason you want to embed data onto an elliptic curve is so you can implement public and secret key crypto systems. For those unfamiliar, the difference between the two will be explained.

Secret key crypto systems have been with us for thousands of years. A single key is used to encrypt and decrypt a message. The best thing we can do to hide information is to make it look as random as possible. People go through a lot of trouble designing secret key computer crypto codes that have "perfect avalanche" [1] and good randomness. Optimal normal basis (or polynomial basis) math looks like scrambled bits, and doing it over an elliptic curve is fundamentally nonlinear. A single bit change in the input causes a nonlinear and very drastic change in the output. Elliptic curves do automatically what symmetric crypto designers have to work very hard at.

Suppose we want to send a new secret key to an agent in Los Angeles. In the old days, we would have to have a "drop." A courier would take the secret key and leave it where the agent could find it and where the courier would not meet the agent. Today, we can use a public key system to hide the secret number on an elliptic curve. All we need to do is transmit the data in the clear, and the agent can recover it through a set of operations. The difficulty of finding the number without knowing the agent's private key is astronomically difficult.

I've been tossing out lots of terms, such as "secret key," "private key," and "public key." There are specific differences, and it can get a bit confusing. The term "secret key" will be used to signify a number that is used for both encrypting and decrypting. This type of cipher is usually referred to as "symmetric," because the same key is needed for both operations.

In 1976, a new method of sharing the secret key was publicly introduced as "public key cryptography." The original concepts proposed using modular exponentiation over a field of two very large primes. It is an asymmetric system, because it takes two keys: one to encrypt and one to decrypt a message. Because the math computations are so long, the "message" is usually just a secret key.

The encryption key is called "public," because anyone can use it to send a secret to a particular agent. The agent has a "private" key, which only he or she knows and which is the matching pair to the public key. On receipt of a cryptogram, the agent can apply his or her private key and decrypt the secret.

For more complete descriptions of the different types of crypto systems, see [1] and [2]. We'll stick to elliptic curves and the associated math. At this time, elliptic curve cryptography is considered the most secure, with some of the best scrutiny by the best minds in the mathematical and crypto fields. For most professionals, understanding the state of the art is what's important, so we'll focus on what it takes to make both good and excellent crypto systems.

6.1 Fundamentals of elliptic curve cryptography

There are several important details that have to be considered when setting up a crypto system. There is no place here to discuss security, because cryptography is not security. Cryptography is just one component of security. Cryptography is the lowest and most important level, and it is important to chose a crypto system appropriate for the security task at hand.

A fundamental question is: How many bits do I need? A 40-bit secret key system can be broken in three hours with the resources of a university computer lab. Recently (June 1997) 56 bits were cracked using the resources of several thousand computers over the Internet. 2^{56} is getting to be a pretty big number: around 72×10^{15}. It will be a while before 64 bits are cracked; this amounts to 18×10^{18}, or about the number of seconds in the age of the universe.

The next question to answer is: How hard do I want to work? For commercial applications we don't really need to keep the NSA or Mossad from reading daily communications. They have better things to worry about than how many processor boards failed to come out of a factory. If we are working for the NSA, then we need to be sure nobody gets access to nuclear weapons launch codes.

The first decision determines how much time it takes to compute an elliptic curve secret key. The time is approximately that of the cube of the number of bits. So if we double the number of bits, it takes about eight times longer to do the calculation. If the calculation is only done once a week, then we may want to opt for a very high number of bits. If the calculation is done once a second, then we have to choose a much lower number. If the time to crack a one-second code is over a week, then this is probably good enough.

The second decision determines how we pick and choose elliptic curves. The number of points on an elliptic curve determines the security level. Calculating the number of points for random curves is difficult. Unless you have a Ph.D. in math and happen to be doing research on the subject, finding the number of points on an arbitrary elliptic curve is not an easy thing to do (see [3]).

For most commercial applications we can risk not knowing the order of a curve. Certicom's contest is with random curves, so there is at least one company putting real money on it. Their first "exercise" of a random 79-bit elliptic curve was cracked after four weeks of work with several 500-MHz processors in December 1997. As of June 1998, 97-bit curves have been cracked after 45 days, using several hundred 600-MHz DEC alpha processors. This gives a real measure of security, which you can use to make judgment calls.

According to the draft IEEE public key cryptographic standard (P1363), you should know the order of the curve and point you use for a crypto system. While this is strictly true for nuclear-grade crypto, it is a bit overwhelming for everyday use. There are many curves listed in various places (and I'll include a few later), so it is possible to choose known curves with known factors.

Some of the protocols also require knowedge of the number of points. That is because these protocols use the point order and mix in modular integer math with the elliptic curve math. For simple key exchange random curves are fine; for advanced digital signature schemes you have to know the order of the curve.

6.2 Choosing an elliptic curve

The first step is to make sure we have more bits to play with than the secret is long. For maximum security, we probably want 2.5 times as many bits as we are trying to hide. The factor of 2 comes from the ability to crack elliptic curves using the square root of the order of the base point, and the factor of 0.5 comes in if you don't know the order of a base point.

For example, let's suppose we want to use a 64-bit secret key. This is better than the 56-bit DES and nowhere near as complex as 128-bit IDEA keys (see [1] for descriptions of DES and IDEA). The closest field size for an optimal normal basis would be between 130 and 148 bits. At the lower end, the public key elliptic curve system would be slightly less secure than the secret key system and would be a point of attack. At the upper end, it's plenty secure but will take longer to compute.

One of the most interesting aspects to come out of elliptic curve research in the past few years is the importance of avoiding supersingular curves. The math can be much faster over these types of curves, because several terms go to 0. However, one research paper [3] says that these curves turned out to be disastrous, since the discrete logarithm problem can be reduced to the discrete logarithm problem over an extension field K of small degree. The curves presented in this book are nonsupersingular and to date require fully exponential algorithms to crack.

We showed in chapter 5 how to multiply an integer k times a point P over an elliptic curve. The cracking process requires finding the integer k only knowing the starting point, P, and the ending point, kP. This is called the "elliptic curve discrete logarithm problem," where "discrete" comes from the finite field basis the mathematics is performed over. The standard method is to compute sets of specific values of an integer multiplier times the original point and then combine these values until a match is found. There are many tricks to this, but suffice it to say that the process is proportional to the square root of the order of the base point. See [4, 50] for a generic description and [5] and [6] for excellent details.

This means we need to increase the field size by 2 bits (a factor of 4) to increase our strength by a factor of 2. If we don't know the order of the curve or base point, then we rely on the structure of numbers to help us. Now, how do we know that the structure of numbers is going to help us? We know this because Hasse's Theorem tells us that the number of points on a curve over F_{2^n} must be somewhere between $2^n - 2^{n/2}$ and $2^n + 2^{n/2}$. For n about 140, the second term is only 2^{70} and can be safely ignored. So we're looking at numbers on the order of 2^{140}—which is about 10^{42}—the number of water molecules in the ocean. This field size is considered intractable by mathematicians (ca. 1990 [7]) and overkill by most reasonable engineers.

The actual security level will be somewhat less than this. There is a reasonable probability that the order of the curve will contain a prime factor on the order of 2^{112}. For a random curve, the security level would be equivalent to DES at 56 bits. A great deal of effort has been expended at finding good curves that have orders with prime factors close to the size of the field, on the order of 2^{n-2}. For maximum security choose those curves!

6.3 Nonsupersingular curves

As shown in chapter 5, nonsupersingular curves have the form:

$$y^2 + xy = x^3 + a_2 x^2 + a_6 \tag{6.1}$$

for F_{2^n} type fields. As shown in [7], specific values of a_6 can give maximum strength curves. If a_2 is 0, then the calculations are a touch faster. When a_2 is nonzero, the curve is called a "twist." An example from [7] is:

$$y^2 + xy = x^3 + x^2 + 1 \tag{6.2}$$

where field sizes 101, 107, 109, 113, and 163 all have order 2 times a very large prime. For the nontwist curve:

$$y^2 + xy = x^3 + 1 \tag{6.3}$$

fields 103, 107, and 131 all have order 4 times a very large prime. Since the order of these curves is known, they make good candidates for high-security applications.

Solinas [8] also works with these curves. He claims the following field sizes for equation (6.2) will also give orders of twice a large prime: 283, 311, 331, 347, and 359. For equation (6.3) he found additional field sizes: 233, 239, 277, 283, 349, and 409. In both cases the upper cutoff was 512 bits. Tables 6.1 and 6.2 present a list of the factors found for some very special curves [7]. The first column is the field size, the second tells which type of optimal normal basis it is (if it is), and the last column gives the order of the curve.

Table 6.1 $E: y^2 + xy = x^3 + x^2 + 1$

Field size	ONB	#E
101	no	2 × 1 26765 06002 28230 88614 28085 08011
107	no	2 × 81 12963 84146 06692 18285 10322 12511
109	no	2 × 324 51855 36584 26701 48744 86564 61467
113	II	2 × 5192 29685 85348 27627 89670 38334 67507
163	no	2 × 5846 00654 93236 11672 81474 17535 98448 34832 91185 74063

Table 6.2 $E: y^2 + xy = x^3 + 1$

Field size	ONB	#E
103	no	4 × 2 53530 12004 56459 53586 25300 67069
107	no	4 × 40 56481 92073 03335 60436 34890 37809
131	II	4 × 6805 64733 84187 69269 32320 12949 34099 85129

The curves in table 6.1 will all have form = 1, a2 = 1, and a6 = 1. Only field size 113 has an optimal normal basis of Type II. The rest must be implemented using polynomial basis. The curves in table 6.2 will all have form = 0 and a6 = 1. Field size 131 is a Type II optimal normal basis; the other two will have to be implemented using polynomial basis.

Table 6.3 shows two curves, which can be implemented with an optimal normal basis. The value of γ is straightforward to calculate in a normal basis. It is the number that, rotated once, equals its own complement. For these curves we have form = 0 and a6 = 0x2A AAAAAAAA AAAAAAAA AAAAAAAA AAAAAAAA for the first curve, and a6 = 0x2AAAAAAA AAAAAAAA AAAAAAAA AAAAAAAA AAAAAAAA. (Note that you can rotate a6 right once and have a correct value as well.)

Table 6.3 $y^2 + xy = x^3 + \gamma, \; \gamma^2 = \gamma + 1$

Field size	ONB	#E
134	II	4 × 54445 17870 73501 54153 44659 58609 44105 99059
158	II	4 × 91 34385 23331 81432 38773 05730 45979 44745 23653 03319

Table 6.4   *E*: $y^2 + xy = x^3 + \gamma x^2 + \gamma$, $\gamma^2 = \gamma + 1$

Field size	ONB	#*E*
118	no	6 × 55384 49982 43714 94566 50574 99908 87769

Table 6.5   *E*: $y^2 + xy = x^3 + \gamma$, $\gamma^3 = \gamma + 1$

Field size	ONB	#*E*
111	no	8 × 324 51855 36584 26723 11495 75723 35741

Table 6.6   *E*: $y^2 + xy = x^3 + x^2 + \gamma$, $\gamma^3 = \gamma + 1$

Field size	ONB	#*E*
141	no	10 × 27 87593 14981 63278 92689 03181 39617 36218 74561
177	no	10 × 191 56194 26082 36107 29479 33791 57473 18375 04813 70807 01777

The curves in tables 6.4, 6.5, and 6.6 must be implemented using polynomial basis. Finding γ for these equations is straightforward but depends on the irreducible polynomial chosen to implement the field. Later in this chapter, we'll solve quadratic equations, and that will show you how to find γ for table 6.4. I'll leave the code for finding γ in tables 6.5 and 6.6 for a later chapter, along with other useful but tangential information.

Table 6.7 $y^2 + xy = x^3 + \gamma x^2 + 1$, $\gamma \in F_{16}$, $Tr(\gamma) = 1$

Field size	ONB	#*E*
148	I	18 × 1982 28846 20916 10945 91407 67798 27981 11637 92081

The final curve, shown in table 6.7, can be implemented using an optimal normal basis of Type I. With a 44-digit prime factor, this curve can be classified as nuclear grade, since it takes on the order of 10^{22} elliptic curve calculations to solve the elliptic curve logarithm problem. At one nanosecond per computation, it will take approximately 300,000 years to find even one secret value. Present processors are about 1 million times slower than this, so this is a candidate for an excellent crypto system.

The value of `form` for this curve is 1, `a6` = 1, and `a2` = 37 repetitions of 4 bits with an odd number of them set. The term $\gamma \in F_{16}$ tells us that there are groups of 4 bits. Since the field size is 148 = 37 × 4, that's how many repetitions we need to create the correct subfield. The possible values of a2 for the curve shown in table 6.7 are shown in table 6.8.

Table 6.8   Values of a2 for Curve in Table 6.7

γ (binary)	a2 (hexadecimal)
0001	11111 11111111 11111111 11111111 11111111
0010	22222 22222222 22222222 22222222 22222222
0100	44444 44444444 44444444 44444444 44444444
1000	88888 88888888 88888888 88888888 88888888
0111	77777 77777777 77777777 77777777 77777777
1011	BBBBB BBBBBBBB BBBBBBBB BBBBBBBB BBBBBBBB
1101	DDDDD DDDDDDDD DDDDDDDD DDDDDDDD DDDDDDDD
1110	EEEEE EEEEEEEE EEEEEEEE EEEEEEEE EEEEEEEE

6.4 Embedding data on a curve

In chapter 5, I showed how to compute sums and multiplications over elliptic curves. But we must first get our data onto a curve, and, if we pick random values, we have to be sure the *x* value we picked is actually one that satisfies the equation of the curve.

Let's rewrite equation (6.1) by converting the right-hand side to a simple form, say $f(x)$. Bring that over to the left-hand side and we have:

$$y^2 + xy + f(x) = 0. \tag{6.4}$$

This is a simple quadratic equation. It turns out to be not so simple to solve over a polynomial basis but very straightforward over an optimal normal basis. Mathematicians consider it trivial, but tracking the code I'm about to present requires a good deal of discipline.

In a Galois Field of F_{2^m}, there are many elements that do not satisfy equation (6.4). This creates a problem. If our data fill all the bits of the field, and these data can't be on the curve, we can't use the crypto system. As I said at the beginning of the chapter, we need more bits in the field than we have in the secret for security reasons. This gives us a chance to change some "don't care" bits in the chosen value of *x*. But which bits?

It turns out that it does not matter which bits we change or how we change them. The "density" of points for any curve over a finite field is almost uniformly distributed. This means we can look at any subsection of the bits as an integer and increment it using simple arithmetic. This method was first proposed by Koblitz [9, 162] and works very well. Usually, if the first guess of x is not on a curve, then the second or third try is. The most I've ever seen a hunt continue is 13, so even 4 spare bits should be sufficient.

This ability to hide the same raw data along with a lot of random garbage is very useful for cryptography. And the more bits of garbage we have to play with, the more difficult the attacker's task is. The programmer's task is to place the raw data along with some random garbage, and then find out if that combination will be on the curve. If not, the garbage is incremented and a test is again performed. Once the values of y—yes, there are two values of y if there is a solution to equation (6.4)—are found, the point P is "on the curve" and we can proceed to hide it.

6.5 *Solving quadratic equations in binary fields*

The first step in solving equation (6.4) is to make a change of variable to eliminate x. Let:

$$y = xz \tag{6.5}$$

in equation (6.4). This gives:

$$(xz)^2 + x^2 z + f(x) = 0. \tag{6.6}$$

By multiplying the entire equation by x^{-2}, we get the simple equation:

$$z^2 + z + c = 0 \tag{6.7}$$

where

$$c = f(x) \cdot x^{-2}. \tag{6.8}$$

According to the mathematicians, equation (6.7) only has a solution when the Trace of c is 0. The Trace function maps F_{2^m} to F_2; it gives us 1 bit as a result. Computing the Trace is simple in a normal basis and a bit more involved for the polynomial basis representation. We'll get to the details of that math in the next section.

Once we know the Trace(c) = 0 in equation (6.7), we can solve for z. It turns out $z + 1$ is also a solution to equation (6.7). To see this, let z be one solution and z' be another solution. If we write equation (6.7) as:

$$\begin{aligned} z(z + 1) &= c \\ z'(z' + 1) &= c \end{aligned} \tag{6.9}$$

and replace z' in the second equation with $z + 1$, we get the first equation. Once we find one solution the other is trivial. Then, putting z and z' in equation (6.5), we recover the two solutions to the quadratic equation and our data are embedded on the curve.

It should be easy to see that once a point is embedded on the curve, the second solution is the negative point. Replace z with $z + 1$ in equation (6.5) and compare this with equation (5.20). From a geometric argument this should be obvious. For elliptic curves over the real numbers, if we draw a vertical line through any x value on the axis, we intersect either no points or two points that are the negative of each other. The same geometry is true over finite fields, but it is difficult to illustrate.

6.6 The Trace function

The first time I learned about a Trace function was with square matrices. It is defined as the sum of the diagonal elements [10, 453]:

$$\text{Trace}(C) = c_{11} + c_{22} + \ldots + c_{nn} \tag{6.10}$$

where C denotes the full matrix and c_{jk} an element in it.

The second time I learned about a Trace function was with finite fields. In a field, F_{2^m}, the Trace is defined as the sum of the $m - 1$ squarings of an element, c, with itself (see [4, 36]):

$$\text{Tr}(c) = c + c^{2^1} + c^{2^2} + \ldots + c^{2^{m-1}} . \tag{6.11}$$

The Trace is a mapping from F_{2^m} to F_2. The final result is a single bit. It turns out that these two definitions are connected, and I'll be taking advantage of that for the polynomial basis representation. For the moment, let's just concentrate on the normal basis representation.

In a normal basis, equation (6.11) is also called a "parity function." It tells us whether the number of bits set is even or odd. To see this, imagine writing element c as a row of bits. Under this row write c^2 as a row of bits. From chapter 4 we know that this is just the first row rotated once. Moving through equation (6.11), each succeeding row k is the rotation of the previous row, $k - 1$. Summing across is the exclusive-or of all the rows. But, notice, every column is the transpose of every row. So we're just taking the exclusive-or of all the bits.

Here is an example. Let $c = 10110$ in F_{2^5}. Then each Trace row from equation (6.11) is:

$$c = 10110$$

$$c^2 = 01101$$

$$c^{2^2} = 11010 \qquad\qquad (6.12)$$

$$c^{2^3} = 10101$$

$$c^{2^4} = 01011.$$

The exclusive-or of all the rows is the same thing as the exclusive-or of all the bits of c. The final result is:

$$\mathrm{Tr}(10110) = 1. \qquad\qquad (6.13)$$

That's a long, drawn-out way to describe a parity bit. We have reduced an m bit field element to a single bit. For a normal basis, computing the Trace will be simple for any element.

Computing the Trace over a polynomial basis has to be done modulo the prime polynomial. Since the result must be a single bit, some combination of an element's coefficients must be exclusive-or(ed) together. If we can find which coefficients should be summed for any given prime polynomial, we only need to sum those bits of any element and we can skip all the squaring and modulo reduction operations of equation (6.11) (saving a lot of processing time).

Because we are dealing with base 2 coefficients, we can store the bits in a simple mask. I call it the "Trace vector," because it is a one-dimensional array of 1-bit coefficients. Let's write the Trace vector as an element in F_{2^m}:

$$t = t_{m-1}x^{m-1} + \ldots + t_1 x + t_0. \qquad\qquad (6.14)$$

To find t in equation (6.14) we simply have to compute equation (6.11) for an arbitrary c modulo the prime polynomial and then match coefficients with equation (6.14). An arbitrary element c will have the same form as equation (6.14); just replace all the t's with c's. Fortunately, there is an easier way, and I thank Richard Pinch for pointing it out to me.

The major thing we need to do is keep track of each coefficient as a variable. The way I do this is to expand each coefficient as an element of F_{2^m}. This creates a matrix: Each row corresponds to a coefficient in the form of equation (6.14), and each column corresponds to a power of x. An initial arbitrary element is then just a diagonal matrix; each coefficient is in front of a single power of x:

$$c = \begin{bmatrix} c_{m-1} & c_{m-2} & \cdots & c_0 \end{bmatrix} \begin{bmatrix} 1 & 0 & \cdots & 0 \\ 0 & 1 & \cdots & 0 \\ \cdots & \cdots & \cdots & \cdots \\ 0 & 0 & \cdots & 1 \end{bmatrix} \begin{bmatrix} x^{m-1} \\ x^{m-2} \\ \cdots \\ 1 \end{bmatrix}. \qquad (6.15)$$

Pinch's Trace algorithm extends the matrix in equation (6.15) upward, with each row representing an additional power of x modulo the prime polynomial. The algorithm attaches rows until we get to a power equal to $2m - 2$. The matrix is no longer square, but the algorithm only looks at m rows at a time. By summing (using exclusive-or) all the values along the diagonal for each square matrix starting at row x^k, we find the coefficient t_k in equation (6.14). Pinch's algorithm makes it clear that the two definitions of Trace equations (6.10) and (6.11) are equivalent. It seems that every possible power of x (modulo the prime polynomial) is summed in a specific order, but it would take a bit of effort to show the relationship between the two definitions.

Here is an example in F_{2^5} for a prime polynomial $x^5 + x^2 + 1$. Starting with $x^0 = 1$ each row is multiplied by x and reduced modulo $x^5 + x^2 + 1$. The resulting matrix looks like this:

0 1 1 0 1 x^8
1 0 1 0 0 x^7
0 1 0 1 0 x^6
0 0 1 0 1 x^5
1 0 0 0 0 x^4
0 1 0 0 0 x^3
0 0 1 0 0 x^2
0 0 0 1 0 x^1
0 0 0 0 1 x^0

Starting at row x^0 and summing the values on the diagonal from bottom right and moving up to the left we find this:

$t_0 = 1$
$t_1 = 0$
$t_2 = 0$
$t_3 = 1$
$t_4 = 0$

To compute the Trace of the previous example (10110) we only need to AND the Trace vector with the number and then sum the resulting bits. In this case, the Trace(10110) modulo $x^5 + x^2 + 1$ is 0.

```
0 1 0 0 1   Trace vector
1 0 1 1 0   example
0 0 0 0 0   result
```

So much for mathematical preliminaries. Figure 6.1 shows the subroutine schematic for this chapter. Both polynomial and normal basis are included as separate paths. While none of the elliptic curve math routines is included here from chapter 5, we need the results of this chapter to make crypto systems work.

I'll first solve the quadratic equation under a normal basis and give all the routines needed to embed data on curves. Then we'll go into the polynomial basis versions. This is where life gets a bit messy, and we'll have to take side trips into matrix inversion and linear equation solving. Fortunately, only 1's and 0's are used, so this is much simpler than anything you may have seen before. The polynomial basis mathematics also requires initialization, and we'll get into that near the end of the chapter.

When we're done, we'll have all the tools necessary to start building cryptographic protocols. So let's write some code.

6.7 Solving quadratic equations in normal basis

Solving a quadratic equation is easy in a normal basis, so let's start there. Here is the beginning of the code: The inputs are the coefficients to the equation $y^2 + ay + b$. The first step is to check if the coefficient of y is 0. If it is, we only need to return the square root of the constant term b as the solution (both solutions are the same in that case). This is just a right shift for a normal basis, so this section is very simple.

```
/*******************************************************************
 *                                                                 *
 *       Routine to solve quadradic equation.  Enter with coeficients *
 *  a and b and it returns solutions y[2]: y^2 + ay + b = 0.       *
 *  If Tr(b/a^2) != 0, returns y=0 and error code 1.               *
 *  If Tr(b/a^2) == 0, returns y[2] and error code 0.              *
 *  If solution fails, returns y=0 and error code 2.               *
 *                                                                 *
 *******************************************************************/

int opt_quadratic(a, b, y)
FIELD2N *a, *b, *y;
{
        INDEX   i, el, bits;
        FIELD2N z, k, a2;
        ELEMENT r, t, mask;

/*  test for a=0. Return y = square root of b.  */
```

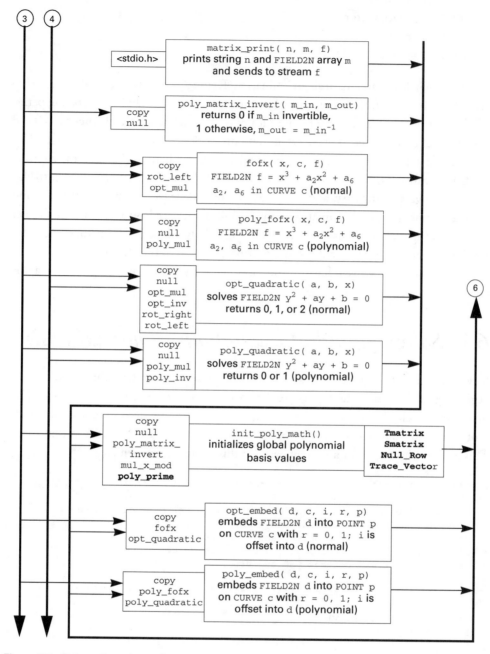

Figure 6.1 Subroutine schematic

```
        r = 0;
        SUMLOOP(i) r |= a->e[i];
        if (!r)
        {
                copy( b, &y[0]);
                rot_right( &y[0]);
                copy( &y[0], &y[1]);
                return(0);
        }
```

The next step is to compute the constant c in equation (6.8). I first compute the inverse of the coefficient a and then square it. This is multiplied with the previous term. The reason for computing the square root of this will become apparent soon.

```
/*  find a^-2  */

        opt_inv( a, &a2);
        rot_left(&a2);

/*  find k=(b/a^2)^.5 */

        opt_mul( b, &a2, &k);
        rot_right(&k);
        r = 0;
```

Since the Trace function is simply a parity operation, the square root doesn't change anything. The first step is to compute the exclusive-or of all the WORDSIZE blocks. The second step is to compute the exclusive-or of all the bits within that ELEMENT. This is a simple loop, which combines the upper half of the block with the lower half and then repeats the operation until we've smashed all the bits down to 1. If the number of bits set was even, then we get 0; otherwise, we'll get a 1.

```
/*  check that Tr(k) is zero.  Combine all words first. */

        SUMLOOP(i)  r ^= k.e[i];

/*  take trace of word, combining half of all the bits each time */

        mask = -1L;
        for (bits = WORDSIZE/2; bits > 0; bits >>= 1)
        {
                mask >>= bits;
            r = ((r & mask) ^ (r >> bits));
        }

/*  if not zero, return error code 1.   */

        if (r)
        {
            null(&y[0]);
            null(&y[1]);
```

```
            return(1);
    }
```

If the Trace was not 0, we return with an error and both y values set to 0. To understand the rest of the code, let's look at some math tricks with normal basis numbers.

Once we have the Trace of c checked out, we have to solve for z in equaiton (6.7). Let's brute force solve for z this way:

$$z = z^{1/2} + c^{1/2}. \tag{6.16}$$

We can do this one bit at a time by considering each bit in equaiton (6.16) as a single equation:

$$z_i = z_{i-1} + c_{i-1}. \tag{6.17}$$

This works, because $z^{1/2}$ is just a right rotation of z, so each bit of c is combined with the same bit of z and the previous bit of z. When i is 0, $i-1$ references the most significant bit of z.

Another useful condition we know is that both z and $z + 1$ are solutions to equation (6.7). In an optimal normal basis, adding 1 is the same as taking a complement. This means that both z and not z are logical solutions to equation (6.7). We can assume the most significant bit is 0 and set $z_0 = c_0$. With this assumption, we can work up the chain of bits with equation (6.17).

The following code implements the solution of equation (6.7) using equation (6.17). The trick here is that we need to keep track of when we cross ELEMENT boundaries. The variable z is the result we're looking for; bits is an index into z, which tracks each bit position; i is the ELEMENT for that bit; and l is the ELEMENT for the next bit. The variable mask is used to set a bit in z if necessary.

```
/*  point is valid, proceed with solution.  mask points to bit i,
which is known, in x bits previously found and k (=b/a^2)^.5.  */

        null(&z);
        mask = 1;
        for (bits=0; bits < NUMBITS ; bits++)
        {

/* source long word could be different than destination  */

            i = NUMWORD - bits/WORDSIZE;
            el = NUMWORD - (bits + 1)/WORDSIZE;

/*  use present bits to compute next one */

            r = k.e[i] & mask;
            t = z.e[i] & mask;
```

```
        r ^= t;
```

/* same word, so just shift result up */

```
        if ( el == i )
        {
           r <<= 1;
           z.e[el] |= r;
           mask <<= 1;
        }
        else
        {
```

/* different word, reset mask and use a 1 */

```
           mask = 1;
           if (r) z.e[el] = 1;
        }
     }
```

/* test that last bit generates a zero */

```
     r = k.e[0] & UPRBIT;
     t = z.e[0] & UPRBIT;
     if ( r^t )
     {
        null(&y[0]);
        null(&y[1]);
        return(2);
     }
```

The variable r holds the value of $z_i + c_i$. If the destination ELEMENT is the same as the source ELEMENT (which it will be most of the time), then r is added to the destination after being shifted once. Otherwise, we only need to check if r is nonzero, and set the least significant bit of the next ELEMENT. At the same time, the mask is adjusted to look at the next bits to be summed.

The only major item to note here is that opt_quadratic() does check to see if the last bit equals the original guess. Assuming the Trace condition is satisfied, it is mathematically impossible for the chain of bit relations to end incorrectly. However, it is always good practice to assume that anything can go wrong—in this case it would probably be a hardware error of some kind.

If anyone does find an error 2 condition return from opt_quadratic(), and it is not a hardware problem, then I can assure you the mathematicians would be very interested. It's more likely that there's a bug in the code somewhere, so double-check it first. But if you do see a case where the math fails, post it to the Net!

To finish the problem, we need to convert back from z to y. This is simple, just multiply by the input x value.

```
/*   convert solution back via y = az */

        opt_mul(a, &z, &y[0]);

/*   and create complementary (z+1) solution y = az + a */

          null (&y[1]);
          SUMLOOP(i) y[1].e[i] = y[0].e[i] ^ a->e[i];

/*   no errors, bye!   */

          return(0);
}
```

So, to recap: To put a random or specific value x onto a given curve, we must solve the quadratic equation (6.4) for y. If there is a solution, we actually have two values of y to choose from. It really doesn't matter which one we pick—for points on a curve one will be the negative of the other. If there is no solution, we must change x until there is. A typical method to embed data onto an elliptic curve over an optimal normal basis might be as follows:

```
/*   embed data onto a curve.
        Enter with data, curve, ELEMENT offset to be used as increment, and
        which root (0 or 1).
        Returns with point having data as x and correct y value for curve.
        Will use y[0] for last bit of root clear, y[1] for last bit of root
        set.
        if ELEMENT offset is out of range, default is 0.
*/

void opt_embed( data, curv, incrmt, root, pnt)
FIELD2N         *data;
CURVE           *curv;
INDEX           incrmt, root;
POINT           *pnt;
{
        FIELD2N         f, y[2];
        INDEX           inc = incrmt;
        INDEX           i;

        if ( (inc < 0) || (inc > NUMWORD) ) inc = 0;
        copy( data, &pnt->x);
        fofx( &pnt->x, curv, &f);
        while (opt_quadratic( &pnt->x, &f, y))
        {
                pnt->x.e[inc]++;
                fofx( &pnt->x, curv, &f);
        }
        copy ( &y[root&1], &pnt->y);
}
```

This function embeds data onto a CURVE. The input incrmt is used to pick out a specific ELEMENT to be incremented while attempting to perform the embedding process. The input root picks out which value of *y* to put into the resulting POINT variable (pnt). This is a generic method for embedding data onto the curve. Enhancements might include a variable amount to increment (which could, for example, pick out regions in an ELEMENT).

The function fofx() used above simply computes the right-hand side of equation (6.1). Using the predefined typedef's from the previous chapter, fofx() looks like this for an optimal normal basis.

```
void fofx(x, curv, f)
FIELD2N *x, *f;
CURVE *curv;
{
        FIELD2N x2,x3;
        INDEX i;

        copy(x, &x2);
        rot_left(&x2);
        opt_mul(x, &x2, &x3);
        if (curv->form) opt_mul(&x2, &curv->a2, f);
                else null(f);
        SUMLOOP(i)
            f->e[i] ^= (x3.e[i] ^ curv->a6.e[i]);
}
```

With the routines fofx() and opt_quadratic() we can ensure that any data value can be put on a chosen curve. The routine opt_embed does this in a very general way and should work for any field size and data storage requirements. If NUMBITS modulo WORDSIZE is less than 6 (or 4, depending on how gutsy you are), then the number of possible values you will try to embed will be less than 64 (or 16 for the brave). While unlikely, it is possible to go into an infinite loop if there are no points on the curve for that small a set of specific field elements. This can be fixed by changing the incrmnt variable to be something other than 0. Again, it will be mathematically interesting if a curve were found with nonuniform density over a large region. If your code goes into an infinite loop in opt_embed, double-check for bugs before posting the amazing discovery to the Net.

6.8 Solving quadratic equations in polynomial basis

Solving equation (6.4) over a polynomial basis is a bit tricky. The first thing we need to do is to look closely at a squaring and modulo reduction operation. Squaring any arbitrary element c would give:

$$c^2 = c_{m-1}x^{2(m-1)} + \ldots + c_1 x^2 + c_0.$$ (6.18)

What this means is that every bit j is moved to location $2j$. For all powers less than half the degree of the prime polynomial, this is a simple shift. For all powers above that, we have to reduce the coefficient modulo the prime polynomial.

If we square equation (6.15), we can keep track of each coefficient in equation (6.18) for any arbitrary value. By summing the resultant matrix of equation (6.18) with equation (6.15), we will have a representation of $z^2 + z$. Let's write it out in math so it will be clear. First, here's equation (6.15) for z:

$$z = \begin{bmatrix} z_{m-1} & z_{m-2} & \cdots & z_0 \end{bmatrix} \begin{bmatrix} 1 & 0 & \ldots & 0 \\ 0 & 1 & \ldots & 0 \\ \ldots & \ldots & \ldots & \ldots \\ 0 & 0 & \ldots & 1 \end{bmatrix} \begin{bmatrix} x^{m-1} \\ x^{m-2} \\ \ldots \\ 1 \end{bmatrix}.$$ (6.19)

Squaring each row and reducing modulo the prime polynomial, we have to get something like this:

$$z^2 = \begin{bmatrix} z_{m-1} & z_{m-2} & \cdots & z_0 \end{bmatrix} \begin{bmatrix} s_{m-1,m-1} & s_{m-1,m-2} & \cdots & s_{m-1,0} \\ \ldots & \ldots & \ldots & \ldots \\ s_{m/2,m-1} & s_{m/2,m-2} & \cdots & 0 \\ \ldots & \ldots & \ldots & \ldots \\ 0 & 0 & \ldots & 1 \end{bmatrix} \begin{bmatrix} x^{m-1} \\ \ldots \\ x^{m/2} \\ \ldots \\ 1 \end{bmatrix}.$$ (6.20)

At the middle of the matrix either $s_{m/2,m-1} = 1$ for m odd, or else $s_{m/2,m-2} = 1$ for m even. Adding the matrices in equations (6.19) and (6.20) together gives us another matrix, which I'll call the T_z matrix. By writing $z^2 + z = T_z z$ in a matrix form, equation (6.7) can be rewritten:

$$T_z z = c.$$ (6.21)

When the coefficient of y is 0 in equation (6.4), we can use equation (6.20) in equation (6.21), compute the inverse of T_z, and find the solution for z from $T_z^{-1} c$. Performing a matrix multiply is a method for computing a square root over a polynomial basis. It sounds weird, but it works really well. I'll go through the details of how the inverse is computed when I get to that subroutine.

Unfortunately, the last row of equations (6.19) and (6.20) are equal. When we add them together, the last row of T_z is 0, and the general matrix of equation (6.21) is not invertible. It is, however, a system of linear equations, and because all the coefficients are either 0 or 1 it is rather easy to solve.

The solution process is similar to the diagonalization process used with computing the inverse of a binary matrix. When all is said and done, the result is a set of basis vectors. For each bit c_k set in equation (6.21) we sum the corresponding row k in the basis vector list to find the correct value of z. I will call the basis vector list "the T matrix."

Since we've lost one equation from the list shown in equation (6.21) (the last row is 0), there is one bit of c that must be a "don't care" bit. The diagonalization process will find this "null row." The Trace function will be our last equation. For some polynomial fields you can replace the last row in T_z with the Trace vector and find an inverse, T_z^{-1}, which will solve equation (6.21). While slick, this method does not work all the time.

We only need to compute the Trace vector, the T matrix, and what I'll call "the S matrix" (for taking square roots) once for any prime polynomial. With these variables initialized we can proceed to solve any quadratic equation, and this will allow us to embed data onto a curve. The first step will be to check the Trace function for 0; the second step will be to use the T matrix to find each coefficient of z.

6.9 Quadratic polynomials: the code

The first step to converting all the above math into code is to recognize that the T matrix is an array of FIELD2N objects. So let's define some globals. Assume that poly_prime has been defined as the prime polynomial for the field in a different file. The new globals are Tmatrix, which we'll use to solve quadratic equations; Smatrix used to compute square roots; Trace_Vector used to mask off the bits for computing the Trace function; and Null_Row, which tells us which row to ignore in Tmatrix.

```
extern      FIELD2N poly_prime;
FIELD2N     Tmatrix[NUMBITS], Smatrix[NUMBITS], Trace_Vector;
INDEX       Null_Row;
```

The first routine inverts a FIELD2N matrix. I call the routine poly_matrix_invert, and it takes an input matrix and an output destination matrix.

The inversion is done in two parts. The first part is Gaussian elimination. In floating-point math this can get tricky, but here we have only 0's and 1's. The process is simpler, because we either have to eliminate a coefficient or we don't, and all values are the same. The second part is to transpose what I call the `Imatrix`. This method of inversion is straightforward and not very efficient. The idea is to create a diagonal matrix, which tracks all the operations on the input matrix including row swaps and sums. Once the input matrix is diagonalized, the intermediate `Imatrix` will contain the transpose of the result we seek. See any book describing matrix inversion or numerical analysis for why this works [11, chapter 10].

To help catch errors, I introduced the variable `found` to make sure there really is a row that has a 1 in it for the column under investigation. The diagonalization process must find a 1 in the column that has the same value as the row we are on. Here `src_mask` and `rowdex`, respectively, keep track of the bit and ELEMENT offset for the diagonal bit of interest. At any row we'll have the condition that all previous rows have been diagonalized; therefore, we can't use them again. So the search moves through the rest of the input matrix, but only if that bit is not already set in the row being tested. The first thing to check is the diagonal bit: We might get lucky and not have to search at all.

```
/*  Subroutine to invert a binary matrix.  The method is brute force but
        simple. Start with a diagonal matrix in I, and for each row operation
        in mat_in that eliminates non diagonal terms, do the same in I.   The
        result is that mat_in = 1/I (transpose) and I = 1.  We then have to
        transpose I back into mat_out to get the correct result.

        Returns 0 if matrix invertible, row number of zero column if not
        invertible. If non zero return, assume output matrix is garbage
*/

INDEX poly_matrix_invert( mat_in, mat_out)
FIELD2N mat_in[NUMBITS], mat_out[NUMBITS];
{
        INDEX           row, col, i, j, rowdex, found, error;
        ELEMENT         src_mask, dst_mask;
        FIELD2N         dummy, Imatrix[NUMBITS];

/*  Create Imatrix as diagonalized  */

        for ( row=0; row<NUMBITS; row++)
        {
                null( &Imatrix[row]);
                Imatrix[row].e[NUMWORD - row/WORDSIZE] = 1L << (row%WORDSIZE);
        }
        error = 0;  /* hope this is return value  */

/*  Diagonalize input matrix.  Eliminate all other bits in each column.
        First find a column bit that is set, and swap with diagonal
        row if needed.
*/
```

```
           for ( row = 0; row < NUMBITS; row ++)
           {
                   rowdex = NUMWORD - row/WORDSIZE;
                   src_mask = 1L << (row % WORDSIZE);

/*  find a row of input matrix which has col = row bit set.
    First see if we get lucky, then do search.
*/
                   found = 0;
                   if ( !(mat_in[row].e[rowdex] & src_mask))
                   {
                           for (j = row+1; j<NUMBITS; j++)
                           {                         /*  found one, swap rows  */
                                   if ( mat_in[j].e[rowdex] & src_mask)
                                   {
                                           copy( &Imatrix[j], &dummy);
                                           copy( &Imatrix[row], &Imatrix[j]);
                                           copy( &dummy, &Imatrix[row]);
                                           copy( &mat_in[j], &dummy);
                                           copy( &mat_in[row], &mat_in[j]);
                                           copy( &dummy, &mat_in[row]);
                                           found = 1;
                                           break;
                                   }
                           }
                   }
                   else found = 1;
```

Once a row is found that does have a bit set in the diagonal column, it is swapped with the current row that does not have that bit set. This is also done in the Imatrix, so the answer will still be correct. (This is standard matrix mathematics; swapping rows on both sides of an equation does not change the list of equations.) If a row is not found, then the matrix is not invertible. In that case, we don't want to do anything for that column. Most of the time, everything will proceed to eliminate all other 1's in that column.

Following is the code listing that proceeds to eliminate all other 1's not on the diagonal. The scan is over all rows except the one we are on (i == row check). If the column bit is clear, we do nothing; if it is set, then both the Imatrix and mat_in matrix are summed with the diagonal row to eliminate the bit.

```
/*  eliminate all other terms in this column  */

           if (found)
           {
               for ( i=0; i<NUMBITS; i++)
               {
                   if ( i == row) continue;
                   if ( mat_in[i].e[rowdex] & src_mask)
                   {
                       SUMLOOP(j)
                       {
```

```
                        Imatrix[i].e[j] ^= Imatrix[row].e[j];
                        mat_in[i].e[j] ^= mat_in[row].e[j];
                }
        }
    }
}                          /*  end column eliminate   */
    else error = row;
}                          /*  end diagonalization    */
```

At this point the `mat_in` matrix is diagonal, and we can transpose the `Imatrix`. If the `error` value is not zero, then the diagonalization process failed. I simply save the value of this row for the return. Another choice would be to return immediately.

The last thing we have to do is transpose the `Imatrix` back into the output matrix. This is a brute-force, one-bit-at-a-time operation. The variable `src_mask` picks off the bit in the `Imatrix`, and the variable `dst_mask` marks off the bit in the resulting `mat_out` matrix. We start by nulling out every row in `mat_out`, and only flip bits if we need to.

```
/*  Next step is to transpose diagonalized matrix.  This completes the
        inversion process.  Clear mat_out to begin with. */

        for (row=0; row<NUMBITS; row++) null(&mat_out[row]);
        for (col = 0; col<NUMBITS; col++)
        {
                j = NUMWORD - col/WORDSIZE;
                src_mask = 1L << (col % WORDSIZE);
                for (row = 0; row<NUMBITS; row++)
                {
                        if (Imatrix[row].e[j] & src_mask)
                        {
                                i = NUMWORD - row/WORDSIZE;
                                dst_mask = 1L << (row  % WORDSIZE);
                                mat_out[col].e[i] |= dst_mask;
                        }
                }
        }
        return(error);
}
```

When a matrix is not invertible, it helps to at least print it out. Here is a simple routine I used to help find a problem with F_{2^5}. Readers can manipulate all this to their hearts' desire.

```
/*  print field matrix.  an array of FIELD2N of length NUMBITS is assumed.  The
    bits are printed out as a 2D matrix with an extra space every 5 characters.
*/

void matrix_print( name, matrix, file)
FIELD2N matrix[NUMBITS];
char *name;
```

```
FILE *file;
{
    INDEX i,j;

    fprintf(file,"%s\n",name);
    for (i = NUMBITS-1; i>=0; i--)
    {
        if (i%5==0) fprintf(file,"\n");/* extra line every 5 rows   */
        for (j = NUMBITS-1; j>=0; j--)
        {
            if ( matrix[i].e[NUMWORD - j/WORDSIZE] & (1L<<(j%WORDSIZE)))
                fprintf(file,"1");
            else fprintf(file,"0");            /* extra space every 5 */
            if (j%5==0) fprintf(file," ");  /* characters   */
        }
        fprintf(file,"\n");
    }
    fprintf(file,"\n");
}
```

The following function is used to compute the global values $\texttt{Smatrix}$, $\texttt{Tmatrix}$, $\texttt{Trace\_Vector}$, and $\texttt{Null\_Row}$. Since this only needs to be done once for any given $\texttt{poly\_prime}$, I gave it the name $\texttt{init\_poly\_math()}$. If the $\texttt{Smatrix}$ gets computed correctly, the function returns 0. If there is an error attempting to invert the $\texttt{Smatrix}$, the routine returns with the row where the error occurred. For $\texttt{poly\_prime}$ irreducible this should never happen.

There are several internal variables used in each different section. The routine starts by defining all these variables. The first chunk of code computes the $\texttt{Trace}$ matrix. This is the $2m - 2$ by m matrix of Pinch's algorithm set up as an array of $\texttt{FIELD2N}$ values.

```
INDEX init_poly_math()
{
        INDEX           i, j, error, k, sum, row, rowdex, found, nulldex;
        ELEMENT         src_mask;
        FIELD2N         x, c, dummy;
        FIELD2N         Trace[2*NUMBITS], Tz[NUMBITS], T2[NUMBITS];

/*  Create Trace_Vector for computing the trace in polynomial basis.
        Given any input c = c_m*x^m + ... + c_1*x + c_0  the Trace_Vector
        will mask off and sum the correct coefficients of a_i.  The
        following method was suggested by Richard Pinch (rgep@dpmms.cam.ac.uk)
*/

/*  step 1 Build a list of powers of x modulo poly_prime from 0 to 2n-2 */

        null( &Trace[0]);
        Trace[0].e[NUMWORD] = 1L;
        for (i=1; i<2*NUMBITS-1; i++)
                mul_x_mod( &Trace[i-1], &poly_prime, &Trace[i]);
```

With that array built, setting up the `Trace_Vector` is easy. Starting with term x^0 the INDEX variable i keeps track of each coefficient in `Trace_Vector`. The INDEX variable k keeps track of each row in the `Trace` matrix from which we are extracting a diagonal value. The ELEMENT variable `src_mask` tracks each bit across the diagonal, and INDEX variable j tracks the ELEMENT that `src_mask` is in. The variable sum is the parity of the terms on the diagonal. If sum ends up set, bit i in `Trace_Vector` is set. This is the core of Pinch's algorithm.

```
/*  step 2: Sum diagonals of nxn matrix using each row as a starting
        point.  Each sum amounts to the trace vector coefficient for that
        power of x.
*/
        null( &Trace_Vector);
        for (i=0; i<NUMBITS; i++)
        {
                sum = 0;
                j = NUMWORD;
                src_mask = 1;
                for ( k=i; k<i+NUMBITS; k++)
                {
                        if ( Trace[k].e[j] & src_mask) sum ^= 1;
                        src_mask <<= 1;
                        if (!src_mask)
                        {
                                src_mask = 1;
                                j--;
                        }
                }
                if (sum) Trace_Vector.e[NUMWORD - i/WORDSIZE] |=
                                1L << (i % WORDSIZE);
        }
```

The next major step is to compute the S and T matrices. Since the `Trace` matrix contains every power of x modulo `poly_prime` that we need, all we have to do is put the correct rows in the right place. The `T2` matrix holds the square of every power of x in each row, and the `Tz` matrix holds $x^2 + x$ modulo `poly_prime` in each row. Inverting the `T2` matrix to get the `Smatrix` is just one subroutine. If an error occurs, there is no point in continuing; something is drastically wrong. Either `poly_prime` is not really a prime polynomial or there is a bug in the code.

```
/*  Next compute Tz = z^2 + z matrix.  We already have every power of x in
        the Trace matrix, so each row of Tz is two rows from Trace.  Do
        partial inversion to get Tmatrix.
*/
        for ( i=0; i<NUMBITS; i++)
        {
                SUMLOOP(j)
                {
```

```
                    Tz[i].e[j] = Trace[i].e[j] ^ Trace[i<<1].e[j];
                    T2[i].e[j] = Trace[i<<1].e[j];
            }
    }

/*  Invert T2 matrix to get special square root matrix (called Smatrix)  */

    if (error = poly_matrix_invert( T2, Smatrix))
    {
            printf("Can not invert square root matrix.  Null row = %d\n",
                        error);
            return(error);
    }
```

The next step appears to be an "almost inversion" process on the `Tz` matrix. The algorithm starts out the same as inversion: Create a diagonal matrix alongside the original matrix and try to diagonalize `Tz`, performing every row operation on both. The differences are that we expect to hit a null row and we don't need an intermediate matrix, because there is no transpose to perform. When we are done diagonalizing `Tz`, we'll have what we need in the `Tmatrix` to solve any quadratic (that can be solved) for all polynomials modulo `poly_prime`.

```
/*  Create a set of basis vectors for use in finding roots of z^2 + z = c
        This is similar to the matrix inversion, but there is no transpose and
        the row order is different.  Exactly how this works is not clear to me,
        but Prof. Pinch gets it and it works.
*/

/*  Create Tmatrix as diagonalized  */

    for ( row=0; row<NUMBITS; row++)
    {
        null( &Tmatrix[row]);
        Tmatrix[row].e[NUMWORD - row/WORDSIZE] = 1L << ( row % WORDSIZE);
    }
```

As with the matrix inversion, we need to find a row with its column bit set to create a diagonal. The following code is copied from the matrix inversion, but I've added the variable `nulldex`. The problem is to match the null row with a null column. Variable `nulldex` tells me where I left the null row, so that when I do find a null column I can set the null row and null column to pivot around the diagonal. This makes my life much easier in the long run.

```
/*  Semi diagonalize input matrix.
        First find a column bit that is set, and swap with diagonal
        row if needed.  Then eliminate all bits below it.
*/

    Null_Row = 0;
```

```
                nulldex = 0;
                for ( row = 0; row < NUMBITS; row++)
                {
                        rowdex = NUMWORD - row/WORDSIZE;
                        src_mask = 1L << (row % WORDSIZE);

/*  find a row of input matrix which has col = row bit set.
     First see if we get lucky, then do search.
*/
                        found = 0;
                        if ( !(Tz[row].e[rowdex] & src_mask))
                        {
                                for (j = row+1; j<NUMBITS; j++)
                                {
                                        if ( Tz[j].e[rowdex] & src_mask)
                                        {   /*  found one, swap rows  */
                                                copy( &Tmatrix[j], &dummy);
                                                copy( &Tmatrix[row], &Tmatrix[j]);
                                                copy( &dummy, &Tmatrix[row]);
                                                copy( &Tz[j], &dummy);
                                                copy( &Tz[row], &Tz[j]);
                                                copy( &dummy, &Tz[row]);
                                                found = 1;
                                        /*  keep track of original null row */
                                                if (row == nulldex) nulldex = j;
                                                break;

                                        }
                                }
                        }
                        else found = 1;
```

Yet another difference is the order of row operations. Once the diagonal bit is set, each column is cleared for the "downward" bits from the diagonal. This eliminates all coefficients in one direction only and amounts to solving a set of linear equations ([11, 498]). When we're all done with this step, the `Null_Row` variable will be set equal to the null column (a "don't care" coefficient) and the last row, with only 1 bit set in its last column.

```
/*  eliminate all other terms below diagonal in this column  */

                        if (found)
                        {
                                for ( i=row+1; i<NUMBITS; i++)
                                {
                                        if ( Tz[i].e[rowdex] & src_mask)
                                        {
                                                SUMLOOP(j)
                                                {
                                                        Tmatrix[i].e[j] ^= Tmatrix[row].e[j];
                                                        Tz[i].e[j] ^= Tz[row].e[j];
                                                }
                                        }
                                }
```

```
                }
        }                       /*  end column eliminate  */
        else
        {               /*  mark null row and swap position with original  */
        Null_Row = row;
        copy( &Tmatrix[nulldex], &dummy);
        copy( &Tmatrix[row], &Tmatrix[nulldex]);
        copy( &dummy, &Tmatrix[row]);
        copy( &Tz[nulldex], &dummy);
        copy( &Tz[row], &Tz[nulldex]);
        copy( &dummy, &Tz[row]);
        }
    }                           /*  end diagonalization  */
```

Starting from the last row, all the coefficients in the "upward" direction are then cleared from the diagonal. This amounts to back-solving the set of linear equations. Matrix `Tz` is then diagonalized, and the `Tmatrix` consists of a set of basis vectors, which we'll use to solve quadratic equations.

```
/*  finally eliminate all other terms above diagonal except for
        Null_Row.  Result is a set of basis vectors which converts
        c to z and z^2 + z = c.
*/

        for ( row = NUMBITS-1; row > 0; row--)
        {
                if (row == Null_Row) continue;

                rowdex = NUMWORD - row/WORDSIZE;
                src_mask = 1L << (row % WORDSIZE);

                for (i = row-1; i>=0; i--)
                {
                        if (Tz[i].e[rowdex] & src_mask)
                        {
                                SUMLOOP(j)
                                {
                                        Tmatrix[i].e[j] ^= Tmatrix[row].e[j];
                                        Tz[i].e[j] ^= Tz[row].e[j];
                                }
                        }
                }
        }                       /*  end column eliminate  */
        return(0);
}
```

The above code solves a system of linear equations. The equations came from an expansion of each coefficient of a power of x in an arbitrary variable z taken modulo the prime polynomial. While it sounds messy, all we are doing is searching for set bits in a particular place and then using exclusive-or to eliminate all other bits in that same place.

The parallel matrix starts out diagonal and ends up holding the answer. Once we have the generic solution, we can use it to find any specific solution.

Inverting the Smatrix worked, because the z^2 matrix has as many equations as unknowns. Inverting the T_z matrix does not work, because we have the Trace condition to satisfy. This additional equation has to exist, since the last row in $z^2 + z$ cancels to 0. For any set of coefficients we must first compute c from equation (6.8), check that the Trace(c) = 0, and then use all bits set in c (except for the null row bit) to determine what z is. So much for the description, let's see some details.

6.10 Using the T matrix

Just as with the normal basis quadratic solver, the polynomial basis version returns error code 0 if there are solutions and error code 1 if not. Since there is nothing else to check, there is no such thing as an error code 2. The following routine uses equation (6.4) as input (copied here):

$$y^2 + xy + f(x) = 0 \qquad\qquad (6.22)$$

for the coefficient names and outputs two y values if there is a solution. If the input coefficient x is 0, the routine jumps to the end and performs a square root of $f(x)$. If x is not 0, we can calculate c as follows:

```
INDEX poly_quadratic( x, f, y)
FIELD2N *x, *f, y[2];
{
        FIELD2N        c, z, dummy;
        FIELD2N        test1, test2;
        INDEX          i, j, k;
        ELEMENT        sum, mask;

/*  first check to see if x is zero  */

        sum = 0;
        SUMLOOP(i) sum |= x->e[i];

        if (sum)
        {
/*  compute c = x^-2 * f  */

                copy (x, &c);
                poly_mul(&c, x, &dummy);         /*  get x^2  */
                poly_inv(&dummy, &z);
                poly_mul( f, &z, &c);
```

The next step is to compute the Trace(c). This is the "dot product" of the Trace_Vector and c; a binary multiplication uses AND—the sum is XOR. We've seen the summation code before. While easy to code, the number of bits set in the Trace_Vector is usually small, so this tends to be wasteful of processor time.

```
/*   verify that trace of c = 0.   If not, no solution
         is possible.   */

                sum = 0;
                SUMLOOP(i) sum ^= c.e[i] & Trace_Vector.e[i];
                mask = ~0;
                for (i = WORDSIZE/2; i > 0; i >>= 1)
                {
                        mask >>= i;
                        sum = ((sum & mask) ^ (sum >> i));
                }
```

If the Trace is 1, there is no solution. Clear the y values and return error code 1.

```
    /* if last bit is set, there is no solution to equation.
    This eliminates half the points in the field, which might
    make sense to a mathematician.
    */
                if (sum)
                {
                        null( &y[0]);
                        null( &y[1]);
                        return(1);
                }
```

For Trace equals 0, we get to use the Tmatrix and compute z from c. The first step is to eliminate the null row bit from c. Then, for every bit k in c that is set, we add row k of the Tmatrix to the solution for z. Calling the Tmatrix "a set of basis vectors" should now make sense; each possible bit in c has a specific solution for the given prime polynomial.

```
/*   clear out null row bit.   that part of matrix will not work.   */

                j = NUMWORD - Null_Row / WORDSIZE;
                c.e[j] &= ~( 1L << (Null_Row % WORDSIZE));

/*   for every bit set in c, add that row of Tmatrix to solution.   */

                null( &z);
                mask = 1;
                j = NUMWORD;
                for (i=0; i<NUMBITS; i++)
                {
                        if ( c.e[j] & mask)
                                SUMLOOP(k) z.e[k] ^= Tmatrix[i].e[k];
```

```
                    mask <<= 1;
                    if ( !mask)
                    {
                            mask = 1;
                            j--;
                    }
            }
```

Inside the loop, j keeps track of the ELEMENT index and mask tracks the bit within that ELEMENT. As usual, when mask goes to 0, j is decremented.

The last step for a full solution is the same as in a normal basis. The first solution, y[0], is set to x times z; the second solution, y[1], is set to x times $z + 1$.

```
/*  compute final solution using input parameters.  */

            poly_mul( x, &z, &y[0]);
            SUMLOOP(i) y[1].e[i] = y[0].e[i] ^ x->e[i];
            return(0);
    }
```

If the input x value in equation (6.22) is 0, we need to compute the square root of $f(x)$. Fortunately, this is easy because we have already precomputed the Smatrix. We multiply the Smatrix times f as a column vector to find z as a column vector. This amounts to the dot product of each row of the Smatrix with f for each bit of z. After that, z is copied to both values of y. Then the routine exits with no error.

```
    else
    {
/*  x input was zero.  Return y = square root of f. Process
    involves ANDing each row of Smatrix with f and summing
    all bits to find coefficient for that power of x */

        null( &z);
        for (j = 0; j<NUMBITS; j++)
        {
            sum = 0;
            SUMLOOP(i) sum ^= Smatrix[j].e[i] & f->e[i];
            if (sum)
            {
                mask = -1L;
                for (i = WORDSIZE/2; i > 0; i >>= 1)
                {
                    mask >>= i;
                    sum = ((sum & mask) ^ (sum >> i));
                }
            }
            if (sum) z.e[NUMWORD - j/WORDSIZE] |= (1L << j%WORDSIZE);
        }
        copy( &z, &y[0]);
        copy( &z, &y[1]);
        return(0);
```

```
        }
}
```

Solving the quadratic equation over a polynomial basis is far more involved than solving it over a normal basis. The initialization is the most time-consuming part, but it only needs to be done once. The biggest drawback for hardware or firmware is the amount of data storage. If embedding data on a curve is needed on a smart card, then the normal basis representation will consume fewer resources. For any other application data storage won't be a problem.

6.11 Embedding data using polynomial basis

To embed data onto an elliptic curve over a polynomial basis, we use the same techniques as with an optimal normal basis. The first step is to compute the right-hand side of equation (6.1). Here's an example.

```
/*  compute f(x) = x^3 + a_2*x^2 + a_6 for non-supersingular elliptic curves
*/

void poly_fofx( x, curv, f)
FIELD2N *x, *f;
CURVE *curv;
{
        FIELD2N         x2, x3;
        INDEX           i;

        copy ( x, &x3);
        poly_mul( x, &x3, &x2);          /*  get x^2  */
        if (curv->form) poly_mul ( &x2, &curv->a2, f);
        else null( f);
        poly_mul( x, &x2, &x3);          /*  get x^3  */
        SUMLOOP (i) f->e[i] ^= ( x3.e[i] ^ curv->a6.e[i] );
}
```

It is really the same thing as the optimal normal basis version, but squaring must be done via the prime polynomial. The structure of the calling routine is the same.

Then, to actually embed data onto the curve, we perform the following function:

```
/*  embed data onto a curve.
    Enter with data, curve, ELEMENT offset to be used as increment, and
    which root (0 or 1).
    Returns with point having data as x and correct y value for curve.
    Will use y[0] for last bit of root clear, y[1] for last bit of root set.
    if ELEMENT offset is out of range, default is 0.
*/

void poly_embed( data, curv, incrmt, root, pnt)
```

```
FIELD2N     *data;
CURVE       *curv;
INDEX       incrmt, root;
POINT       *pnt;
{
    FIELD2N    f, y[2];
    INDEX      inc = incrmt;
    INDEX      i;

    if ( (inc < 0) || (inc > NUMWORD) ) inc = 0;
    copy( data, &pnt->x);
    poly_fofx( &pnt->x, curv, &f);
    while (poly_quadratic( &pnt->x, &f, y))
    {
        pnt->x.e[inc]++;
        poly_fofx( &pnt->x, curv, &f);
    }
    copy ( &y[root&1], &pnt->y);
}
```

This is identical to the optimal normal basis version; all I've done is replace the calls with their polynomial basis versions. Once the polynomial math package is initialized, calling the routines is easy. It does tend to be a bit slower than the optimal normal basis version in this implementation. So be my guest and improve the code!

6.12 Summary of quadratic solving

The point of all this math and code is to embed data onto curves. Once we have data on a curve, we can begin to manipulate these data in a cryptographically significant manner. It is important to remember that the data you want to embed on the curve must use fewer bits than the field size to ensure a selection of x values, which will be on the curve. Modify the *_embed routines to suit your application.

The choice of curve can be random or it can be a very specific one. For moderate security random curves are perfectly adequate. For high-security, curves of known order and no simple attack are necessary. These high security types of curves have been presented in this chapter. For those who want to use random curves and find the order, see [3] and references therein. Other methods of choosing known curves are given in the IEEE P1363 standard.

This book cannot hope to explain all the possible high-speed shortcuts found over the past few years that can greatly speed up polynomial basis calculations over elliptic curves. The interested reader is urged to read [12–14] for more details. Once the mathematics presented here is understood, these additional references should be easy to digest.

6.13 References

1 B. Schneier, *Applied Cryptography*, 2d ed. (New York: John Wiley & Sons, 1996).

2 A. Salomaa, *Public Key Cryptography* (Berlin: Springer-Verlag, 1990).

3 R. Lercier and F. Morain, "Counting the Number of Points on Elliptic Curves over Finite Fields: Strategies and Performances," in *EUROCRYPT '95* (Berlin: Springer-Verlag, 1995).

4 A. J. Menezes, *Elliptic Curve Public Key Cryptosystems* (Boston: Kluwer Academic Publishers, 1993).

5 P. C. van Oorschot and M. J. Wiener, "Parallel Collision Search with Cryptanalytic Applications" (Nortel, Ottawa, Canada, September 23, 1996, internal paper).

6 M. J. Wiener and R. J. Zuccherato, "Faster Attacks on Elliptic Curve Cryptosystems" (Entrust Technologies, Ottawa, Canada, April 8, 1988, internal paper).

7 N. Koblitz, "CM—Curves with Good Cryptographic Properties," *CRYPTO '91* (New York: Springer-Verlag, 1992), 279.

8 J. A. Solinas, "An Improved Algorithm for Arithmetic in a Family of Elliptic Curves," in *CRYPTO '97* (New York: Springer-Verlag, 1997).

9 N. Koblitz, *Introduction to Elliptic Curves and Modular Forms* (New York: Springer-Verlag, 1993).

10 E. Kreyszig, *Advanced Engineering Mathematics* (New York: John Wiley & Sons, 1962).

11 C. R. Wylie, *Advanced Engineering Mathematics*, 4th ed. (New York: McGraw-Hill, 1975).

12 R. Schroeppel, H. Orman, and S. O'Mally, "Fast Key Exchange with Elliptic Curve Systems," TR-95-03 (Tucson, AZ: University of Arizona, Computer Sciences Department, 1995). (Also appears in *CRYPTO '95* [New York: Springer-Verlag, 1995].)

13 D. Beauregard, "Efficient Algorithms for Implementing Elliptic Curve Public Key Schemes" (Master's thesis, Worcester Polytechnic Institute, Worcester, MA, 1996).

14 E. De Win, A. Bosselaers, S. Vandenberghe, P. De Gersem, and J. Vandewalle, "A Fast Software Implementation for Arithmetic Operations in GF (2^n)," *ASIACRYPT '96* (Berlin: Springer-Verlag, 1996), 65–76.

C H A P T E R   7

Simple protocols

7.1 Introduction   166

7.2 Random bit generator   168

7.3 Choosing random curves   171

7.4 Protocols   174

7.5 References   197

7.1 Introduction

Now wait a minute, you're thinking, where is the crypto in the previous chapters? We have covered all the math of finite fields, elliptic curves, and the basics of getting real data onto a curve, but we have yet to actually hide any data. This chapter will show you how to do that. It is called, "Simple protocols," because the schemes presented in this chapter utilize only one type of math package. In the next chapters, we'll combine hash functions and integer routines with polynomial or normal basis for more complex protocols.

Koblitz [1] mentions two schemes that we'll cover in this chapter and one that I'll save until later. These are basic protocols, which will work for most applications. We'll also discuss one of the more advanced ideas covered by the IEEE P1363 draft standard for public key cryptography. All these protocols are used for secret sharing. They are a way to send a symmetric key over unsecure networks.

As in the previous chapter, I will use the term "public key" for data that are visible to everyone and "private key" for data held by a single individual. While a private key is also secret, a "secret key" has to be shared between two computers to encrypt and decrypt long messages quickly. A private key remains secret to the person holding it. In the next chapter, I'll give an example of an elliptic curve encryption scheme first described in the November 1995 draft of the IEEE P1363 document.

The three protocols suggested by [1] are called Diffie-Hellman, Massey-Omura, and ElGamal. The original inventors of these schemes did not foresee the elliptic curve version, but their names are still attached to the basic idea. I'll cover Diffie-Hellman and ElGamal in this chapter. For Massey-Omura we also need modular arithmetic (over integers), so I'll discuss it in chapter 9. Massey-Omura is a multipass protocol, which means we need to send several points in the clear to complete the process. For closely coupled systems this is not a problem, but for long-range communications it may be.

The subroutine schematic for this chapter is shown in figure 7.1. All the previous mathematical subroutines are needed to implement the protocols. The polynomial and normal basis versions are very similar; you just need to replace one or the other to complete a protocol. After introducing a random bit generator, we'll get into example protocols. Detailed examples of how to use the subroutines along with real data are also included.

The first step in any protocol is the creation of a secret. The process of creating a secret is a security problem that goes far beyond the scope of this book. For the examples that follow, I will assume "secrets" as known inputs. In the real world, getting the secret from the user into the computer is an interesting challenge. One of the most useful ways to test a cryptographic system is with random input data. Therefore, I'll preface this

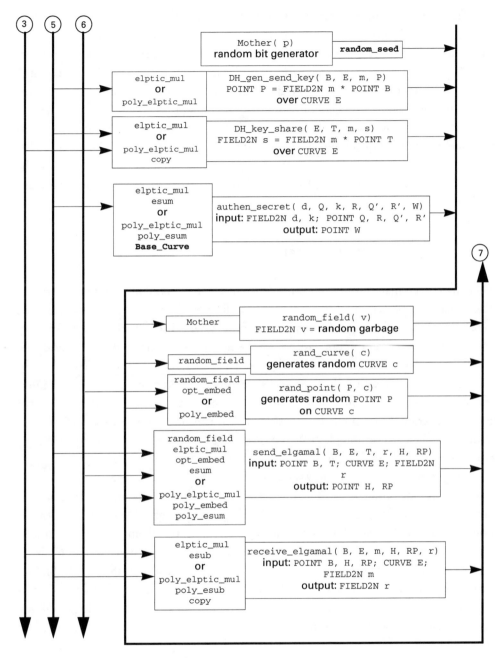

Figure 7.1 Subroutine schematic

chapter with a few routines that cover one of my favorite pseudorandom bit algorithms. Later, I'll put randomization to a different use in constructing crypto systems.

The second step in any protocol is the selection of public key parameters. For elliptic curve protocols this means choosing the curve and some base point on the curve. As an initial point of reference, it took over a month for mathematical researchers using several 500-MHz processors to crack the first Certicom 79-bit challenge in December 1997. This challenge was based on random curves and points. For normal communication conditions—practical telephony, Internet e-mail, and Web pages—random curves that give at a minimum several hours of security for the resources of even large corporations are perfectly adequate. For better security you need to pick known curves. Either the curves given in the previous chapter or an alternate method can be used (see the appendix to IEEE P1363). Now, let's take a look at picking random bits to create random curves.

7.2 Random bit generator

There have been many words and programs written about random number generators. The concept of random has little meaning in a digital computer, because it is designed to reproduce the same output for any given input. What is useful for cryptographic purposes is that an attacker can not easily guess the next bit knowing all the previous data.

George Marsaglia has been working in the area of random number generation for about 30 years. His recent DIEHARD tests are useful for determining if a random number generator is bad. It's almost impossible for any test to determine if a random number generator is good, but as long as one is not bad it can be considered useful. For more reading see [2] and visit the pLab Web pages (`http://random.mat.sbg.at/literature`), as well as Marsaglia's Web page (`http://stat.fsu.edu/~geo`).

The routine presented here was developed by Dr. Marsaglia several years ago. He reports the repeat period to be approximately 2^{250}, which is far beyond anything anyone can guess. Starting with a 32-bit seed seems risky at first sight. One can argue that it would be easy to tabulate all possible starting values and run them for several hundred rounds to compare with any particular use. Even if this were possible (several terabytes of storage would be required), it would not be helpful. The reason is that the 32-bit pattern will be repeated 2^{218} times. It would be difficult to tell where a pattern was a repeat seed and where it was an initial seed. This won't stop the NSA from trying, so if you need nuclear-grade security you may wish to do a great deal of research into random bit generators.

Here is Marsaglia's code. He calls it the "Mother" of all random bit generators. I've turned off the floating-point output in this copy; it's obvious how to turn it back on.

```
/*  random seed is accessible to everyone, not best way, but functional.  */
```

```
unsigned long random_seed;

/*  below is from Mother code, till end of mother.  Above is all my fault.  */

#include <string.h>

static short mother1[10];
static short mother2[10];
static short mStart=1;

#define m16Long 65536L                          /* 2^16 */
#define m16Mask 0xFFFF          /* mask for lower 16 bits */
#define m15Mask 0x7FFF              /* mask for lower 15 bits */
#define m31Mask 0x7FFFFFFF      /* mask for 31 bits */
#define m32Double  4294967295.0  /* 2^32-1 */

/* Mother ********************************************************

|       George Marsaglia's The mother of all random number generators

|            producing uniformly distributed pseudo random 32 bit values with

|             period about 2^250.

|    The arrays mother1 and mother2 store carry values in their
|            first element, and random 16 bit numbers in elements 1 to 8.
|            These random numbers are moved to elements 2 to 9 and a new
|            carry and number are generated and placed in elements 0 and 1.
|    The arrays mother1 and mother2 are filled with random 16 bit values
|            on first call of Mother by another generator.  mStart is the
|               switch.

|    Returns:
|    A 32 bit random number is obtained by combining the output of the
|            two generators and returned in *pSeed.  It is also scaled by
|            2^32-1 and returned as a double between 0 and 1

|    SEED:
|    The inital value of *pSeed may be any long value

|    Bob Wheeler 8/8/94

|    removed double return since I don't need it.  mgr
*/


void Mother(unsigned long *pSeed)
{
        unsigned long   number,
                        number1,
                        number2;
        short           n,
                        *p;
        unsigned short sNumber;
```

```
                    /* Initialize motheri with 9 random values the first time */
        if (mStart) {
                sNumber= *pSeed&m16Mask;    /* The low 16 bits */
                number= *pSeed&m31Mask;    /* Only want 31 bits */

                p=mother1;
                for (n=18;n--;) {
                        number=30903*sNumber+(number>>16);
                                /* One line multiply-with-cary */
                        *p++=sNumber=number&m16Mask;
                        if (n==9)
                                p=mother2;
                }
                /* make cary 15 bits */
                mother1[0]&=m15Mask;
                mother2[0]&=m15Mask;
                mStart=0;
        }
                /* Move elements 1 to 8 to 2 to 9 */
        memmove(mother1+2,mother1+1,8*sizeof(short));
        memmove(mother2+2,mother2+1,8*sizeof(short));

                /* Put the carry values in numberi */
        number1=mother1[0];
        number2=mother2[0];

                /* Form the linear combinations */
number1+=1941*mother1[2]+1860*mother1[3]+1812*mother1[4]+1776*mother1[5]+
        1492*mother1[6]+1215*mother1[7]+1066*mother1[8]+12013*mother1[9];

number2+=1111*mother2[2]+2222*mother2[3]+3333*mother2[4]+4444*mother2[5]+
        5555*mother2[6]+6666*mother2[7]+7777*mother2[8]+9272*mother2[9];

                /* Save the high bits of numberi as the new carry */
        mother1[0]=number1/m16Long;
        mother2[0]=number2/m16Long;
                /* Put the low bits of numberi into motheri[1] */
        mother1[1]=m16Mask&number1;
        mother2[1]=m16Mask&number2;

                /* Combine the two 16 bit random numbers into one 32 bit */
        *pSeed=(((long)mother1[1])<<16)+(long)mother2[1];

                /* Return a double value between 0 and 1
        return ((double)*pSeed)/m32Double;   */
}
```

It is clear that the internal state of the generator determines the output. The initial seed is used to create the initial internal state, so this should be as random as possible to begin with. The source of random data can be interval timings between keystrokes or it can be 32 coin flips. While slower, the latter is easy to implement without access to special timing or hardware calls.

It should be noted that the internal state of the random bit generator (any random bit generator, not just the above example) should be secure from outside access. The RAM storage should be locked-down memory, which is purged after use, and the seed value should be in a hidden file if saved for the next invocation. This is a point of security: If the internal state of the random bit generator is known, then the signature protocols (in the following chapters) will be easy to attack. No matter how you implement a random bit generator, it should be considered a security risk and programmed accordingly.

The routine that calls `Mother` to fill in a `FIELD2N` variable is very simple. This particular invocation assumes the word size of the machine is less than or equal to the 32-bit random seed value. For machine words larger than this, another random generator, which fills each word in one shot, is probably going to be more useful than multiple calls to `Mother`.

```
/*  Generate a random bit pattern which fits in a FIELD2N size variable.
        Calls Mother as many times as needed to create the value.
*/

void random_field( value)
FIELD2N *value;
{
        INDEX   i;

        SUMLOOP(i)
        {
                Mother( &random_seed);
                value->e[i] = random_seed;
        }
        value->e[0] &= UPRMASK;
}
```

There is far more to know about random bit generators. The statistical analysis of these algorithms is very sophisticated, and there are many books that discuss this topic. We'll leave that to the experts. Suffice it to say that a great deal of work has gone into random bit generators, and to get a job done all we have to do is copy one.

7.3 Choosing random curves

Choosing good curves is hard. A "good" curve for cryptographic purposes is not the same thing as a good curve for factoring purposes. For cryptography we want the order of the curve to contain the largest prime number possible. From Hasse's Theorem (see chapter 5) we do know that the order of an elliptic curve (called *#E* by mathematicians) lies in the range:

$$2^n - 2\sqrt{2^n} + 1 \le \#E \le 2^n + 2\sqrt{2^n} + 1 \qquad (7.1)$$

where *n* is the number of bits in the field (NUMBITS in the code). If *n* is 64, the range of the cardinality is:

$$0 \times 100020001 > \#E > 0 \times \text{FFFE001}. \qquad (7.2)$$

Since most of us don't think in hexadecimal, that converts to:

$$1.844674407 \times 10^{19} > \#E > 1.8446744 \times 10^{19} \qquad (7.3)$$

in decimal. Since the quantity of numbers in the range of equation (7.3) is only $2^{34} = 1.7179869 \times 10^{10}$, one could actually brute-force search for the largest primes. Matching such a cardinality to a particular curve is nontrivial.

The overall security of an elliptic curve crypto system is proportional to the square root of the largest prime factor of the curve order. So, our random 64-bit curve is equivalent to approximately a 20-bit symmetric key to someone who actually knows how to implement the square root methods described in [3, 50], [4], and [5].

The distribution of curve order appears to be related to field structure. For fields over F_{2^p} where *p* is prime, curve orders tend to have a large prime factor. For fields over F_{2^m} with *m* having many factors, curve orders tend to be smooth (meaning many small factors). For *m* with only two factors, it is possible to find both good and bad curves. For random curves it appears that using fields of F_{2^p} has a higher probability of being secure. (See [6] for examples.)

Here is some code to create a random curve. It's really simple.

```
/*  generate a random curve for a given field size.
        Enter with pointer to storage space for returned curve.
        Returns with curve.form = 0, curve.a2 = 0 and curve.a6
        as a random bit pattern.  This is for the equation

            y^2 + xy = x^3 + a_2x^2 + a_6
*/

void rand_curve ( curv)
CURVE *curv;
{
        curv->form = 0;
        random_field( &curv->a6);
        null( &curv->a2);
}
```

Since the curve is random, setting the coefficient of x^2 to 0 does not matter. But if we know the cardinality (such as those curves described in [7]), this term may be necessary. The only reason to do this rather than generate two random bit fields is that the elliptic curve calculations are slightly faster.

When we generate a random point on a curve, we usually want that point to belong to the largest possible group on the curve. That group size will be the largest prime factor of the order of the curve. A point at random will most likely be in that largest group. If you don't know the cardinality of the curve, you won't know. The larger the largest prime factor, the higher the probability that a random point will be in that group.

For medium-security situations, this does not matter. For high-security situations, it matters a lot. The way to check the order of a random point is to multiply by the factors of the order of the curve plus 1 and check to see if you get the starting point back. If you do, you know the order of the point must have one of the factors you multiplied by. Mathematically:

$$P = (n+1)P \qquad (7.4)$$

where n is the order of the point P that is on the curve.

The odds of being unlucky enough to choose a point on a "smooth" curve with lots of small factors is fairly small if you choose a prime value for NUMBITS. But it's going to happen if you choose many random curves and points. If you use random curves and points, change them often to ensure that the amount of data exposed to a weak combination is low. If you really need security, use known curves!

Here is some code to generate a random point on a chosen curve.

```
/*  generate a random point on a given curve.
        Enter with pointer to curve and one pointer
        to storage space for returned point.  Returns
        one of solutions to above equation. Negate point
        to get other solution.
*/

void rand_point( point, curve)
POINT   *point;
CURVE   *curve;
{
        FIELD2N         rf;

        random_field( &rf);
        opt_embed( &rf, curve, NUMWORD, rf.e[NUMWORD]&1, point);
}
```

All we're doing here is creating a random x value for a point and then forcing it onto the curve. This is random security. Increase your probability of better security by using a higher number for NUMBITS. But be careful: The time it takes to compute an elliptic curve multiply is proportional to NUMBITS^3.

Now that we have a public curve and point and some presumed secret bits, we can look at some of the basic protocols. All these protocols solve the problem of secret sharing and are useful for communication. The last two protocols help with authentication problems.

7.4 Protocols

We will now discuss two of the three major protocols: Diffie-Hellman and ElGamal. The third major protocol, Massey-Omura, will be discussed in chapter 9. After discussing Diffie-Hellman and ElGamal, we will focus on the Menezes-Qu-Vanstone key agreement scheme, which is more advanced than the Diffie-Hellman scheme but includes the Diffie-Hellman protocol as a subset.

7.4.1 Diffie-Hellman

The first scheme is the original public key crypto system proposed for secret sharing. It is called the Diffie-Hellman protocol for the inventors (see [8, chapter 22] for a description). The IEEE proposed standard suggests this as a basic secret-sharing algorithm (called ECKAS-DH, Elliptic Curve Key Agreement Scheme, Diffie-Hellman); but they also have a few other ideas, which are improvements on the Diffie-Hellman scheme, to solve a few interesting problems.

As in most texts on crypto, we have to introduce two people who actually want to communicate with each other. We'll let A be Alicia and B be Brandon. Both Alicia and Brandon chose their own private key to be a random bit pattern in a mutually agreed upon field size. Let k_A be Alicia's key and k_B belong to Brandon. They first agree to use a specific curve, field size, and type of mathematics (polynomial or optimal normal basis). Usually those decisions are made by the programmer, but however it gets done it will be public information. The elliptic curve is one that satisfies equation (6.1).

They then chose a random base point, B, on the chosen elliptic curve. This too is public. Brandon computes:

$$P_B = k_B B \qquad (7.5)$$

over the chosen elliptic curve and sends it to Alicia. Alicia computes:

$$P_A = k_A B \qquad (7.6)$$

and sends it to Brandon. Then they both compute the shared secret:

$$P_s = k_A(k_B B) = k_B(k_A B).\qquad (7.7)$$

Now, you might think that you have both an x and a y value, which can be used for the shared secret. But, really, only 1 bit of y is necessary, since we could recover the value of y from the elliptic curve equation using the quadratic equation solver code from the previous chapter. For reasonable security it is important to use only the x value from equation (7.7).

Let's see what it takes to implement the Diffie-Hellman protocol using the code from the previous chapters. The first routine really is simple and doesn't need to be a separate subroutine at all. We just need to generate a public key using the chosen curve and base point.

```
/*  Compute a Diffie-Hellman key exchange.

        First routine computes senders public key.
        Enter with public point Base_point which sits on public curve E and
        senders private key my_private.
        Returns public key point My_public = my_private*Base_point to be sent
        to other side.
*/
void DH_gen_send_key( Base_point, E, my_private, My_public)
POINT *Base_point, *My_public;
CURVE *E;
FIELD2N *my_private;
{
        elptic_mul( my_private, Base_point, My_public, E);
}
```

All we do is multiply the private key my_private times the public Base_point to get our public key point My_public. The magic of the mathematics is buried in the elliptic curve multiply. By choosing a large enough field size (greater than 140 bits, for example), we can be reasonably sure that only the NSA could ever hope to begin finding the private key. And, if you choose a curve mentioned in the previous chapter, it is truly impossible to find the private key (for the near future).

Once the public point My_public is computed, it must be sent to the other side. Whoever is going to communicate will send back his or her public key to us. The details of this transmission are left to the application, but let's assume both sides have the same code. To find the shared secret we do the following:

```
/*      Second routine computes shared secret that is same for sender and
        receiver.
        Enter with public point Base_point which sits on public curve E along
        with senders public key their_public and receivers private key
        my_private.
        Returns shared_secret as x component of elliptic multiply.
```

```
*/

void DH_key_share(Base_point, E, their_public, my_private, shared_secret)
POINT *Base_point, *their_public;
CURVE *E;
FIELD2N *my_private, *shared_secret;
{
        POINT   temp;

        elptic_mul( my_private, their_public, &temp, E);
        copy (&temp.x, shared_secret);
}
```

Again, there is not a lot here for a complete routine, but the idea is to use the basic mathematics to create a very simple protocol. Each side will possess the same secret after the exchange is completed, and anyone listening in to the communication will not be able to figure out what that secret is without solving the elliptic curve discrete logarithm problem. The actual number of bits used from the secret can be less than the field size. For most applications this makes sense, and for maximum security it should be at most only half of the field, because the level of security is proportional to the square root of the largest factor in the order of the public point. Obviously the position of the bits that get used should be assumed as public knowledge. The critical issue here is the user's private key, my_private, which must not be revealed. That is a security problem you will have to deal with.

As an example, here is a test routine and its output using normal basis with 131-bit field size. The random bit generator is initialized with a fixed constant, so this test should produce the same results on all implementations. This is a Type II field.

```
main()
{
        FIELD2N         private1, private2, key1, key2;
        CURVE           rnd_crv;
        POINT           Base, P1, P2;

        random_seed = 0x1325fe9b;

#ifdef TYPE2
        genlambda2();
#else
        genlambda();
#endif

        printf("create random curve and point\n\n");

        rand_curve(&rnd_crv);
        print_curve("random curve", &rnd_crv);
        rand_point(&Base, &rnd_crv);
        print_point("Base point", &Base);
```

```
        printf("\ncreate each sides private key\n\n");

        random_field(&private1);
        print_field("Side 1 secret:", &private1);
        random_field(&private2);
        print_field("Side 2 secret:", &private2);

        printf("\nGenerate each sides public key\n\n");

        DH_gen_send_key( &Base, &rnd_crv, &private1, &P1);
        print_point("Side 1 public key", &P1);
        DH_gen_send_key( &Base, &rnd_crv, &private2, &P2);
        print_point("Side 2 public key", &P2);

        printf("\nShow that each side gets the same shared secret\n\n");

        DH_key_share( &Base, &rnd_crv, &P2, &private1, &key1);
        print_field("key 1 is", &key1);
        DH_key_share( &Base, &rnd_crv, &P1, &private2, &key2);
        print_field("key 2 is", &key2);
}
```

The output of the above code is as follows:

```
create random curve and point

random curve
form = 0
a6 :          1 8c6651fd abfdc0c0 ea79f216 9b5f15ed

Base point
x :          2 821b8b1d 13847fd6 e8cbd586 7400e917
y :          1 b91f3605 eca4f933 9c118e9d 1deaf35f


create each sides private key

Side 1 secret: :       7 dcc910af 687ea94c 57b15969 ce792322
Side 2 secret: :       1 b57a7beb 31290e35 d03aef2e abc03aab

Generate each sides public key

Side 1 public key
x :          1 efaf23a0 b4707892  4933883 49ed6980
y :          7 469a18ed 3ef4f782 b58e1078 4f93fcef

Side 2 public key
x :          5 1a98a11e  3ec9a73 4a983ac6 bdbadd55
y :          6 224f65c5 2eaad16a 294591fe 71031b33


Show that each side gets the same shared secret

key 1 is :          5 17e4d32f c2fa5703 3f325785 f23acdfd
```

```
key 2 is :          5 17e4d32f c2fa5703 3f325785 f23acdfd
```

Note that each side has to transmit its public key to the other side before a common secret can be computed. The private keys have to be kept until the secret is created. After that, they can be lost so that new public keys can be generated the next time a communications link is set up.

For polynomial versions of the above code, we just substitute the polynomial elliptic curve subroutine `poly_elptic_mul` for `elpti_mul` in the above routines. There's really no point in calling separate routines; the Diffie-Hellman protocol can be buried anywhere you need it. Here is an example using the same field size but with the polynomial basis routines.

```
main()
{
        FIELD2N        private1, private2, key1, key2;
        CURVE          rnd_crv;
        POINT          Base, P1, P2, P3, P4;
        INDEX          error;

        random_seed = 0x15fe932b;

        if (!irreducible(&poly_prime)) return(0);
        print_field("poly_prime = ", &poly_prime);

        if (error = init_poly_math())
        {
                printf("Can't initialize S matrix, row = %d\n", error);
                return(-1);
        }

        rand_curve(&rnd_crv);
        print_curve("random curve", &rnd_crv);
        rand_point(&Base, &rnd_crv);
        print_point("Base point", &Base);

/*      printf("\ncreate each sides private key\n\n");
*/

        random_field(&private1);
        print_field("Side 1 secret:", &private1);
        random_field(&private2);
        print_field("Side 2 secret:", &private2);

        printf("\nGenerate each sides public key\n\n");

        DH_gen_send_key( &Base, &rnd_crv, &private1, &P1);
        print_point("Side 1 public key", &P1);
        DH_gen_send_key( &Base, &rnd_crv, &private2, &P2);
        print_point("Side 2 public key", &P2);

        printf("\nShow that each side gets the same shared secret\n\n");
```

```
        DH_key_share( &Base, &rnd_crv, &P2, &private1, &key1);
        print_field("key 1 is", &key1);
        DH_key_share( &Base, &rnd_crv, &P1, &private2, &key2);
        print_field("key 2 is", &key2);
}
```

Using a prime polynomial from [8] for $F_{2^{131}}$, the above code generates the following output:

```
poly_prime =  :        8      0      0      0    10d
random curve
form = 0
a6 :          1 830c9705 1c7e0f3f 9888bd5d 5980a3e5

Base point
x :           2 9039e676 6d7f0d1f da25ad06 aec21605
y :           4 7ff08b74 fdc724af bf15389b 3a0f09d0

Side 1 secret: :       7 b2abf428 1ed42e0d 2e3999a8 719f3306
Side 2 secret: :       6 55db41f7 52a8598f b376c901 4fc56eb3

Generate each sides public key

Side 1 public key
x :           5 e6f412d8 829622dd 2a48ba2f 761c6eea
y :           0 140d3641 fc339a4c 44123056 d39addee

Side 2 public key
x :           4 fa58876 fc501f48 e7ce1570 4d92ac8d
y :           2 da0a2d2f 373df235 45c7058e 75978c47


Show that each side gets the same shared secret

key 1 is :     4 23586dbf 3e3c0ea7 63ed2007 f52ee35e
key 2 is :     4 23586dbf 3e3c0ea7 63ed2007 f52ee35e
```

The problem with Diffie-Hellman is fundamental and is called the "man-in-the-middle" attack. Suppose Micah sits in the middle between Alicia and Brandon. He cuts the line and inserts his own computer. He gets Alicia's public key on one side and Brandon's public key on the other. He sends both of them his own public key. Both Brandon and Alicia are unaware that they are communicating through Micah, because they see that they can encrypt and decrypt data equally. Micah decrypts the data from Alicia using his shared secret with her and then reencrypts the data and forwards these data to Brandon. He can even change message data if he wants to wreak havoc.

This attack can be thwarted by several protocols, but the only sure way to eliminate it is to have more than one channel of communication. If the attacker can get in-between your phone and your ISP, the man-in-the-middle attack can be achieved. That's incredibly expensive, so once the public keys in the following protocol are verified they are much more secure than the straight Diffie-Hellman.

7.4.2 ElGamal Protocol

The elliptic curve analog to the original ElGamal public key encryption scheme is not mentioned in the IEEE P1363 draft. It is a very useful protocol for randomly generated curves and points, because it does not require knowledge of the order of the curve, the factors of that number, or the order of the base point. Another advantage is that it is not patented.

The elliptic curve version of ElGamal requires a chosen field size, mathematical basis, and public curve E, which satisfies equation (6.1). Since any nonzero random bit pattern for coefficient a_6 is allowed, we can choose a_2 to be 0. This helps speed up the calculations by 10 percent. Of course, it is always better for high security to use a known curve. But not every application involves protecting nuclear weapons.

A base point, B, which is public, must also be chosen. Both Alicia and Brandon choose some random bit pattern k_A and k_B, respectively. Alicia computes her public key:

$$P_A = k_A B \tag{7.8}$$

and sends it to Brandon. Brandon in turn computes his public key:

$$P_B = k_B B \tag{7.9}$$

and sends it to Alicia. Now, Alicia and Brandon can send messages using these public points in such a way that no one can discover the data without solving the discrete elliptic curve logarithm problem.

For Alicia to send a message to Brandon, she first embeds the message information onto the curve, E, using the embedding method shown in the previous chapter. Let's call this message point P_m. Alicia then chooses a random bit pattern, r, and computes two points:

$$P_r = rB \tag{7.10}$$

and

$$P_h = P_m + rP_B. \tag{7.11}$$

Alicia then sends both points P_r and P_h to Brandon. To extract the message point, Brandon computes:

$$P_s = k_B P_r \tag{7.12}$$

and subtracts this from P_h to get:

$$P_m = P_h - P_s. \qquad (7.13)$$

Let's expand equation (7.13) to see how this works. In equation (7.11) the second term on the right-hand side can be expanded using equation (7.9):

$$rP_B = r(k_B B). \qquad (7.14)$$

The term P_h in equation (7.13) is actually:

$$P_h = P_m + r(k_B B). \qquad (7.15)$$

Putting equation (7.10) into equation (7.12) to expand P_s, and combining this with equation (7.15) into equation (7.13), gives us:

$$P_m = P_m + r(k_B B) - k_B(rB) \qquad (7.16)$$

which is what we want. The only points the attacker sees are P_h, P_A, P_B, and P_r. The nice point about this protocol is that the public keys can stay public; there is no need to change them. Every time data are exchanged, a new random value r is chosen. Neither side needs to remember r, and, if the field size is large enough, it will be very difficult to discover the secret numbers k_B or k_A. This gives us both secret sharing and authentication.

For this protocol a man-in-the-middle attack is possible. Effort placed outside this protocol can effectively eliminate this attack by verifying the public keys via an alternate channel such as a telephone. This gives reasonable security and authentication too.

ElGamal using optimal normal basis.   Assuming a field size has already been chosen and a private key that fits that field size exists, here is the code that implements the ElGamal algorithm. We first have to pick a public curve and public point. For now, we'll take that as a given—for example, we are a newcomer to a company, and we need to create a new public key and transfer some files.

To generate the public key we only need to do the following:

```
elptic_mul( &private_key, &Base_Point, &My_Public, &Public_curve);
```

The real security problem here is the generation of the `private_key`. For the best security, it should never be stored on any medium other than the user's brain. Normally, one uses a hash function (see next chapter) on a pass phrase to create this private key. In the code that follows, we assume proper security precautions protect the private key.

For the sake of simplicity, let's call the other person's public key `Their_public`. We assume some kind of key management system is built in, so that the following code can actually work.

```
/*  Send data to another person using ElGamal protocol. Send Hidden_data and
        Random_point to other side. */

void send_elgamal(
                Base_point, Base_curve,
                Their_public, raw_data,
                Hidden_data, Random_point)
FIELD2N         *raw_data;
POINT           *Base_point, *Their_public, *Hidden_data, *Random_point;
CURVE           *Base_curve;
{
        FIELD2N         random_value;
        POINT           hidden_point, raw_point;

/*  create random point to help hide the data   */

        random_field (&random_value);
        elptic_mul (&random_value, Base_point, Random_point, Base_curve);

/*  embed raw data onto the chosen curve,  Assume raw data is contained in
        least significant ELEMENTs of the field variable and we won't hurt
        anything using the most significant to operate on.
        Uses the first root for y value.
*/

        opt_embed( raw_data, Base_curve, 0, 0, &raw_point);

/*  Create the hiding value using the other person's public key  */

        elptic_mul( &random_value, Their_public, &hidden_point, Base_curve);
        esum( &hidden_point, &raw_point, Hidden_data, Base_curve);
}
```

There are three steps to the transmission side of the protocol. The first step is to generate a random FIELD2N value, which I call `random_value`. We need to hide this value and send it to the other person. The hiding operation is the elliptic curve multiply call.

The second step is to embed the data onto the `Base_curve`. This method is described in chapter 6.

The third step is to hide the embedded data somewhere on the elliptic curve. To do this, we first multiply our random value times the receiver's public key and then add this value to the embedded data. The resulting hidden data point and random point are then sent to the other side.

Here is the code that the other side executes. It is very simple, since all we have to do is multiply our own private key times the random point and then subtract that result from the hidden point.

```
/*  Recieve data from another person using ElGamal protocol. We get
        Hidden_data and Random_point and output raw_data. */

void receive_elgamal(
                Base_point, Base_curve,
                my_private, Hidden_data, Random_point,
                raw_data)
FIELD2N         *my_private, *raw_data;
POINT           *Base_point, *Hidden_data, *Random_point;
CURVE           *Base_curve;
{
        POINT   hidden_point, raw_point;

/*  compute hidden point using my private key and the random point  */

        elptic_mul( my_private, Random_point, &hidden_point, Base_curve);
        esub( Hidden_data, &hidden_point, &raw_point, Base_curve);
        copy(&raw_point.x, raw_data);
}
```

Here is an example test routine to exercise the above code. Obviously, there is some communication that has to take place for these subroutines to be useful, but this test should give you an idea of how to set up the calls. Only one side is implemented, but the code is symmetric for all users.

```
main()
{
     FIELD2N    private1, private2, send_data, get_data;
     CURVE      Public_Curve;
     POINT      Base_Point, Their_public, Hidden_data, Random_point;

     random_seed = 0x139b25fe;

#ifdef TYPE2
     genlambda2();
#else
     genlambda();
#endif

     printf("create Base curve and point\n\n");

     rand_curve(&Public_Curve);
     print_curve("Public curve", &Public_Curve);
     rand_point(&Base_Point, &Public_Curve);
     print_point("Base point", &Base_Point);

     printf("\ncreate side 2's private key\n\n");
```

```
        random_field(&private2);
        print_field("Side 2 secret:", &private2);

        printf("\nGenerate side 2's public key\n\n");
        elptic_mul( &private2, &Base_Point, &Their_public, &Public_Curve);
        print_point("Side 2 public key", &Their_public);

        printf("\nCreate message data\n\n");
        random_field( &send_data);

        printf("\nHide data on curve and send from side 1 to side 2\n\n");
        send_elgamal( &Base_Point, &Public_Curve, &Their_public,
                          &send_data, &Hidden_data, &Random_point);
        print_point("Hidden data", &Hidden_data);
        print_point("Random point", &Random_point);
```

Now, side 1 (Alicia) sends the points `Hidden_data` and `Random_point` to side 2 (Brandon). This transmission can be direct or "compressed." The compressed version would include one bit for the *y* component, and the receive side would have to use the quadratic solver to recover the full *y* component. The tradeoff for this is transmission time cost versus CPU time cost and obviously depends on the application. In any case, once the points are received, Brandon computes the following:

```
        printf("\nRecover transmitted message\n\n");
        receive_elgamal( &Base_Point, &Public_Curve, &private2,
                          &Hidden_data, &Random_point, &get_data);
        print_field("sent data     ", &send_data);
        print_field("received data", &get_data);
}
```

Using field size with NUMBITS = 130 (a Type I field), I get the following output:

```
create Base curve and point

Public curve
form = 0
a6 :        0 5e629417 3dbdf669 b9fca0fe cd2165b0

Base point
x :        0 358df1ea 9ebc2e42 2fbec069 dde73d2c
y :        3 1eebc63e 37208618 ad902976 ee82a35c


create each sides private key

Side 1 secret: :        0 d2a3e242 4ce7401a 58e0e961 b20afcdf
Side 2 secret: :        1 99d659e8 3428a5da 9b130925 aed734d8

Generate side two public key

Side 2 public key
x :        0 e0ae7fb0 154fb309 99998f28 e45f667d
```

```
y :         1 c2f9ccaa    56e652 2a511643 4b2f90f3


Create message data


Hide data on curve and send from side 1 to side 2

Hidden data
x :        0  9ff62e2 874e9f23 642d0439 679cc775
y :        3 79559912 efbc58b4 931f4e98 d71225ce

Random point
x :        3 4ed89630 908268d0 c5791005 1eb7b27b
y :        0 17a3093e da5ee5f6 8df265c6 2cadc4a1


Recover transmitted message

sent data     :     2 f93ff6c8 e42f891b d8aeabdf cd419f2f
received data :     2 f93ff6c8 e42f891b d8aeabdf cd419f2f
```

In this example I got lucky—the random data fit on the curve on the first try. A good test that shows how random the hidden point is compared to the transmitted data is to flip just one bit in the `sent data` for every possible bit position and compare the hidden data using the same `Random_point`. This will give you a good idea of how well elliptic curve math really does scramble bits.

ElGamal: polynomial basis. The polynomial basis code is identical except for a change in lower-level function calls. Since it's been described previously, here's the ElGamal send routine for polynomial basis mathematics.

```
void send_elgamal(
            Base_point, Base_curve,
            Their_public, raw_data,
             Hidden_data, Random_point)
FIELD2N     *raw_data;
POINT       *Base_point, *Their_public, *Hidden_data, *Random_point;
CURVE       *Base_curve;
{
      FIELD2N      random_value;
      POINT        hidden_point, raw_point;

/*  create random point to help hide the data  */

      random_field (&random_value);
      poly_elptic_mul (&random_value, Base_point, Random_point, Base_curve);

/*  embed raw data onto the chosen curve,  Assume raw data is contained in
       least significant ELEMENTs of the field variable and we won't hurt
       anything using the most significant to operate on.
```

```
        Uses the first root for y value.
*/

        poly_embed( raw_data, Base_curve, 0, 0, &raw_point);

/*  Create the hiding value using the other person's public key  */
        poly_elptic_mul( &random_value, Their_public,
                                &hidden_point, Base_curve);
        poly_esum( &hidden_point, &raw_point, Hidden_data, Base_curve);
}
```

And here is the receive version. It's a one-to-one copy of the normal basis version, only changing the low-level routines.

```
void receive_elgamal(
                Base_point, Base_curve,
                my_private, Hidden_data, Random_point,
                raw_data)
FIELD2N         *my_private, *raw_data;
POINT           *Base_point, *Hidden_data, *Random_point;
CURVE           *Base_curve;
{
        POINT   hidden_point, raw_point;

/*  compute hidden point using my private key and the random point  */

        poly_elptic_mul( my_private, Random_point, &hidden_point, Base_curve);
        poly_esub( Hidden_data, &hidden_point, &raw_point, Base_curve);
        copy(&raw_point.x, raw_data);
}
```

Finally, here is an example that calls the above routines. As with the normal basis routines, I set the field size to NUMBITS = 130 and took the prime polynomial from [8]. It is also copied from the normal basis version. However, the end data look different. Here is the main test routine.

```
main()
{
        FIELD2N   private1, private2, send_data, get_data;
        CURVE     Public_Curve;
        POINT     Base_Point, Their_public, Hidden_data, Random_point;
        INDEX     error;

        random_seed = 0x932b15fe;

        if (!irreducible(&poly_prime)) return(0);
        print_field("poly_prime = ", &poly_prime);

        if (error = init_poly_math())
        {
            printf("Can't initialize S matrix, row = %d\n", error);
            return(-1);
```

```
    }

    printf("create Base curve and point\n\n");

    rand_curve(&Public_Curve);
    print_curve("Public curve", &Public_Curve);
    rand_point(&Base_Point, &Public_Curve);
    print_point("Base point", &Base_Point);

    printf("\ncreate side 2's private key\n\n");

    random_field(&private2);
    print_field("Side 2 secret:", &private2);

    printf("\nGenerate side 2's public key\n\n");
    poly_elptic_mul( &private2, &Base_Point, &Their_public, &Public_Curve);
    print_point("Side 2 public key", &Their_public);

    printf("\nCreate message data\n\n");
    random_field( &send_data);

    printf("\nHide data on curve and send from side 1 to side 2\n\n");
    send_elgamal( &Base_Point, &Public_Curve, &Their_public,
                    &send_data, &Hidden_data, &Random_point);
    print_point("Hidden data", &Hidden_data);
    print_point("Random point", &Random_point);
```

The points `Hidden_data` and `Random_point` are transmitted to the side 2. Side 2 then computes the following:

```
    printf("\nRecover transmitted message\n\n");
    receive_elgamal( &Base_Point, &Public_Curve, &private2,
                        &Hidden_data, &Random_point, &get_data);
    print_field("sent data     ", &send_data);
    print_field("received data", &get_data);
}
```

The output from the above code looks like this:

```
poly_prime =  :          4       0       0       0       9
create Base curve and point

Public curve
form = 0
a6 :          1 63323eab 10fc68f8 254d4d11 d2d518f2

Base point
x :          0 f3814df5 5d0be8bb a913fcdb 91edee60
y :          2 e2eb8a2a 849d0f77 2cf8106e 488148b8


create side 2's private key
```

```
Side 2 secret: :        2 295d85ac 44043edd 3a0f94f6 e0caf9a7

Generate side 2's public key

Side 2 public key
x :         2 84b09f64 6928e8e7 5d3b6b95 38a4849f
y :         1 32b78d28 3b91e459 6bc593d3 7d43ad0e


Create message data


Hide data on curve and send from side 1 to side 2

Hidden data
x :         1 5410c452 e6dd9399 ccc0050a 16ddfac7
y :         1 8f0ceab7 178d6bff a56c365e 1ed38358

Random point
x :         2 9cceeacd fbbfbc1f e2a9adf6 f6ecd6c5
y :         0 2a5e79e4 935115c3 769f3e89  bc54bb8


Recover transmitted message

sent data    :     0 8591c5e5 3935d4dc 3d80d402 741aa073
received data :    3 8591c5e5 3935d4dc 3d80d402 741aa073
```

The sent data are different from the received data, because we were unlucky. The raw data did not fit on the curve, and the embedding routine was instructed to increment offset 0. We were lucky, because there are only 2 bits available in the upper ELE-MENT and we hit the curve anyway. This is probably dangerous (because we could have gone into an infinite loop), so change your code to fit the field size and application.

7.4.3 Menezes-Qu-Vanstone key agreement scheme

This key-sharing scheme is more advanced than the Diffie-Hellman scheme, but it includes the Diffie-Hellman protocol as a subset. The idea of the Menezes-Qu-Vanstone (MQV) scheme is to prevent the man-in-the-middle attack and to perform authentication of the key holders. In addition, it ensures that if a particular message were cracked, it would take an equal amount of effort to crack any other message between the same two users. Since this is exceptionally useful, I will present two different versions. The first will be based on a mathematical description of a 1996 draft description of MQV. In the next chapter, I'll describe the 1997 draft description.

I will use the same terminology as the August 1996 IEEE P1363 draft standard to describe MQV. There are two sides to the communication and each side has two keys, so that makes four points we have to keep track of. The other side's key data will be followed by a prime sign (′) and our side will not. For example, each side generates an ephemeral random key: R on our side and R' on the other side.

All calculations occur over the same elliptic curve, E, which satisfies equation (6.1). The base point is called P, and our public key (or public point) is:

$$Q = dP \tag{7.17}$$

where d is our private key. The other side has public key Q', and we do not know the other side's private key, d'.

This scheme uses the x component of the public key points to compute modular math. This ties the ephemeral data (random noise preferred) to the public key data in a way that only the owner of the key can compute. I'll first go through the scheme, then describe how it works, and finally give the code that will execute it.

The IEEE standard describes this as ECKAS-MQV, which means "Elliptic Curve Key Agreement Scheme—Menezes-Qu-Vanstone version." The input includes the following public parameters:

E—the elliptic curve coefficients
P—the base point
n—the order of the curve
Q and Q'—the permanent public keys of this and the other side, respectively
R and R'—the ephemeral public keys of this and the other side, respectively

While the standard specifies that we need to know the order of the curve, the code following this section won't use it. We can get away with this, because calculations over the elliptic curve end up being modulo the order of the base point. Thus, the following code does not meet the standard, but it can be very useful in medium-security applications. I'll show the code that implements the standard in the advanced protocols of chapter 9.

In addition to the curve parameters, we specify that the (x,y) pair data, which compose a point, are distributed and symbolized as follows:

$$Q' = (a',b') \tag{7.18}$$

$$R' = (x',y') \tag{7.19}$$

$$Q = (a,b) \tag{7.20}$$

$$R = (x,y) = kP. \tag{7.21}$$

The output of the scheme is a shared secret, t, which is a FIELD2N-size block of bits. Both sides will have t, but no one seeing the data in-between will know what these data are or how to find them. Nor will they be able to spoof the key to become a passthrough, such as the man-in-the-middle attack of Diffie-Hellman. More importantly, if an attacker does find t for a particular transmission, it will not help him or her crack previous transmissions. This is known as "perfect forward secrecy."

The standard specifies the first calculation as:

$$s = k + xad \quad \mod n. \tag{7.22}$$

This combines the ephemeral random data k with the private key d and both the ephemeral and public point's x values. The value s is a private term and should not be leaked outside the key generation process.

The next step is to compute the point U from the other side's data using the formula:

$$U = R' + x'a'Q'. \tag{7.23}$$

The shared secret is then the x component of the point:

$$W = sU. \tag{7.24}$$

At this stage, both sides will have the same value of W and no one else will be able to compute it, because no one else knows the private keys. Let's see how it works.

First, let's multiply equation (7.22) by the base point P. This gives us:

$$sP = kP + xa(dP). \tag{7.25}$$

We can substitute equations (7.17) and (7.21) into equation (7.25) to see that:

$$sP = R + xaQ. \tag{7.26}$$

If we replace every term on the right-hand side of equation (7.26) with its primed cousin (the other side's data) we get the point U', which the other side computes from our data. But U does not equal U'. To see how both sides derive the same key, let's expand equation (7.24) using equations (7.22) and (7.23):

$$W = (k + xad)(R' + x'a'Q'). \tag{7.27}$$

In addition, we know that both R' and Q' are derived from the base point P, so we can expand equation (7.27) as follows:

$$W = (k + xad)(k' + x'a'd')P. \tag{7.28}$$

It is now clear that both sides have the same value of W. At its core this is simply the Diffie-Hellman key exchange shown previously. The twist is that we've protected our communications from attack and have included verification. If an attacker does not know d or d', he or she cannot spoof the shared secret. Further, the shared secret is different every time the two sides communicate, because random values k and k' have been introduced on each side. Even if an attacker finds your private key, he or she must still solve the discrete elliptic curve logarithm problem to find k and k' for each message.

MQV: the code—simple version.   The above math works assuming we know the order of the curve. For those of you who are rapidly changing keys, moving lots of data, and don't have time to pick the perfect curve or simply feel that a random curve is plenty good enough, the following code eliminates the necessity of having to do modular integer mathematics. All the modularity is done automatically by the cyclical structure of the elliptic curve. Let's start at the top of the code.

```
/*      MQV method to establish shared secret.
           Enter with other servers permenent (other_Q) and ephemeral (other_R)
           keys, this servers permenent key (skey, pkey)
           and ephemeral (dkey, dpoint) keys.
           Returns shared secret point W.  Only W.x is useful as key, and further
           checks may be necessary to confirm link established.
*/

CURVE Base_curve;
```

This version of the mathematics assumes that the `Base_curve` is global. This may make sense in some applications and not in others. Whatever your project is, the important part is to be sure the mathematics works. Since this protocol is symmetric (both sides do exactly the same calculations), it should be easy to test. Note that the routine returns the entire secret point W rather than just the shared secret t.

```
void authen_secret( d, Q, k, R, other_Q, other_R, W)
FIELD2N *d, *k;
POINT  *Q, *R, *other_Q, *other_R, *W;
{
        POINT S, T, U;

/*  compute U = R' + x'a'Q' from other sides data */

        elptic_mul(&other_Q->x, other_Q, &S, &Base_curve);
        elptic_mul(&other_R->x, &S, &T, &Base_curve);
        esum(other_R, &T, &U, &Base_curve);
```

At this point we have equation (7.23). The next step is to compute equation (7.24). This takes four elliptic curve multiplies and one elliptic curve sum. Not very efficient, but it works nicely for random curves.

```
/* compute (k + xad)U the hard way.  Need modulo math routines to make this
        quicker, but no need to know point order this way.
```

```
*/
        elptic_mul(d, &U, &S, &Base_curve);
        elptic_mul(&Q->x, &S, &T, &Base_curve);
        elptic_mul(&R->x, &T, &S, &Base_curve);
        elptic_mul(k, &U, &T, &Base_curve);
        esum(&S, &T, W, &Base_curve);
}
```

In this version of the MQV protocol, we need to compute the other side's point first. With that, we multiply by our private key, our ephemeral key, and the *x* components of both *Q* and *R*. This does exactly the same modular mathematics as the standard version, but we let the curve do the work rather than worrying about what the curve order actually is.

Here is an example using the above code with the normal basis routines.

```
main()
{
        FIELD2N         private1, private2, ephemeral1, ephemeral2;
        POINT           Base_Point, My_public, Their_public;
        POINT           My_random, Their_random;
        POINT           Shared_Secret1, Shared_Secret2;

        random_seed = 0x25f139be;

#ifdef TYPE2
        genlambda2();
#else
        genlambda();
#endif

        printf("create Base curve and point\n\n");

        rand_curve(&Base_curve);
        print_curve("Public curve", &Base_curve);
        rand_point(&Base_Point, &Base_curve);
        print_point("Base point", &Base_Point);

        printf("\ncreate each sides private key\n\n");

        random_field(&private1);
        print_field("Side 1 secret:", &private1);
        random_field(&private2);
        print_field("Side 2 secret:", &private2);

        printf("\nGenerate each sides public key\n\n");
        elptic_mul( &private1, &Base_Point, &My_public, &Base_curve);
        print_point("Side 1 public key", &My_public);
        elptic_mul( &private2, &Base_Point, &Their_public, &Base_curve);
        print_point("Side 2 public key", &Their_public);

        printf("\nCreate each sides ephemeral data\n\n");
```

```
random_field( &ephemeral1);
elptic_mul( &ephemeral1, &Base_Point, &My_random, &Base_curve);
print_point("Side 1 random point", &My_random);
random_field( &ephemeral2);
elptic_mul( &ephemeral2, &Base_Point, &Their_random, &Base_curve);
print_point("Side 2 random point", &Their_random);
```

In a real system, the base curve and point will be preestablished, and both sides will generate their public keys independently. The ephemeral data also depend on the base curve and point but will never be stored. In most cases the public key data can be stored in a database. The private key should never be stored, and, once the secret between both sides has been established, the random ephemeral data should be destroyed. Again, this is a security problem that depends on the operating system, as well as other factors.

Once the data have been exchanged, both sides compute the same secret using the same subroutine, but with different data.

```
printf("\nExchange data and compute shared secret\n\n");
authen_secret(&private1, &My_public, &ephemeral1, &My_random,
                &Their_public, &Their_random, &Shared_Secret1);
print_point("Side 1 shared secret", &Shared_Secret1);
authen_secret(&private2, &Their_public, &ephemeral2, &Their_random,
                &My_public, &My_random, &Shared_Secret2);
print_point("Side 2 shared secret", &Shared_Secret2);
}
```

Using NUMBITS = 134, the above code generates the following output:

```
create Base curve and point

Public curve
form = 0
a6 :       e 94bc2131 964024bb 53d7b20d 5e6b6d82

Base point
x :        2 e5d56efc ec98fe8f 3e605f32 e3319f8b
y :       3a c3dbca42 fda8b67f d3f20989 b0289e82


create each sides private key

Side 1 secret: :      28 719c8ee4 2fd38bb3 940eea4b cc81e426
Side 2 secret: :      21 26a4835c a8cd968e 42b82947 ce298dc9

Generate each sides public key

Side 1 public key
x :        b c91ffea9  b1695e2 4e6f5ab4 8d09058a
y :       31 2bda8e9b 58681842 d736aea0 a999a3bc

Side 2 public key
x :       33   327233e cc2be2db 1155acc4 1d4d10f5
```

```
y :         3 25c1ef11 627393b4 d52ac689 58cc9c5f
```

```
Create each sides ephemeral data

Side 1 random point
x :        1f 60167f47  8f95138 7a83032f ee6fa013
y :         1 44fc318d c595d4f0 d8901ecb  72899cb

Side 2 random point
x :         c daa92cbd 3e88ebdd ae44999a 637c2bbc
y :        25 a7b8fd28 85a331be 862e68cc 7baba80d


Exchange data and compute shared secret

Side 1 shared secret
x :         c 3b05faf3 d763a550 1529a3ae df90b225
y :        30 499b3465 6de5d419 48870852 f3298dcd

Side 2 shared secret
x :         c 3b05faf3 d763a550 1529a3ae df90b225
y :        30 499b3465 6de5d419 48870852 f3298dcd
```

Now, let's change all the normal basis subroutines to polynomial basis routines and do the same thing. Here is the polynomial version of the MQV key-sharing protocol.

```
void authen_secret( d, Q, k, R, other_Q, other_R, W)
FIELD2N *d, *k;
POINT  *Q, *R, *other_Q, *other_R, *W;
{
        POINT S, T, U;

/*  compute U = R' + x'a'Q' from other sides data */

        poly_elptic_mul(&other_Q->x, other_Q, &S, &Base_curve);
        poly_elptic_mul(&other_R->x, &S, &T, &Base_curve);
        poly_esum(other_R, &T, &U, &Base_curve);

/* compute (k + xad)U the hard way.  Need modulo math routines to make this
        quicker, but no need to know point order this way.
*/

        poly_elptic_mul(d, &U, &S, &Base_curve);
        poly_elptic_mul(&Q->x, &S, &T, &Base_curve);
        poly_elptic_mul(&R->x, &T, &S, &Base_curve);
        poly_elptic_mul(k, &U, &T, &Base_curve);
        poly_esum(&S, &T, W, &Base_curve);
}
```

And here is a test routine that shows how it works.

```
main()
```

```c
{
        FIELD2N    private1, private2, ephemeral1, ephemeral2;
        POINT      Base_Point, My_public, Their_public;
        POINT      My_random, Their_random;
        POINT      Shared_Secret1, Shared_Secret2;
        INDEX      error;

        random_seed = 0x1932b5fe;

        if (!irreducible(&poly_prime)) return(0);
        print_field("poly_prime = ", &poly_prime);

        if (error = init_poly_math())
        {
            printf("Can't initialize S matrix, row = %d\n", error);
            return(-1);
        }

        printf("create Base curve and point\n\n");

        rand_curve(&Base_curve);
        print_curve("Public curve", &Base_curve);
        rand_point(&Base_Point, &Base_curve);
        print_point("Base point", &Base_Point);

        printf("\ncreate each sides private key\n\n");

        random_field(&private1);
        print_field("Side 1 secret:", &private1);
        random_field(&private2);
        print_field("Side 2 secret:", &private2);

        printf("\nGenerate each sides public key\n\n");
        poly_elptic_mul( &private1, &Base_Point, &My_public, &Base_curve);
        print_point("Side 1 public key", &My_public);
        poly_elptic_mul( &private2, &Base_Point, &Their_public, &Base_curve);
        print_point("Side 2 public key", &Their_public);

        printf("\nCreate each sides ephemeral data\n\n");
        random_field( &ephemeral1);
        poly_elptic_mul( &ephemeral1, &Base_Point, &My_random, &Base_curve);
        print_point("Side 1 random point", &My_random);
        random_field( &ephemeral2);
        poly_elptic_mul( &ephemeral2, &Base_Point, &Their_random, &Base_curve);
        print_point("Side 2 random point", &Their_random);

        printf("\nExchange data and compute shared secret\n\n");
        authen_secret(&private1, &My_public, &ephemeral1, &My_random,
                      &Their_public, &Their_random, &Shared_Secret1);
        print_point("Side 1 shared secret", &Shared_Secret1);
        authen_secret(&private2, &Their_public, &ephemeral2, &Their_random,
                      &My_public, &My_random, &Shared_Secret2);
        print_point("Side 2 shared secret", &Shared_Secret2);
}
```

The field size is 134, and the prime polynomial is from [8]. The initial random seed is again different, but the result is the same: The math actually works!

```
poly_prime =  :        40        0        0 2000000        1
create Base curve and point

Public curve
form = 0
a6 :        36 fc01a2ea 920ff4e4 789cf04b e39e9302

Base point
x :         8 cf0ec27f ab882021 af8e5bea 99f1b1a7
y :        2d 36f8d3df 68986941 b00014a3 f4476bd3

create each sides private key

Side 1 secret: :         6 6cfa64f5 395b5064 4411772e 19516028
Side 2 secret: :        31 9ddf9500  adbf0aa ddc0cead 57fb0487

Generate each sides public key

Side 1 public key
x :        30 78a02db2 40b61609 f058d2c4 e26f8f0f
y :        31 1042706b 49f361c3  5394183  a79c7b9

Side 2 public key
x :        31   576c077 23f7b3e1 46181f6b 537606b5
y :        19 9d6e6ce0 e8dff93b  7ea9c96 5e9a9df0


Create each sides ephemeral data

Side 1 random point
x :         2 4004939b 5536468e 6a0e902d abca915a
y :        23 49a8d6cb 9a8dca90 c6f6eeb4  ad0400b

Side 2 random point
x :        1e d8ce7420 2183c1ee e67855df c97d40a6
y :        25 20db317c f28928b9   faed5d 795ba496


Exchange data and compute shared secret

Side 1 shared secret
x :         2 50cf3acf 97b541ef 4302dda4 eee740a4
y :        14 3f8094af a1103030 61ab0843 80045f90

Side 2 shared secret
x :         2 50cf3acf 97b541ef 4302dda4 eee740a4
y :        14 3f8094af a1103030 61ab0843 80045f90
```

The point of this version is to show that there are a great many ways to implement the mathematics for any given application. Understanding the math will allow you much greater flexibility in creating useful code instead of calling canned subroutines. The MQV protocol is an excellent example of why this attitude can be exceptionally useful.

So much for simple protocols. In the next chapter, we will add a hash function to create a simple elliptic curve encryption scheme. It's really Diffie-Hellman with a symmetric key, but it's in the standard. After that we can look at combining the integer math routines of chapter 2 with the above protocols to create the Massey-Omura and MQV key exchange protocols. Then we'll look at signature protocols, which combine both the hash functions and the integer math routines with all the elliptic curve routines. Now that you understand the basics, the combinations should be easy.

7.5 References

1 N. Koblitz, *A Course in Number Theory and Cryptography* (New York: Springer-Verlag, 1987).

2 D. E. Knuth, *Seminumerical Algorithms* (Reading, MA: Addison-Wesley, 1981).

3 A. J. Menezes, *Elliptic Curve Public Key Cryptosystems* (Boston: Kluwer Academic Publishers, 1993).

4 P. C. van Oorschot and M. J. Wiener, "Parallel Collision Search with Cryptanalytic Applications" (Nortel, Ottawa, Canada, September 23, 1996, internal paper).

5 M. J. Wiener and R. J. Zuccherato, "Faster Attacks on Elliptic Curve Cryptosystems" (Entrust Technologies, Ottawa, Canada, April 8, 1998, internal paper).

6 D. Beauregard, "Efficient Algorithms for Implementing Elliptic Curve Public Key Schemes" (Master's thesis, Worcester Polytechnic Institute, Worcester, MA, 1996).

7 N. Koblitz, "CM—Curves with Good Cryptographic Properties," *CRYPTO '91* (New York: Springer-Verlag, 1992), 279.

8 B. Schneier, *Applied Cryptograpy*, 2d ed. (New York: John Wiley & Sons, 1996).

CHAPTER 8

Elliptic curve encryption

8.1 Introduction to ECES   200

8.2 Mask generation function   202

8.3 Hash function SHA-1   203

8.4 Mask generation: the code   210

8.5 ECES: the code   212

8.6 References   219

8.1 Introduction to ECES

This chapter introduces the combination of elliptic curve mathematics and a hash function. The idea is to use public keys to create a useful secret key for direct encryption. Originally introduced in the November 1995 draft of the P1363 standard, the elliptic curve form has been dropped from later drafts. Because the order of the curve is not required, it is a reasonable protocol for some applications. This type of encryption is still being proposed for the integer factorization schemes.

The subroutine schematic for this chapter is shown in figure 8.1. After some preliminary mathematics we'll get into SHA-1, which is one of the hash functions recommended in the P1363 standard. From there we'll cover the key generation protocols, which are used to create random points for the encryption algorithm. The mask generation function is common to both polynomial and normal basis versions.

As with the ElGamal and MQV protocols, the elliptic curve encryption scheme assumes a public curve and base point. Let's assume that an elliptic curve that satisfies equation (7.1) and base point P are already chosen. To send a message, Alicia generates a random value k and requests Brandon's public point $B = bP$. She then computes:

$$R = kP \qquad\qquad (8.1)$$

and

$$S = kB. \qquad\qquad (8.2)$$

The x component of S is the secret key. This is fed into a mask generation function, and the resultant mask is exclusive-or(ed) with the message. Alicia then sends this encrypted message, as well as the point R to Brandon.

To decrypt the message, Brandon computes:

$$S = bR. \qquad\qquad (8.3)$$

Just as with the Diffie-Hellman protocol, both sides have the same shared secret. But in this case, only one person's key is needed. While this meets the specification of the protocol, the same mask generator can be used with any shared key scheme. If authentication is desired, the MQV protocol might be used to create the shared secret.

The original specification listed the following steps for the Elliptic Curve Encryption Scheme (ECES) for a message M.

1 Generate a one-time key pair *(R, k)* from the public elliptic curve parameters using the Elliptic Curve Key Generation Protocol (ECKGP). The standard specifies that point R be converted to a byte string for transmission compatibility. I'll skip that and leave R as a POINT.

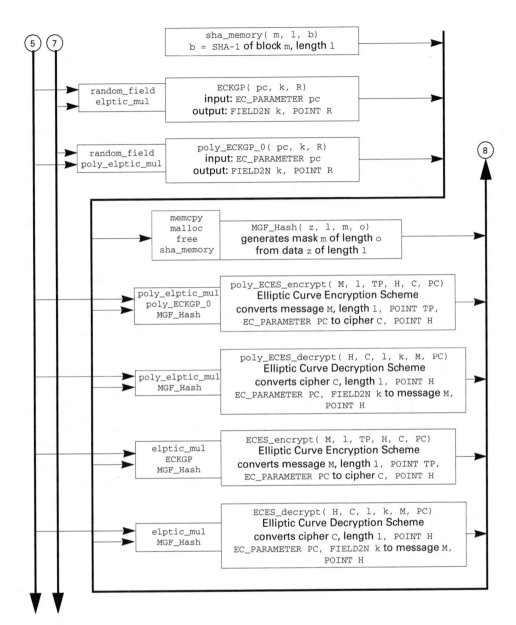

Figure 8.1   Subroutine schematic

2 Use the x component of $S = kB$ as a string X. B is the recipient's public key and is defined using the public elliptic curve parameters.

3 Generate a mask Y, which is the same number of bytes as the input message using the string X with the Mask Generation Function (MGF).

4 Compute the Encrypted Message (EM) as the exclusive-or of Y with M.

The final step is to concatenate the point R as a string of bytes with the encrypted message. My example does not do that, but for real-world transmission this is trivial.

Since there are two forms of the underlying field, I'll give both versions of the encryption schemes along with examples. But the first item we need to discuss is the mask generation function.

8.2 Mask generation function

The IEEE P1363 standard describes the mask generation function in terms of bytes (octets, officially). The input is a key that must be less than $2^{61} - 4$ bytes, which seems fairly ridiculous but it does set an upper limit. A 32-bit counter is concatenated with the key and a hash of the whole mess is performed. The output of the hash function is always a fixed length, and this number of bytes defines the output block size.

To create a mask of the desired length, the counter is incremented and the hash recomputed. The outputs from the hash function are concatenated until the desired number of bytes has been generated. Obviously, a good hash function is required. The standard recommends the use of either SHA-1 or RIPEMD-160. Both of these have an output of 160 bits, so either one will work equally well with the mask generation function.

The standard proceeds to describe the MGF-hash as follows: Given a hash function with output length `hLen`, an input byte string `Z` of length `zLen`, and a desired output length of `oLen` bytes, create a string `mask` of `oLen` bytes. The standard states that the input length should be less than $2^{61} - 4$, but I'll ignore that limit. The only error my routine specifies is a memory allocation problem. It also specifies that the routine should return an error if the required `oLen` is greater than `hLen` times 2^{32}. That is not a problem for 32-bit inputs. I suggest that if you must meet the standard, you will need to work with 64-bit or larger inputs.

The November 1997 standard specifically instructed the following:

1 Check that `zLen` $< 2^{61} - 4$ and `oLen` $< 2^{32} \times$ `hLen`. Exit with error if not.

2 Let `counter = 0`. Let `cThreshold = ceiling( oLen / hLen )`.

3 Let `M` be an empty string.

4 Convert `counter` to byte string `C` of length 4.

5 Compute `H = hash( Z || C )` (of length `hLen`).

6 Let `M = M || H`.

7 Increment `counter` by 1. If `counter` < `cThreshold`, go to step 4.

8 Output `oLen` bytes of `M` as the desired `mask`.

In their terminology, two parallel bars mean "concatenate." The `hash()` function used here is SHA-1. Let's start at the bottom and work our way back up to the ECES.

8.3 Hash function SHA-1

Dr. James J. Gillogly (senior cryptographer, Mentat Inc.) has kindly let me reproduce his version of SHA-1. For more information see either FIPS-PUB 180-1 from the U.S. government or [1]. The hash function takes an arbitrary number of bytes for input and mashes the bits to create a fixed-length output. The idea is to ensure that a single bit flip anywhere in the input will give a completely different output. That's why concatenating a counter with the key should work.

Here is Jim's version of SHA-1, along with a few external routines. Only the routine `sha_memory()` is needed, because all the following code is executed with data in RAM, but you may want to use the hash algorithm for other purposes.

```
/* Implementation of NIST's Secure Hash Algorithm (FIPS 180)
 * Lightly bummed for execution efficiency.
 *
 * Jim Gillogly 3 May 1993
 *
 * 27 Aug 93: imported LITTLE_ENDIAN mods from Peter Gutmann's implementation
 * 5 Jul 94: Modified for NSA fix
 *
 * Compile: cc -O -o sha sha.c
 *
 * To remove the test wrapper and use just the nist_hash() routine,
 *      compile with -DONT_WRAP
 *
 * To reverse byte order for little-endian machines, use -DLITTLE_ENDIAN
 *
 * To get the original SHA definition before the 1994 fix, use -DVERSION_0
 *
 * Usage: sha [-vt] [filename ...]
 *
 *      -v switch: output the filename as well
 *      -t switch: suppress spaces between 32-bit blocks
 *
 *      If no input files are specified, process standard input.
 *
 * Output: 40-hex-digit digest of each file specified (160 bits)
 *
 * Synopsis of the function calls:
 *
 *   sha_file(char *filename, unsigned long *buffer)
 *      Filename is a file to be opened and processed.
 *      buffer is a user-supplied array of 5 or more longs.
 *      The 5-word buffer is filled with 160 bits of non-terminated hash.
 *      Returns 0 if successful, non-zero if bad file.
```

```
 *
 *   void sha_stream(FILE *stream, unsigned long *buffer)
 *       Input is from already-opened stream, not file.
 *
 *   void sha_memory(char *mem, long length, unsigned long *buffer)
 *       Input is a memory block "length" bytes long.
 *
 * Caveat:
 *       Not tested for case that requires the high word of the length,
 *       which would be files larger than 1/2 gig or so.
 *
 * Limitation:
 *       sha_memory (the memory block function) will deal with blocks no longer
 *       than 4 gigabytes; for longer samples, the stream version will
 *       probably be most convenient (e.g. perl moby_data.pl | sha).
 *
 * Bugs:
 *       The standard is defined for bit strings; I assume bytes.
 *
 * Copyright 1993, Dr. James J. Gillogly
 * This code may be freely used in any application.
 */

/* #define LITTLE_ENDIAN */

/* #define VERSION_0 */  /* Define this to get the original SHA definition */

#include <stdio.h>
#include <memory.h>
#include <string.h>              /*  for Mac/Metrowerks  */

#define VERBOSE

/*#define TRUE  1               commented out for Mac/Metrowerks
#define FALSE 0
*/
#define SUCCESS 0
#define FAILURE -1
#define ONT_WRAP

int sha_file();                         /* External entries */
void sha_stream(), sha_memory();

static void nist_guts();

#ifndef ONT_WRAP        /* Using just the hash routine itself */

#define HASH_SIZE 5     /* Produces 160-bit digest of the message */


main(argc, argv)
int argc;
char **argv;
{
```

```
        unsigned long hbuf[HASH_SIZE];
        char *s;
        int file_args = FALSE;   /* If no files, take it from stdin */
        int verbose = FALSE;
        int terse = FALSE;

#ifdef MEMTEST
        sha_memory("abc", 31, hbuf);              /* NIST test value from appendix A */
        if (verbose) printf("Memory:");
        if (terse) printf("%081x%081x%081x%081x%081x\n",
            hbuf[0], hbuf[1], hbuf[2], hbuf[3], hbuf[4]);
        else printf("%081x %081x %081x %081x %081x\n",
            hbuf[0], hbuf[1], hbuf[2], hbuf[3], hbuf[4]);
#endif

        for (++argv; --argc; ++argv)              /* March down the arg list */
        {
            if (**argv == '-')                    /* Process one or more flags */
                for (s = &(*argv)[1]; *s; s++)    /* Obfuscated C contest entry */
                    switch(*s)
                    {
                        case 'v': case 'V':
                            verbose = TRUE;
                            break;
                        case 't': case 'T':
                            terse = TRUE;
                            break;
                        default:
                            fprintf(stderr, "Unrecognized flag: %c\n", *s);
                            return FALSE;
                    }
            else                                  /* Process a file */
            {
                if (verbose) printf("%s:", *argv);
                file_args = TRUE;                 /* Whether or not we could read it */

                if (sha_file(*argv, hbuf) == FAILURE)
                    printf("Can't open file %s.\n", *argv);
                else
                    if (terse) printf("%081x%081x%081x%081x%081x\n",
                        hbuf[0], hbuf[1], hbuf[2], hbuf[3], hbuf[4]);
                    else printf("%081x %081x %081x %081x %081x\n",
                        hbuf[0], hbuf[1], hbuf[2], hbuf[3], hbuf[4]);
            }
        }
        if (! file_args)    /* No file specified */
        {
            if (verbose) printf("%s:", *argv);
            sha_stream(stdin, hbuf);

            if (terse) printf("%081x%081x%081x%081x%081x\n",
                hbuf[0], hbuf[1], hbuf[2], hbuf[3], hbuf[4]);
            else printf("%081x %081x %081x %081x %081x\n",
                hbuf[0], hbuf[1], hbuf[2], hbuf[3], hbuf[4]);
```

```
        }
    return TRUE;
}


#endif ONT_WRAP

#ifdef LITTLE_ENDIAN       /* Imported from Peter Gutmann's implementation */

/* When run on a little-endian CPU we need to perform byte reversal on an
   array of longwords.  It is possible to make the code endianness-
   independant by fiddling around with data at the byte level, but this
   makes for very slow code, so we rely on the user to sort out endianness
   at compile time */

static void byteReverse( unsigned long *buffer, int byteCount )
    {
    unsigned long value;
    int count;

    byteCount /= sizeof( unsigned long );
    for( count = 0; count < byteCount; count++ )
        {
        value = ( buffer[ count ] << 16 ) | ( buffer[ count ] >> 16 );
        buffer[ count ] = ( ( value & 0xFF00FF00L ) >> 8 ) |
               ( ( value & 0x00FF00FFL ) << 8 );
        }
    }
#endif /* LITTLE_ENDIAN */

union longbyte


{
    unsigned long W[80];            /* Process 16 32-bit words at a time */
    char B[320];                    /* But read them as bytes for counting */
};

sha_file(filename, buffer)          /* Hash a file */
char *filename;
unsigned long *buffer;
{
    FILE *infile;

    if ((infile = fopen(filename, "rb")) == NULL)
    {
        int i;

        for (i = 0; i < 5; i++)
            buffer[i] = 0xdeadbeef;
        return FAILURE;
    }
    (void) sha_stream(infile, buffer);
    fclose(infile);
    return SUCCESS;
```

```
}

void sha_memory(mem, length, buffer)      /* Hash a memory block */
char *mem;
unsigned long length;
unsigned long *buffer;
{
    nist_guts(FALSE, (FILE *) NULL, mem, length, buffer);
}

void sha_stream(stream, buffer)
FILE *stream;
unsigned long *buffer;
{
    nist_guts(TRUE, stream, (char *) NULL, 01, buffer);
}

#define f0(x,y,z) (z ^ (x & (y ^ z)))                 /* Magic functions */
#define f1(x,y,z) (x ^ y ^ z)
#define f2(x,y,z) ((x & y) | (z & (x | y)))
#define f3(x,y,z) (x ^ y ^ z)

#define K0 0x5a827999                                 /* Magic constants */
#define K1 0x6ed9eba1
#define K2 0x8f1bbcdc
#define K3 0xca62c1d6

#define S(n, X) ((X << n) | (X >> (32 - n)))      /* Barrel roll */

#define r0(f, K) \
    temp = S(5, A) + f(B, C, D) + E + *p0++ + K; \
    E = D;  \
    D = C;  \
    C = S(30, B); \
    B = A;  \
    A = temp

#ifdef VERSION_0
#define r1(f, K) \
    temp = S(5, A) + f(B, C, D) + E + \
        (*p0++ = *p1++ ^ *p2++ ^ *p3++ ^ *p4++) + K; \
    E = D;  \
    D = C;  \
    C = S(30, B); \
    B = A;  \
    A = temp
#else                    /* Version 1: Summer '94 update */
#define r1(f, K) \
    temp = *p1++ ^ *p2++ ^ *p3++ ^ *p4++; \
    temp = S(5, A) + f(B, C, D) + E + (*p0++ = S(1,temp)) + K; \
    E = D;  \
    D = C;  \
    C = S(30, B); \
    B = A;  \
```

```
        A = temp
#endif

static void nist_guts(file_flag, stream, mem, length, buf)
int file_flag;                      /* Input from memory, or from stream? */
FILE *stream;
char *mem;
unsigned long length;
unsigned long *buf;
{
    int i, nread, nbits;
    union longbyte d;
    unsigned long hi_length, lo_length;
    int padded;
    char *s;

    register unsigned long *p0, *p1, *p2, *p3, *p4;
    unsigned long A, B, C, D, E, temp;

    unsigned long h0, h1, h2, h3, h4;

    h0 = 0x67452301;                              /* Accumulators */
    h1 = 0xefcdab89;
    h2 = 0x98badcfe;
    h3 = 0x10325476;
    h4 = 0xc3d2e1f0;

    padded = FALSE;
    s = mem;
    for (hi_length = lo_length = 0; ;)   /* Process 16 longs at a time */
    {
        if (file_flag)
        {
            nread = fread(d.B, 1, 64, stream);   /* Read as 64 bytes */
        }
        else
        {
            if (length < 64) nread = length;
            else             nread = 64;
            length -= nread;
            memcpy(d.B, s, nread);
            s += nread;
        }
        if (nread < 64)    /* Partial block? */
        {
            nbits = nread << 3;                   /* Length: bits */
            if ((lo_length += nbits) < nbits)
                    hi_length++;                  /* 64-bit integer */

            if (nread < 64 && ! padded)  /* Append a single bit */
            {
                    d.B[nread++] = 0x80; /* Using up next byte */
                    padded = TRUE;       /* Single bit once */
            }
        }
```

```
                    for (i = nread; i < 64; i++) /* Pad with nulls */
                            d.B[i] = 0;
                    if (nread <= 56)    /* Room for length in this block */
                    {
                            d.W[14] = hi_length;
                            d.W[15] = lo_length;
#ifdef LITTLE_ENDIAN
                    byteReverse(d.W, 56 );
#endif /* LITTLE_ENDIAN */
                    }
#ifdef LITTLE_ENDIAN
                    else byteReverse(d.W, 64 );
#endif /* LITTLE_ENDIAN */
            }
            else    /* Full block -- get efficient */
            {
                    if ((lo_length += 512) < 512)
                            hi_length++;     /* 64-bit integer */
#ifdef LITTLE_ENDIAN
                    byteReverse(d.W, 64 );
#endif /* LITTLE_ENDIAN */
            }

            p0 = d.W;
            A = h0; B = h1; C = h2; D = h3; E = h4;

            r0(f0,K0); r0(f0,K0); r0(f0,K0); r0(f0,K0); r0(f0,K0);
            r0(f0,K0); r0(f0,K0); r0(f0,K0); r0(f0,K0); r0(f0,K0);
            r0(f0,K0); r0(f0,K0); r0(f0,K0); r0(f0,K0); r0(f0,K0);
            r0(f0,K0);

            p1 = &d.W[13]; p2 = &d.W[8]; p3 = &d.W[2]; p4 = &d.W[0];

                        r1(f0,K0); r1(f0,K0); r1(f0,K0); r1(f0,K0);
            r1(f1,K1); r1(f1,K1); r1(f1,K1); r1(f1,K1); r1(f1,K1);
            r1(f1,K1); r1(f1,K1); r1(f1,K1); r1(f1,K1); r1(f1,K1);
            r1(f1,K1); r1(f1,K1); r1(f1,K1); r1(f1,K1); r1(f1,K1);
            r1(f1,K1); r1(f1,K1); r1(f1,K1); r1(f1,K1); r1(f1,K1);
            r1(f2,K2); r1(f2,K2); r1(f2,K2); r1(f2,K2); r1(f2,K2);
            r1(f2,K2); r1(f2,K2); r1(f2,K2); r1(f2,K2); r1(f2,K2);
            r1(f2,K2); r1(f2,K2); r1(f2,K2); r1(f2,K2); r1(f2,K2);
            r1(f2,K2); r1(f2,K2); r1(f2,K2); r1(f2,K2); r1(f2,K2);
            r1(f3,K3); r1(f3,K3); r1(f3,K3); r1(f3,K3); r1(f3,K3);
            r1(f3,K3); r1(f3,K3); r1(f3,K3); r1(f3,K3); r1(f3,K3);
            r1(f3,K3); r1(f3,K3); r1(f3,K3); r1(f3,K3); r1(f3,K3);
            r1(f3,K3); r1(f3,K3); r1(f3,K3); r1(f3,K3); r1(f3,K3);

            h0 += A; h1 += B; h2 += C; h3 += D; h4 += E;

            if (nread <= 56) break; /* If it's greater, length in next block */
        }
    buf[0] = h0; buf[1] = h1; buf[2] = h2; buf[3] = h3; buf[4] = h4;
}
```

For my purposes, the `main` function is not needed, so the variable `ONT_WRAP` is defined. This gets its name from the −D option in most compilers. Since all the work is done at byte level, big- and little-endian versions matter. I've tested the routine on a big-endian computer; set the variables appropriately for your machine.

8.4 Mask generation: the code

With the above code, we can now look at the mask generation function. Our inputs are a key that is a `char` variable derived from a `FIELD2N` structure, its length, and the desired length of output. The output is a filled `char` block of the desired length, assuming no errors. The routine returns 0 for no error and 1 if it cannot allocate enough memory to compute the hash of the key plus counter combination.

```
/*  Create simple Mask Generation Function for IEEE P1363 standard  */

#include <stdio.h>
#include <stdlib.h>
#include <string.h>

extern void sha_memory();
int MGF_Hash();

/*  MGF-Hash

        As described in section 13.2.1 of 21 Sept. 1997 P1363 draft.
        Assumes 32 bit inputs, no size error returned.
        This version calls Jim Gilogly's implementation of SHA-1.

        Input:
                        BYTE string Z of length zLen
                        pointer to output area (BYTE) mask
                        number of bytes desired in output oLen
        Output:
                        mask filled with oLen bytes of garbage,
                        returns 0 for no error,
                        returns 1 if not enough memory available
*/

int MGF_Hash( Z, zLen, mask, oLen)
unsigned char *Z, *mask;
unsigned long zLen, oLen;
{
        unsigned char *catspace, *catpoint;
        int           tbyte, counter;
        unsigned long cThreshold = oLen/20;
        unsigned long *M, temp[5];

        M = (unsigned long*) mask;
```

The variable M points to our output block. Since the hash function works with unsigned long data, the pointer is created in these terms. We'll deal with the last block as a special case, since the number of bytes may be different from a fully formed hash block.

The routine first computes cThreshold = oLen/20. This is the number of times we can call sha_memory for complete 160-bit mask outputs. The variable tbyte is used to hold oLen % 20, the number of bytes we need from the last call to sha_memory. The variable temp is used to hold those last few bytes.

```
/*  establish enough memory space to do the hashing with counter  */

        catspace = malloc( zLen + 4);
        if ( !catspace) return(1);
        memcpy ( catspace, Z, zLen);
        catpoint = catspace + zLen;
```

The first step is to allocate enough memory to concatenate the counter with the key. If we can't get enough space, we have to give up. I also mark the point in the allocated RAM for the counter. The standard specifies that the counter be placed at the end of the input key; the variable catpoint is the marker.

```
/*  create main block of mask data  */

        for ( counter = 0; counter < cThreshold; counter++)
        {
                *catpoint = (counter >> 24) & 0xFF;
                *(catpoint+1) = (counter >> 16) & 0xFF;
                *(catpoint+2) = (counter >> 8) & 0xFF;
                *(catpoint+3) = counter & 0xFF;
                sha_memory( catspace, zLen+4, M);
                M += 5;
        }
```

The basic requirement here is to ensure the counter is concatenated with the key. This is formed in big-endian order one byte at a time. The order does not really matter but consistency does. So long as sender and receiver do the same order, the final mask will be identical. The mask pointer M is incremented to point at the next 160-bit block to be filled.

```
/*  finish up any uneven multiples of a single hash step  */

        if ( tbyte = oLen % 20)
        {
                *catpoint = (counter >> 24) & 0xFF;
                *(catpoint+1) = (counter >> 16) & 0xFF;
                *(catpoint+2) = (counter >> 8) & 0xFF;
                *(catpoint+3) = counter & 0xFF;
                sha_memory( catspace, zLen+4, temp);
```

```
                memcpy( M, temp, tbyte);
        }
        free ( catspace);
        return (0);
}
```

The last chunk of code is performed only if the number of bytes requested is not an even multiple of 160 bits. A temporary storage holds the result of the hash, and the number of bytes needed is copied to the mask. That's all there is to the mask generating function; now let's look at the encryption code.

8.5   ECES: the code

For Alicia to send a message to Brandon, she first gets Brandon's public key. This requires a common curve and base point. For the purposes of this chapter, I'll introduce a new structure called EC_PARAMETER. In the next chapter, I'll add more to this structure, but for now the following is sufficient.

```
typedef struct
{
        CURVE           crv;
        POINT           pnt;
} EC_PARAMETER;
```

The elliptic curve parameter structure holds a curve structure and a point structure, which are common to all users of the protocol. For this particular encryption protocol, users could have their own curve and base point along with their public key point, which hides their private key. This makes the public key quite a bit larger, but this might make sense for some applications.

For both polynomial and normal basis routines, I will introduce some of the IEEE standard. This includes an elliptic curve key generating protocol subroutine. For this chapter the subroutine is trivial, but I'll expand on it later when we add integer math routines.

Let's start with a polynomial basis example and follow with the normal basis code.

8.5.1 Polynomial basis

The first routine we need is a simple random bit generator and an elliptic curve multiply. We'll see this in a different version later, but for now here is a basic routine to generate a random value and point from a given set of EC_PARAMETERs.

```
/*  Generate a key pair, a random value plus a point.
        This was called ECKGP for Elliptic Curve Key Generation
        Primitive in an early draft of IEEE P1363.
```

```
           Input:  Base point on curve (pnt, crv)

           Output: secret key k and random point R
*/

void poly_ECKGP_0( pnt_crv, k, R)
POINT   *R;
EC_PARAMETER *pnt_crv;
FIELD2N *k;
{
        random_field( k);
        poly_elptic_mul( k, &pnt_crv->pnt, R, &pnt_crv->crv);
}
```

With this subroutine, the polynomial version of the elliptic curve encryption
scheme is only a few calls. Calling the encryption routine requires pointers to the message, a value for the number of bytes, the receiver's public key, and the elliptic curve
parameters. A pointer to the encoded message area is also required.

```
/*  ECES, Elliptic Curve Encryption Scheme
        Present in an original draft, absent from recent ones
        of the IEEE P1363 standard.

        Input:  pointer to message Message, length message_Len,
                    recipient's public key their_pub_point,
                    pointer to encrypted message Encoded_Message
                    and public elliptic curve parameters public_curve.

        Output: point hidden_point and encrypted message space filled.

        This deviates from the standard since the point and
        encrypted message are not concatenated.
*/

void poly_ECES_encrypt( Message, message_Len, their_pub_point,
                hidden_point, Encoded_Message, public_curve)
char *Message, *Encoded_Message;
unsigned long message_Len;
POINT *their_pub_point, *hidden_point;
EC_PARAMETER *public_curve;
{
        FIELD2N one_time_key;
        POINT one_time_point;
        char *m, *em;
        unsigned long i;

/*  generate one time key and hide it on public curve  */

        poly_ECKGP_0( public_curve, &one_time_key, hidden_point);

/*  create shared secret value (this is DH basicly)  */

        poly_elptic_mul( &one_time_key, their_pub_point,
```

```
                              &one_time_point, &public_curve->crv);

/*  use shared secret to create mask for raw data   */

        MGF_Hash( (char*)&one_time_point.x, sizeof(FIELD2N),
                        Encoded_Message, message_Len);

/*  exclusive or input data with mask data    */

        m = Message;
        em = Encoded_Message;
        for (i=0; i<message_Len; i++) *em++ ^= *m++;
}
```

The random value should be completely destroyed to prevent any attacker from decrypting the message. The secret key is used once and then it too can be destroyed. The hidden_point is sent in the clear to the recipient. With the recipient's private key he or she can regenerate the secret key as shown below.

```
/*  decrypt message from ECES.

        Input:   Point hidden_point and encrypted message Encoded_Message of
                 length message_Len, secret key my_secret_key and elliptic
                 curve parameters public_curve.

        Output: message Message of length message_Len.

*/

void poly_ECES_decrypt( hidden_point, Encoded_Message,
                                          message_Len, my_secret_key,
                                          Message, public_curve)
POINT *hidden_point;
char *Encoded_Message, *Message;
unsigned long message_Len;
FIELD2N *my_secret_key;
EC_PARAMETER *public_curve;
{
        char *m, *em;
        POINT one_time_point;
        unsigned long i;

/*  create shared secret   */

        poly_elptic_mul( my_secret_key, hidden_point,
                                        &one_time_point, &public_curve->crv);

/*  create mask data   */

        MGF_Hash( (char*)&one_time_point.x, sizeof(FIELD2N),
                                        Message, message_Len);

/*  exclusive or input data with mask data   */
```

```
                m = Message;
                em = Encoded_Message;
                for (i=0; i<message_Len; i++) *m++ ^= *em++;
        }
```

As you can see, the decryption function is really simple. The shared secret is created, fed into the mask function, and the message is decrypted. An example run of the above subroutines is as follows:

```
main()
{
        FIELD2N         test1, test2, test3, test4;
        POINT           key, ephemeral_key;
        EC_PARAMETER Base;
        char            data_block[1024], encrypt_block[1024];
        char            decrypt_block[1024];
        INDEX           i, error;

        random_seed = 0x1932b5fe;

        if (!irreducible(&poly_prime)) return(0);
        print_field("poly_prime = ", &poly_prime);

        if (error = init_poly_math())
        {
                printf("Can't initialize S matrix, row = %d\n", error);
                return(-1);
        }

        printf("create Base curve and point\n\n");

        rand_curve(&Base.crv);
        print_curve("Public curve", &Base.crv);
        rand_point(&Base.pnt, &Base.crv);
        print_point("Base point", &Base.pnt);
```

Once the base curve and point are selected, we need to generate a public key. For this example, any random set is allowed, so I just call the simple key generating function. In real life the user's key should be created from a pass phrase by passing it through a hash function such as SHA-1. If created in this manner, the user's private key is never stored on any medium other than his or her own brain. If properly understood by the user, this creates the maximum possible security.

```
        poly_ECKGP_0( &Base, &test3, &key);
        print_field("receiver's secret value ", &test3);
        print_point("receiver's public point ",&key);
        for (i=0; i<1024; i++) data_block[i] = i;
```

The message for this test is a byte block of integers repeating every 256 bytes. Since the result matches this input, it's clear that it worked.

```
        poly_ECES_encrypt( data_block, 1024, &key, &ephemeral_key,
encrypt_block, &Base);
        print_point("transmitted public key", &ephemeral_key);
        print_field("encrypt data", (FIELD2N*) encrypt_block);
        poly_ECES_decrypt( &ephemeral_key, encrypt_block, 1024, &test3,
decrypt_block, &Base);
        print_field("decrypt data", (FIELD2N*) decrypt_block);

}
```

And the output is as follows:

```
poly_prime =   :        40          0          0  2000000          1
create Base curve and point

Public curve
form = 0
a6 :         36 fc01a2ea 920ff4e4 789cf04b e39e9302

Base point
x :          8 cf0ec27f ab882021 af8e5bea 99f1b1a7
y :         2d 36f8d3df 68986941 b00014a3 f4476bd3

receiver's secret value  :          6 6cfa64f5 395b5064 4411772e 19516028
receiver's public point
x :         30 78a02db2 40b61609 f058d2c4 e26f8f0f
y :         31 1042706b 49f361c3  5394183  a79c7b9

transmitted public key
x :         31  576c077 23f7b3e1 46181f6b 537606b5
y :         19 9d6e6ce0 e8dff93b  7ea9c96 5e9a9df0

encrypt data : b5653d42 9c657019 5535d1c3 43bf6c22  95c5d19
decrypt data :    10203  4050607  8090a0b  c0d0e0f 10111213
```

The output is leading 0 suppressed, so the first byte is 00, followed by 01, 02, and 03. Even knowing the message, an attacker would have a very difficult time reconstructing the key from the mask. The only attack that makes sense is to recover the private key from the receiver's public point. With a large enough field size, this can be made intractable for a long time.

8.5.2 Normal basis

The normal basis encryption routines are essentially identical to the polynomial basis versions with calls to normal basis math being substituted. The normal basis simple version of the elliptic curve key generation protocol is as follows:

```
void ECKGP( pub_crv, k, R)
EC_PARAMETER *pub_crv;
FIELD2N *k;
POINT *R;
```

```
{
        random_field( k);
        elptic_mul( k, &pub_crv->pnt, R, &pub_crv->crv);
}
```

The normal basis encryption routine is then identical to the polynomial basis routine, as follows:

```
void ECES_encrypt( Message, message_Len, their_pub_point, hidden_point,
                              Encoded_Message, public_curve)
char *Message, *Encoded_Message;
unsigned long message_Len;
POINT *their_pub_point, *hidden_point;
EC_PARAMETER *public_curve;
{
        FIELD2N one_time_key;
        POINT one_time_point;
        char *m, *em;
        unsigned long i;

/*  generate one time key and hide it on public curve  */

        ECKGP( public_curve, &one_time_key, hidden_point);

/*  create shared secret value (this is DH basicly)  */

        elptic_mul( &one_time_key, their_pub_point,
                        &one_time_point, &public_curve->crv);

/*  use shared secret to create mask for raw data  */

        MGF_Hash( (char*)&one_time_point.x, sizeof(FIELD2N),
                        Encoded_Message, message_Len);

/*  exclusive or input data with mask data  */

        m = Message;
        em = Encoded_Message;
        for (i=0; i<message_Len; i++) *em++ ^= *m++;
}
```

The decryption routine is just as simple; it's a copy from the polynomial basis version changing the low-level routines.

```
void ECES_decrypt( hidden_point, Encoded_Message, message_Len,
                        my_secret_key, Message, public_curve)
POINT *hidden_point;
char *Encoded_Message, *Message;
unsigned long message_Len;
FIELD2N *my_secret_key;
EC_PARAMETER *public_curve;
{
        char *m, *em;
```

```
        POINT one_time_point;
        unsigned long i;

/*  create shared secret  */

        elptic_mul( my_secret_key, hidden_point,
                      &one_time_point, &public_curve->crv);

/*  create mask data  */

        MGF_Hash( (char*)&one_time_point.x, sizeof(FIELD2N), Message,
message_Len);

/*  exclusive or input data with mask data  */

        m = Message;
        em = Encoded_Message;
        for (i=0; i<message_Len; i++) *m++ ^= *em++;
}
```

And here is an example that calls the above routines for testing.

```
main()
{
        FIELD2N         test1, test2, test3, test4;
        POINT           key, ephemeral_key;
        EC_PARAMETER Base;
        char            data_block[1024], encrypt_block[1024];
        char            decrypt_block[1024];
        int   i, j;

        random_seed = 0x1325fe9b;

#ifdef TYPE2
        genlambda2();
#else
        genlambda();
#endif

        Base.crv.form = 0;
        null(&Base.crv.a2);
        one(&Base.crv.a6);
        print_curve("koblitz 131", &Base.crv);

        random_field(&test2);
        print_field("random field", &test2);
        random_point( &Base.crv, &Base.pnt);
        print_point(" Base point ",&Base.pnt);
        ECKGP( &Base, &test3, &key);
        print_field("random value ", &test3);
        print_point("hidden point ",&key);
        for (i=0; i<1024; i++) data_block[i] = i;
        ECES_encrypt( data_block, 1024, &key, &ephemeral_key,
                        encrypt_block, &Base);
```

```
      print_field("encrypt data", (FIELD2N*) encrypt_block);
      ECES_decrypt( &ephemeral_key, encrypt_block, 1024,
                      &test3, decrypt_block, &Base);
      print_field("decrypt data", (FIELD2N*) decrypt_block);
}
```

For this example I picked a very secure Koblitz curve. While not necessary, it shows the ease of choosing Koblitz curves over a normal basis. Even though this protocol is simple, it can be very secure. Assuming the transmission path is known, of course: A man-in-the-middle attack is pretty simple if the public key is not verified by an alternate channel.

The output of the previous example is as follows:

```
koblitz 131
form = 0
a6 :          7 ffffffff ffffffff ffffffff ffffffff

random field :        1 8c6651fd abfdc0c0 ea79f216 9b5f15ed
 Base point
x :          2 821b8b1d 13847fd6 e8cbd586 7400e914
y :          1 6cfc8391 f626e140 6596373e 703af872

random value  :        7 dcc910af 687ea94c 57b15969 ce792322
hidden point
x :          4 339ac4b3 4d890513 111e5dbc a3c3ecd4
y :          6 be25ef5a 7163cc3a f72ffa64 a1445e09

encrypt data : a164df45 50a298fd 94b8b1ce ec19d6d1 8b2419c1
decrypt data :    10203  4050607  8090a0b  c0d0e0f 10111213
```

The above routines are interesting, but the IEEE standard is a bit more complicated. The structure for EC_PARAMETER does not include the base point order, and none of the algorithms presented so far uses any integer math. In the next two chapters, we'll look at key agreement and signature schemes that require integer math, as well as the elliptic curve math. In the case of signatures, we'll also need the hash algorithm presented in this chapter.

So, let's first look at some advanced protocols for key sharing. Both Massey-Omura and Menezes-Qu-Vanstone in all their glory are coming up!

8.6 References

1 B. Schneier, *Applied Cryptography*, 2d ed. (New York: John Wiley & Sons, 1996).

C H A P T E R   9

Advanced protocols, key exchange

9.1 Preliminaries for key exchange   222

9.2 Polynomial solution to $\gamma^3 = \gamma + 1$ 226

9.3 Massey-Omura protocol   234

9.4 MQV: the standard   244

9.5 References   254

9.1 Preliminaries for key exchange

The key exchange schemes I'll talk about now include the elliptic curve version of Massey-Omura and the Menezes-Qu-Vanstone secret key agreement schemes. Both these schemes require the use of modular integer arithmetic, as well as modular polynomial or normal basis mathematics. Although the mathematics of integers and binary fields is completely different, there are many similarities when seen as a Galois Field.

Figure 9.1 illustrates the subroutine schematic for this chapter. As you can see, the subroutines that incorporate the key exchange protocols require all the mathematical and cryptographic subroutines discussed in previous chapters. Some of the routines described in chapter 8 are rewritten here to use new structures.

I will first describe a few simple routines for conversions to and from the different structures used by integers and binary fields. From there I'll define some new structures to hold key data and common public parameters and rewrite the key generation routines of the previous chapter. Then we'll take a side trip into solutions of linear equations for polynomial basis curves, because we need to know the order of the curve. After that I'll go into the meat of the key exchange algorithms.

A very simple yet important pair of functions is the conversion between integer and binary field representations. For the code described in this book, the representations are quite different. Only half of an ELEMENT is used to hold a chunk of integer. So the conversion is simply an expansion, when changing a bit string from FIELD2N to BIGINT, and a compression, when going the other way.

Here is the conversion from binary field to integer.

```
void field_to_int( a, b)
FIELD2N *a;
BIGINT *b;
{
        INDEX           i, j;

        int_null( b);
        for (i=NUMWORD; i>=0; i--)
        {
                j = INTMAX - ((NUMWORD - i)<<1);
                b->hw[j] = a->e[i] & LOMASK;
                j--;
                b->hw[j] = (a->e[i] & HIMASK) >> HALFSIZE;
        }
}
```

This routine moves from the least significant ELEMENT to the most significant, converting each one into two half-size chunks. The variable j keeps track of which ELEMENT each half ends up in relative to the BIGINT definition. Similarly, the conversion from integer to binary field is as follows:

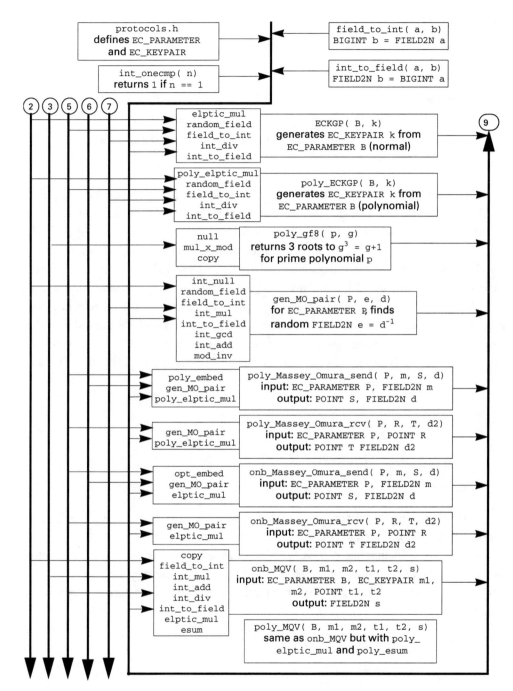

Figure 9.1   Subroutine schematic

```
void int_to_field( a, b)
BIGINT *a;
FIELD2N *b;
{
        INDEX i, j;

        SUMLOOP(i)
        {
                j = (i + MAXLONG) << 1;
                b->e[i] = a->hw[j+1] | (a->hw[j] << HALFSIZE);
        }
}
```

Here I just concatenate two halves into a single ELEMENT. The INDEX j is computed relative to the FIELD2N storage size, since the integer has to have four times as many ELEMENTS. It's not quite a factor of 4, because NUMBITS is not usually an even multiple of 2. So I add MAXLONG to get an offset and then double this for the half words.

Both of the key agreement protocols described in the following text share some basic properties. In the IEEE standard these are called the "elliptic curve parameters" and "function subroutines." As stated in the previous chapter, we need to add a few more structures to the EC_PARAMETER structure. These values include the order of the base point, as well as a term called the "cofactor." The order of the curve can be found by multiplying the cofactor value with the order of the base point. I'll define the new version of the structure as follows:

```
typedef struct
{
        CURVE           crv;
        POINT           pnt;
        FIELD2N         pnt_order;
        FIELD2N         cofactor;
} EC_PARAMETER;
```

Even if you use the previous code with this new structure, there should not be any problems; the point order and cofactor are simply ignored.

For the key exchange algorithms, we create a lot of random private keys and multiply them by the base point. I call these an EC_KEYPAIR, because they are used as private and public versions of a key. The structure I use to pass these values between routines is as follows:

```
typedef struct
{
        FIELD2N         prvt_key;
        POINT           pblc_key;
} EC_KEYPAIR;
```

Associated with any EC_KEYPAIR are the EC_PARAMETERs. Usually the elliptic curve parameters are set up "permanently" for any particular application. Especially for authentication, the elliptic curve parameters must remain constant for long periods of time, because many users will be creating EC_KEYPAIRs and won't want to change them too often. Because the curve order must be known for the following protocols, you'll know how secure you are. A good measure of security is the time to crack the Certicom challenges, so it's worthwhile keeping track of how many of those problems have been solved.

The elliptic curve key generation routine of the previous chapter needs to be modified for use with the routines in this chapter. The standard requires that the random value used to create the private key be less than the order of the base point in the elliptic curve parameters. This is easy to do; we first generate some random bit pattern and mask it down to the size of a FIELD2N variable. This value is reduced modulo the point order to ensure the standard is met.

Here is the normal basis version for the ECKGP routine mentioned in the IEEE P1363 draft.

```
void ECKGP( Base, Key)
EC_PARAMETER            *Base;
EC_KEYPAIR              *Key;
{
        BIGINT          key_num, point_order, quotient, remainder;
        FIELD2N         rand_key;

/*  ensure random value is less than point order  */

        random_field( &rand_key);
        field_to_int( &rand_key, &key_num);
        field_to_int( &Base->pnt_order, &point_order);
        int_div( &key_num, &point_order, &quotient, &remainder);
        int_to_field( &remainder, &Key->prvt_key);

        elptic_mul( &Key->prvt_key, &Base->pnt, &Key->pblc_key, &Base->crv);
}
```

I'll actually be converting the order of the point many times in the following routines. You could argue that it takes less time to specify the EC_PARAMETER structure with the order of the point stored as a BIGINT, but I felt that saving space was more important. Change this to suit your application.

This is not all that complicated, but it means we must now link all our subroutines into one library. While the integer routines stay the same, if we choose to use polynomial basis math instead of normal basis, we'll have to call the following routine instead:

```
void poly_ECKGP( Base, Key)
EC_PARAMETER            *Base;
EC_KEYPAIR              *Key;
{
        BIGINT          key_num, point_order, quotient, remainder;
        FIELD2N         rand_key;
```

```
/*  ensure random value is less than point order  */

        random_field( &rand_key);
        field_to_int( &rand_key, &key_num);
        field_to_int( &Base->pnt_order, &point_order);
        int_div( &key_num, &point_order, &quotient, &remainder);
        int_to_field( &remainder, &Key->prvt_key);

        poly_elptic_mul( &Key->prvt_key, &Base->pnt,
                         &Key->pblc_key, &Base->crv);
}
```

While only one line of code is different, there is a tremendous amount of difference in how the two routines operate at the lower levels of math. At the higher level, they are completely the same. As usual, I wrote the normal basis version first and left off the onb_ before the name of the subroutine. For the highest-level routines, the same inputs are used in the same order, and the only difference will be the onb_ or poly_ in the start of the routine name.

The assumption for the protocols in this and the next chapter is that we already know the parameters a^2 and a^6 of the public curve. Since finding these for some versions of polynomial basis examples listed in chapter 6 requires some additional calculation, I'm going to take a slight detour here and discuss a subroutine that solves for γ in the Koblitz curves from tables 6.5 and 6.6 in chapter 6.

9.2 Polynomial solution to $\gamma^3 = \gamma + 1$

The Koblitz curves from tables 6.5 and 6.6 can only be used with polynomial basis mathematics. Because they offer very good security with reasonable field size, it is worthwhile understanding how to create the a_6 value for any prime polynomial.

The curves are based on F_{2^3}, and the coefficient a_6 is given as:

$$\gamma \in F_{2^3} \qquad \gamma^3 = \gamma + 1. \tag{9.1}$$

To solve for γ in equation (9.1) for any prime polynomial, we have to know a few math tricks. Again, thanks to Richard Pinch for pointing these out to me. The most important trick is to multiply equation (9.1) by γ to get:

$$\gamma^4 + \gamma^2 + \gamma = 0. \tag{9.2}$$

This trivial operation performs magic for us. Taking the square of an element in a base 2 field is a linear operation. By linear I mean:

$$(a + b)^2 = a^2 + b^2. \tag{9.3}$$

We saw this before in chapter 6. Equation (9.2) can be solved with standard techniques for linear equations. We will find four solutions: one is 0, two are independent, and the last is the sum of those.

The solution process is similar to what we did in chapter 6 for the quadratic equation. We first compute a table of all powers of x (modulo the prime polynomial) that could be present in γ. Since we're going to γ^4, we need four times NUMBITS storage, actually (4 * (NUMBITS - 1)). With that table it is easy to construct the sum of all the terms in equation (9.2).

The matrix representation of γ, which we get from these operations, gives us rows proportional to a specific coefficient and columns proportional to a specific power of x. Since the coefficients are the unknowns, we can transpose the matrix and work with rows proportional to specific powers of x and columns proportional to the coefficients we wish to find.

We'll find out that we have two more equations than we have unknowns, so there must be two independent vectors that satisfy all the equations. This will give us null columns when we try to lower-diagonalize the matrix through Gaussian elimination. These null columns are arbitrary variables. See [1, chapter 10] for a detailed explanation of this method.

All the other coefficients will be found in terms of these two variables. The only possible values of these variables are (0, 0), (0, 1), (1, 0), and (1, 1). The first gives us 0 for a solution we knew we could ignore. The last is the sum of the previous two.

Let's look at a simple example. Over F_{2^6} take the prime polynomial as:

$$x^6 + x + 1. \tag{9.4}$$

Writing just the coefficients of all the powers of x modulo the above polynomial, we obtain the lookup table shown in table 9.1.

Table 9.1 Lookup Table

Power	Coefficient
0	0 0 0 0 0 1
1	0 0 0 0 1 0
2	0 0 0 1 0 0
3	0 0 1 0 0 0
4	0 1 0 0 0 0
5	1 0 0 0 0 0
6	0 0 0 0 1 1
7	0 0 0 1 1 0

Table 9.1 Lookup Table (continued)

Power	Coefficient
8	0 0 1 1 0 0
9	0 1 1 0 0 0
10	1 1 0 0 0 0
11	1 0 0 0 1 1
12	0 0 0 1 0 1
13	0 0 1 0 1 0
14	0 1 0 1 0 0
15	1 0 1 0 0 0
16	0 1 0 0 1 1
17	1 0 0 1 1 0
18	0 0 1 1 1 1
19	0 1 1 1 1 0
20	1 1 1 1 0 0

The next step is to form a matrix representing equation (9.2) using the lookup table shown in table 9.1. This is the same thing we did in chapter 6. Each row is a specific coefficient: The top row in equation (9.5) is the sum of rows 5, 10, and 20 from table 9.1. The next row down is the sum of rows 4, 8, and 16, and so on to fill the whole matrix.

$$
\begin{bmatrix} \gamma_5 & \gamma_4 & \gamma_3 & \gamma_2 & \gamma_1 & \gamma_0 \end{bmatrix}
\begin{bmatrix}
1 & 0 & 1 & 1 & 0 & 0 \\
0 & 0 & 1 & 1 & 1 & 1 \\
0 & 0 & 1 & 1 & 1 & 0 \\
0 & 1 & 1 & 0 & 0 & 0 \\
0 & 1 & 0 & 1 & 1 & 0 \\
0 & 0 & 0 & 0 & 0 & 1
\end{bmatrix}
\begin{bmatrix}
x^5 \\ x^4 \\ x^3 \\ x^2 \\ x \\ 1
\end{bmatrix} = 0
\tag{9.5}
$$

Since we need to find the coefficients to γ, we can transpose equation (9.5) and write out one equation for each power of x in terms of all the coefficients:

$$
\begin{bmatrix} x^5 & x^4 & x^3 & x^2 & x & 1 \end{bmatrix}
\begin{bmatrix}
1 & 0 & 0 & 0 & 0 & 0 \\
0 & 0 & 0 & 1 & 1 & 0 \\
1 & 1 & 1 & 1 & 0 & 0 \\
1 & 1 & 1 & 0 & 1 & 0 \\
0 & 1 & 1 & 0 & 1 & 0 \\
0 & 1 & 0 & 0 & 0 & 1
\end{bmatrix}
\begin{bmatrix}
\gamma_5 \\ \gamma_4 \\ \gamma_3 \\ \gamma_2 \\ \gamma_1 \\ \gamma_0
\end{bmatrix} = 0
\tag{9.6}
$$

CHAPTER 9 ADVANCED PROTOCOLS, KEY EXCHANGE

The top row is obvious, $\gamma_5 = 0$. But it is not obvious to a computer program. So let's lower-diagonalize the above matrix to get:

$$
\begin{array}{llllll}
1 & 0 & 0 & 0 & 0 & 0 \\
0 & 1 & 1 & 1 & 0 & 0 \\
0 & 0 & 1 & 1 & 0 & 1 \\
0 & 0 & 0 & 1 & 1 & 0 \\
0 & 0 & 0 & 0 & 0 & 0 \\
0 & 0 & 0 & 0 & 0 & 0 .
\end{array}
\qquad (9.7)
$$

The last two rows have gone to 0, which means the last two coefficients are variables. We can create two solutions with these variables. The solutions are vectors, and equation (9.7) shows us how to combine the two variables to find the solution vectors. The solution vectors can be written:

$$
\begin{bmatrix}
\gamma_{0,5} \\
\gamma_{0,4} \\
\gamma_{0,3} \\
\gamma_{0,2} \\
0 \\
1
\end{bmatrix}
\qquad
\begin{bmatrix}
\gamma_{1,5} \\
\gamma_{1,4} \\
\gamma_{1,3} \\
\gamma_{1,2} \\
1 \\
0
\end{bmatrix} .
\qquad (9.8)
$$

Row 2 in equation (9.7) tells us that $\gamma_2 = \gamma_1$. Using this relationship in equation (9.8), we find that $\gamma_{0,2} = 0$ and $\gamma_{1,2} = 1$. This is called back-solving the matrix and is a standard technique for the solutions to linear equations (see [1]). What we're doing here is much simpler, because all the values are 0 or 1. With the two solutions to equation (9.8) found, the third solution will be their sum. The final answer is:

$$
\begin{bmatrix}
0 \\
1 \\
1 \\
0 \\
0 \\
1
\end{bmatrix}
\qquad
\begin{bmatrix}
0 \\
0 \\
1 \\
1 \\
1 \\
0
\end{bmatrix}
\qquad
\begin{bmatrix}
0 \\
1 \\
0 \\
1 \\
1 \\
1
\end{bmatrix} .
\qquad (9.9)
$$

It is easy to verify that $x^3 + x^2 + x$ cubed is equal to itself plus 1 modulo the prime polynomial in equation (9.4). So much for examples we can do by hand; let's see how to do this in C.

Here is the header to a subroutine that performs the previous calculations for a given prime polynomial. The routine assumes the input is a prime polynomial and that the field size has a factor of 3 in it. It will probably fail miserably if these conditions are not met. The output consists of three FIELD2N values packed one after the other.

```
/********************************************************************
*                                                                  *
*               periferal functions useful for setting up polynomial *
*        math but not called routinely.                            *
*                                                                  *
********************************************************************/

#include "field2n.h"
#include "poly.h"

/*  for given irreducible polynomial solve g^3 = g + 1.
        Useful for GF(8^n) Koblitz curves.
        Trick is to lineraize equation into form g^4 + g^2 + g = 0.
        This is linear because (a + b)^(2^n) = a^(2^n) + b^(2^n).
        There are four solutions: one is zero, two are found as
        independent vectors and the third is their sum.

    \   Input:  pointers to irreducble polynomial and g[3]
        Output: g[0], g[1], and g[3] = g[0] + g[1] filled in
*/

void poly_gf8( prime, g)
FIELD2N   *prime, g[3];
{
        FIELD2N         gamma_matrix[NUMBITS], solve[NUMBITS];
        FIELD2N         power_table[4*NUMBITS], temp;
        INDEX           row, column, i, j, found, vector;
        ELEMENT         tobit, frombit, bit, null_check;
```

The first step is to build a lookup table holding all the powers of x we'll need. This sets the first entry to 1 and then multiplies each succeeding entry by x modulo the input prime to get the next entry in the table.

```
/*  step 1:  compute all powers of x modulo prime polynomial
        with simple function */

        null( &power_table[0]);
        power_table[0].e[NUMWORD] = 1L;
        for (row = 1; row < 4*NUMBITS; row++)
                mul_x_mod( &power_table[row-1], prime, &power_table[row]);
```

The next step is to compute equation (9.2) using the lookup table shown in table 9.1. This amounts to copying one of the diagonal rows and summing it with the rows that have 2 and 4 times the diagonal row number.

```
/*   step 2:   sum powers of rows to create g^4 + g^2 + g
         coefficients matrix.
*/
         for( row=0; row < NUMBITS; row++)
         {
                 copy( &power_table[row], &gamma_matrix[row]);
                 SUMLOOP (i) gamma_matrix[row].e[i] ^=
                         power_table[row<<1].e[i] ^ power_table[row<<2].e[i];
         }
```

Next I transpose the γ matrix. The first operation is to clear the result matrix (called solve), and the next operation is to set the bits that need it. Each row and column of the source gamma_matrix is tested, and, if set, the corresponding column and row in the solve matrix is set.

```
/*   step 3:   transpose matrix and work with single powers of x */
         for ( row=0; row < NUMBITS; row++)  null( &solve[row]);
         for ( row=0; row < NUMBITS; row++)
         {
                 bit = 1L << (row % WORDSIZE);
                 i = NUMWORD - (row/WORDSIZE);
                 frombit = 1;
                 j = NUMWORD;
                 for ( column = 0; column < NUMBITS; column++)
                 {
                         if (gamma_matrix[row].e[j] & frombit)
                                                 solve[column].e[i] |= bit;
                         frombit <<= 1;
                         if ( !frombit)
                         {
                                 frombit = 1;
                                 j--;
                         }
                 }
         }
```

The next step is to lower-diagonalize the solve matrix to eliminate terms. This is similar to what we did in chapter 6, but now there is no diagonal matrix holding the solution. If the diagonal bit is not set, we search all rows below the present one until we find one that is set and swap it with the present one.

```
/*   step 4: lower diagonalize solve matrix.
         2 columns will go null, search for null rows instead
         of diagnalizing. */

         vector = 0;      /*  set up solution space  */
         null( &g[0]);
         null( &g[1]);

         for (column = NUMBITS - 1; column > 0; column--)
```

```
{
        bit = 1L << (column % WORDSIZE);
        i = NUMWORD - column/WORDSIZE;
        if ( !(bit & solve[column].e[i]) )
        {
        /*  go look for a bit set in this column  */

                found = 0;
                for (row = column - 1; row >= 0; row--)
                {
                        if ( bit & solve[row].e[i])
                        {
                                copy ( &solve[row], &temp);
                                copy ( &solve[column], &solve[row]);
                                copy ( &temp, &solve[column]);
                                found = 1;
                                break;
                        }
                }
        }
        else found = 1;
    /*  and eliminate any set bits below it  */
```

If the diagonal bit is set, the elimination process is the same as previously.

```
        if (found)
        {
                for ( row = column-1; row >=0; row--)
                {
                        if (solve[row].e[i] & bit)
                                SUMLOOP (j)
                                solve[row].e[j] ^= solve[column].e[j];
                }
        }
        else
```

Along the way two rows will go to 0. When I find a null column (i.e., a column with no bits set at or below the diagonal), I try to find a matching null row to swap it with. I then call that row a variable and set one bit in a solution vector. The counter vector is bumped to make sure both solutions are started with only one variable.

```
        {
    /*  if null column, see if we have null row to match it.  */

                null_check = 0;
                SUMLOOP (j) null_check |= solve[column].e[j];
                if ( null_check)
                {
                /*  search for a null row to put here  */

                        for ( row = column-1; row >=0; row--)
                        {
```

```
                    null_check = 0;
                    SUMLOOP (j) null_check |= solve[row].e[j];
                    if ( !null_check)
                    {
                            copy ( &solve[row], &temp);
                            copy ( &solve[column], &solve[row]);
                            copy ( &temp, &solve[column]);
                            break;
                    }
                }
            }

    /*  mark this vector with column bit, and use next vector */

                g[vector].e[i] |= bit;
                vector++;
            }
        }
```

When lower diagonalization is finished, I have to check if the second vector had a solution. That's because the last bit is never checked. If the last bit was set, then we must have already found a variable. The reason is that the last bit set means $\gamma_0 = 0$. If the last bit is clear, then γ_0 is a variable, and the last bit in the second solution vector must be set.

```
/*  last row may be null and not marked.  if INDEX vector < 2,
        set g[1] = 1
*/
        if (vector < 2) g[1].e[NUMWORD] = 1;
```

The last major procedure is to back-solve the matrix using the known variables. The 0 row is already given, so we start at the first row and work up the matrix 1 bit at a time. For each bit set on the diagonal, we have to add all the bits in the solution vector that are set in the row. This really is back-solving: substitution of all the known coefficients to find the next one. Since there are two vector solutions, the same sum is performed twice.

```
/*  find two solution vectors by back solving matrix.  use bits
        previoiusly solved to find bits not yet solved.  Initial vectors
        come from assuming g0 and g1 are variables.
*/

        for ( row=1; row<NUMBITS; row++)
        {
            tobit = 1L << (row % WORDSIZE);
            j = NUMWORD - (row/WORDSIZE);

            /*  check to see if diagonal bit is set  */

            if (solve[row].e[j] & tobit)
```

```
        {
                for (column = row-1; column >= 0; column--)
                {
                        frombit = 1L << (column % WORDSIZE);
                        i = NUMWORD - column/WORDSIZE;
                        if ( solve[row].e[i] & frombit)
                        {
                                if (g[0].e[i] & frombit) g[0].e[j] ^= tobit;
                                if (g[1].e[i] & frombit) g[1].e[j] ^= tobit;
                        }
                }
        }
    }

/*  last step:  g[2] = g[1] + g[0]  */

    SUMLOOP (i) g[2].e[i] = g[0].e[i] ^ g[1].e[i];
}
```

When all is said and done, we get the third solution by summing the first two. From these three roots we can pick any one to be the a_6 value for a Koblitz curve. The order of the curve will be known, and the following routines can be easily implemented.

9.3 Massey-Omura protocol

To thwart the man-in-the-middle attack, one can use the Massey-Omura multipass protocol for key sharing. This requires the use of a math package such as freelip or the code from chapter 2. It also assumes you know the order of the public curve. So, let's pick one of the curves described in [2] and make that assumption valid.

The idea behind the Massey-Omura protocol is to take advantage of the cyclical nature of a Galois Field. Let's call the order of the chosen elliptic curve N. If we find a value e between 1 and N that is relatively prime to N, then from chapter 2 we know that gcd$(e, N) = 1$. We can use an inversion algorithm to find:

$$d = e^{-1} \mod N .$$

(9.10)

To combine the field of integers modulo N with elliptic curves over binary fields, we have to know that the modular mathematics we do over integers is identical to the properties of the mathematics over elliptic curves. Using e and d from equation (9.10) and any point P on an elliptic curve we can compute:

$$Q = eP$$
$$R = dQ.$$

(9.11)

We will find that $R = P$. The Massey-Omura protocol takes advantage of this and the intractability of finding factors of given points with respect to a known base point.

Let's go back to Alicia and Brandon. Alicia picks e_A and computes d_A. Similarly, Brandon picks e_B and computes d_B. For both of them, e is their "encryption" key and d is their "decryption" key, since $ed = 1 \bmod N$.

Alicia embeds her message onto some point P_m using the `opt_embed` or `poly_embed` functions of chapter 6. She then multiplies this message point by her secret value e_A to get the point:

$$P_1 = e_A P_m. \tag{9.12}$$

Alicia then sends this point to Brandon. Brandon can't make heads or tails of this yet, so he computes:

$$P_2 = e_B P_1 \tag{9.13}$$

and sends this back to Alicia. If Micah intercepts either of these points, there is nothing he can do to get out the original data P_m. However, Brandon still does not know what P_m is either, so he sends P_2 back to Alicia. Alicia then computes:

$$P_3 = d_A P_2 \tag{9.14}$$

and returns this point back to Brandon. Now, magic has happened. Let's expand equation (9.14) and see what it is:

$$P_3 = d_A P_2 = d_A(e_B P_1) = d_A(e_B(e_A P_m)). \tag{9.15}$$

The magic occurs because the order of the curve is N, and we already know that $d_A e_A = 1$ modulo N. The effect of Alicia's multiplication is to undo her first operation. So she returns point P_3, which now only contains Brandon's encryption key times the message point, to him:

$$P_3 = e_B P_m. \tag{9.16}$$

On receipt of P_3 Brandon multiplies by d_B to undo his factor and recover the message data:

$$P_m = d_B(e_B P_m). \tag{9.17}$$

This whole algorithm uses a single elliptic curve, which is known. It foils the man-in-the-middle attack, but at the expense of a lot of communication. Only `elptic_mul()` (or `poly_elptic_mul`) is required for every step, but there are a lot of data that need to be moved around between processors, and the initial setup of the factors *e* and *d* requires large integer math routines.

9.3.1 Massey-Omura: the code

The first thing we need to do for the Massey-Omura protocol is create a pair of BIGINTs, which are inverses of each other and relatively prime to the order of the elliptic curve. Since both sender and receiver need to create a pair, both sides in a transmission require the use of the same routine. I call it gen_MO_pair, and it is the same for both normal and polynomial basis routines.

Relatively prime numbers are, of course, easy to check; we just use the binary greatest common divisor routine from chapter 2 and verify that the output is 1. Since this test has to be done in an if statement, it makes sense to create a routine that compares a BIGINT to 1. Here is that routine.

```
/*  function to compare BIGINT value to 1.
        Returns 1 if it is, 0 otherwise.
*/

INDEX int_onecmp( number)
BIGINT *number;
{
        INDEX   i;

        if ( number->hw[INTMAX] > 1) return (0);
        for ( i=0; i<INTMAX; i++)
                if ( number->hw[i]) return (0);
        if (number->hw[INTMAX]) return (1);
        return (0);
}
```

This is a very easy test: If the last ELEMENT is greater than 1, we know immediately to return 0. If it is 1, we have to check all the other ELEMENTS in the structure. The last line would only be executed if the number is 0, which can't happen in a perfect world.

With this it is easy to create a pair of numbers that are inverses and relatively prime to the order of a given curve. Since all curves over F_{2^m} must have even order, we start with an odd number and increment by 2 to search for a random value that will work.

```
void gen_MO_pair ( Public, e, d)
EC_PARAMETER        *Public;
FIELD2N             *e, *d;
{
        FIELD2N         garbage;
        BIGINT          gcd_check, crv_order, pnt_order, cfactor;
        BIGINT          search, en, de;

/*  since 2 is always a factor, stay odd while hunting  */
```

```
            int_null( &search);
            search.hw[INTMAX] = 2;

/*  compute curve order   */

            field_to_int( &Public->pnt_order, &pnt_order);
            field_to_int( &Public->cofactor, &cfactor);
            int_mul( &cfactor, &pnt_order, &crv_order);
```

The first calculation finds the curve order from the base point order (assumed to be a large prime number) by multiplying with the cofactor. For those applications that need speed, the curve order can be computed once and saved somewhere.

```
/*  find random value prime to curve order.  EC curves over
       GF(2^n) are always even  */

            random_field( &garbage);
            garbage.e[NUMWORD] |= 1L;
            field_to_int( &garbage, &en);
            int_gcd( &en, &crv_order, &gcd_check);
```

To create an odd random number, I just call the random number generator to fill a FIELD2N variable and set the last bit. After converting to an integer, I check to see if the random number is relatively prime to the curve order.

```
/*  hunt for value that is relatively prime to curve order  */

            while ( !int_onecmp( &gcd_check))
            {
                    int_add( &search, &en, &en);
                    int_gcd( &en, &crv_order, &gcd_check);
            }
```

If the result of the gcd calculation is not 1, the random number is incremented by 2 and checked again. For curves of large prime order with small cofactors this loop is rarely entered.

```
/*  compute an inverse to complete the pair  */

            mod_inv( &en, &crv_order, &de);
            int_to_field( &en, e);
            int_to_field( &de, d);
}
```

The last step computes the inverse of the random value modulo the curve order. The integer representations are then compressed back to FIELD2N structures.

With the above subroutine, the initial send routine is trivial. The input message is embedded on the given public curve and multiplied by one number from the random pair generated previously. The second number is returned for the second transmission.

```
/*   Massey-Omura secret sharing protocol, sender side.
        Computes an encryption, decryption pair (e, d) and
        embeds data on public curve (Pub_crv).
        Output is e*Pm and d.
*/

void poly_Massey_Omura_send( Pub_crv, message, send_point, decrypt)
EC_PARAMETER          *Pub_crv;
FIELD2N               *message, *decrypt;
POINT                 *send_point;
{
        POINT           msg;
        FIELD2N         e;

/*   embed data on given curve.  Change increment or field size to
        ensure trouble free operations.
*/
        poly_embed( message, &Pub_crv->crv, 0, 0, &msg);

/*   create random encryption and decryption pair  */

        gen_MO_pair( Pub_crv, &e, decrypt);

/*   compute point to transmit  */

        poly_elptic_mul( &e, &msg, send_point, &Pub_crv->crv);
}
```

The normal basis version is basically identical.

```
void onb_Massey_Omura_send( Pub_crv, message, send_point, decrypt)
EC_PARAMETER          *Pub_crv;
FIELD2N               *message, *decrypt;
POINT                 *send_point;
{
        POINT           msg;
        FIELD2N         e;

/*   embed data on given curve.  Change increment or field size to
        ensure trouble free operations.
*/
        opt_embed( message, &Pub_crv->crv, 0, 0, &msg);

/*   create random encryption and decryption pair  */

        gen_MO_pair( Pub_crv, &e, decrypt);

/*   compute point to transmit  */

        elptic_mul( &e, &msg, send_point, &Pub_crv->crv);
}
```

The receive side also has to generate a pair of numbers and then perform an elliptic curve multiply. This subroutine takes only two lines of code in polynomial basis version.

```
/*  Massey-Omura secret sharing protocol, receiver side.
        input: senders point (rcv_point), public curve (Pub_crv).
        generates encrypt, decrypt pair,
        output: e*rcv_point (step2), decrypt
*/

void poly_Massey_Omura_rcv( Pub_crv, rcv_point, step2, decrypt)
EC_PARAMETER            *Pub_crv;
POINT                   *rcv_point, *step2;
FIELD2N                 *decrypt;
{
        FIELD2N         e;

/* create encrypt, decrypt pair  */

        gen_MO_pair (Pub_crv, &e, decrypt);

/*  compute point to transmit back  */

        poly_elptic_mul ( &e, rcv_point, step2, &Pub_crv->crv);
}
```

It appears as follows in the normal basis version:

```
void onb_Massey_Omura_rcv( Pub_crv, rcv_point, step2, decrypt)
EC_PARAMETER            *Pub_crv;
POINT                   *rcv_point, *step2;
FIELD2N                 *decrypt;
{
        FIELD2N         e;

/* create encrypt, decrypt pair  */

        gen_MO_pair (Pub_crv, &e, decrypt);

/*  compute point to transmit back  */

        elptic_mul ( &e, rcv_point, step2, &Pub_crv->crv);
}
```

Let's look at two examples. The above routines are called to set things up, and then both sides must perform another multiply with data they receive from a transmission. Since this is just a single elliptic multiply, there's no need for a special subroutine. The first example is with a normal basis.

```
main()
{
        EC_PARAMETER            Base;
        FIELD2N                 side1_dcrpt, side2_dcrpt, message;
```

```
        POINT                   P1, P2, P3, P4;
        BIGINT                  prime_order;
        POINT                   temp;
```

The following curve order is from table 6.1 in chapter 6. It's a Type II normal basis. The coefficients of a_2 and a_6 are 1.

```
        char string1[MAXSTRING] ="519229685853482762789670383467507";

#ifdef TYPE2
        genlambda2();
#else
        genlambda();
#endif

        random_seed = 0xBEC0D1F5;

/*  compute curve order from Koblitz data  */

        ascii_to_bigint(&string1, &prime_order);
        int_to_field( &prime_order, &Base.pnt_order);
        null( &Base.cofactor);
        Base.cofactor.e[NUMWORD] = 2;

/*  create Koblitz curve  */

        Base.crv.form = 1;
        one(&Base.crv.a2);
        one(&Base.crv.a6);
        print_curve("Koblitz 113", &Base.crv);
```

From there a random point is found. Since the only cofactor is 2, we can guarantee that the chosen point order has the large prime factor by simply doubling the random point. This is not strictly necessary for this protocol.

```
/*  create base point of known order with no cofactor  */

        rand_point( &temp, &Base.crv);
        print_point("random point", &temp);
        edbl( &temp, &Base.pnt, &Base.crv);
        print_point(" Base point ",&Base.pnt);

/*  test Massey Omura protocol
        create dummy message        */

        random_field( &message);
```

The message can be anything. It just has to be flexible enough to be embedded on a curve—that is, a few bits flipped in a given location shouldn't matter. The first side embeds the message on the curve and sends the first point.

```
/*  sender transmits first point  */

        onb_Massey_Omura_send( &Base, &message, &P1, &side1_dcrpt);
        print_point("First point sent", &P1);
```

The second side generates a pair of values and returns a multiple of the first side's point.

```
/*  receiver replies with second point  */

        onb_Massey_Omura_rcv( &Base, &P1, &P2, &side2_dcrpt);
        print_point("second point returned", &P2);
```

The first side undoes its original number and sends it back.

```
/*  sender decrypts their portion and returns third point  */

        elptic_mul( &side1_dcrpt, &P2, &P3, &Base.crv);
        print_point("third point sent", &P3);
```

And finally the second side undoes its original multiply and finds the message.

```
/*  receiver decrypts message  */

        elptic_mul( &side2_dcrpt, &P3, &P4, &Base.crv);
        print_point("message recived", &P4);
        print_field("z ", &message);
        printf("compared to message sent\n");

}
```

Example output of the above code looks like this:

```
Koblitz 113
form = 1
a2 :    1ffff ffffffff ffffffff ffffffff
a6 :    1ffff ffffffff ffffffff ffffffff

random point
x :     1563e ed5bd6a9 8941ae48 bc047792
y :      4fbc d8d3e80b 837ac64f 6fd86594

 Base point
x :       d48 181d5f83 c7803439 e60f21d9
y :      1aa3 b524941a edddf53 247e7eb7

First point sent
x :     154b9 4b0f93e5 7dcee749 474907a9
y :      ab31 370b4eaf 25f6fb12 1801b5e5

second point returned
x :      8b7d 85cbbe8a 73cd67be 35371dab
y :      267e 4760122c dfa3c02c be335ac4
```

```
third point sent
x :      2880 52fee677 ea85b780 6e020787
y :      2b00 575524e2 bf82e343  1c02731


message recived
x :      1517d e823c63d fb82eba5 449ce4ec
y :      a5a6 81a81af3 67724c8c d1af9f59


z :      1517d e823c63d fb82eba5 449ce4ec
compared to message sent
```

Again, I got lucky—the original data were on the curve without any searching. Now, here's an example for the polynomial basis routines. For this example I chose the field in table 6.5 in chapter 6. This requires the `poly_gf8` subroutine (after describing it, I'd better use it!), and I chose the second vector for the coefficient a_6.

```
main()
{
        EC_PARAMETER            Base;
        FIELD2N                 root[3];
        FIELD2N                 side1_dcrpt, side2_dcrpt, message;
        POINT                   P1, P2, P3, P4;
        BIGINT                  prime_order;
        POINT                   temp;
        INDEX                   error;
        char string1[MAXSTRING] ="3245185536584267231149575723335741"; /*N 111
*/

        random_seed = 0x1fe9325b;

        if (!irreducible(&poly_prime)) return(0);
        print_field("poly_prime = ", &poly_prime);

        if (error = init_poly_math())
        {
                printf("Can't initialize S matrix, row = %d\n", error);
                return(-1);
        }

/*   compute curve order from Koblitz data   */

        ascii_to_bigint(&string1, &prime_order);
        int_to_field( &prime_order, &Base.pnt_order);
        null( &Base.cofactor);
        Base.cofactor.e[NUMWORD] = 8;

        printf("create Base curve and point\n\n");

        Base.crv.form = 0;
        null(&Base.crv.a2);
        poly_gf8(&poly_prime, root);
        copy( &root[1], &Base.crv.a6);
        print_curve("Public curve", &Base.crv);
```

```
        rand_point(&P1, &Base.crv);
        poly_elptic_mul(&Base.cofactor, &P1, &Base.pnt, &Base.crv);
        print_point("Base point", &Base.pnt);

/*   test Massey Omura protocol
        create dummy message        */
        random_field( &message);

/*   sender transmits first point   */

        poly_Massey_Omura_send( &Base, &message, &P1, &side1_dcrpt);
        print_point("First point sent", &P1);

/*   receiver replies with second point   */

        poly_Massey_Omura_rcv( &Base, &P1, &P2, &side2_dcrpt);
        print_point("second point returned", &P2);

/*   sender decrypts their portion and returns third point   */

        poly_elptic_mul( &side1_dcrpt, &P2, &P3, &Base.crv);
        print_point("third point sent", &P3);

/*   receiver decrypts message   */

        poly_elptic_mul( &side2_dcrpt, &P3, &P4, &Base.crv);
        print_point("message recived", &P4);
        print_field("z ", &message);
        printf("compared to message sent\n");

}
```

Again, I got lucky—the data were directly embedded on the curve. The output from the above code is as follows:

```
poly_prime =  :     8000        0        0      401
create Base curve and point

Public curve
form = 0
a6 :    5b85 d9a7e747 7e0c9615 7fb27dc6

Base point
x :     280b aa055801 cd90187c b281c4b6
y :      7f6 c3efee97 245a1cc5 c3d153a3

First point sent
x :     4b38 a6dbd329 b2de8cd6  a892c46
y :     26ea dde4f72c e06b975f bffbdb2c

second point returned
x :     3d03 265fe939 3301623f 7df7b89d
y :     3afb c636df9d 1b4eb868 ab319503
```

```
third point sent
x :     14e6 a81b9a82 d209d85b a5a5fcfe
y :     4c3a e592a677    18097d b03bbe7f

message recived
x :     7024 afe50ce3 b54cd28 f8176e34
y :     6529 b228c90a 84b5cfcc 133612d1

z :     7024 afe50ce3 b54cd28 f8176e34
compared to message sent
```

The actual data transmission is not shown. This mechanism is fine for a smart card application where there is tight coupling between the two sides and there is little time constraint. For long-range systems such as the Internet, it is not so great, because one might lose a link while setting up a key exchange. Since the attacker does not know either the encryption or decryption keys, there is no way to find out the starting point P_m from any of the transmitted data. However, there is no verification that you know who you are talking to. To get authentication of identity let's look at one more protocol.

9.4 MQV: the standard

In chapter 7, I introduced the mathematics behind the Menezes-Qu-Vanstone (MQV) secret-sharing protocol. The version implemented there does not follow the standard. In this section, I'll give you code that meets the P1363 standard as described in the November 1997 draft. The standard may change, but the following should adapt easily.

The subroutine presented will follow the standard quite closely. The only major difference is that I don't multiply by the cofactor in one step. I found the code did not work for the examples I picked. Because the following code works, it does not appear to be necessary.

The standard defines a term that is half of the logarithm base 2 of the order of the base point. If r is the largest prime factor in the order of curve, then the equation looks like:

$$h = \lceil (\log_2 r)/2 \rceil .$$

(9.18)

For the curves in chapter 6, the cofactor is between 2 and 18. So h is half of NUMBITS for all practical purposes. Technically, it is going to be a touch less, so instead of using the ceiling function of equation (9.18), we can divide NUMBITS by 2 to get close to the value.

The basic mathematics of the standard is the same as described in chapter 7. There is a difference in how the x components of the ephemeral keys are used. The value of h is used to determine how many of the bits to keep in this version.

The standard specifies the steps as follows:

1 Create an integer, t, which is the bottom half of the x component of this side's public ephemeral point.

2 Create an integer, t', which is the bottom half of the x component of the other side's public ephemeral point.

3 Compute an integer $e = (t * \text{this side's secret key} + \text{this side's ephemeral key})$.

4 Compute an elliptic curve point $P = e * (\text{the other side's ephemeral point} + t' * \text{the other side's public key point})$.

5 Output the x component of P as the shared secret.

Let's follow the math so we can compare this to the previous method. We can use the same variables as in the previous chapter and derive the above steps mathematically. The first step is:

$$t = x \quad \bmod 2^b \tag{9.19}$$

and

$$t' = x' \quad \bmod 2^b. \tag{9.20}$$

Both t and t' then have bit b set according to the standard. This adds 2^b to each value and forces a nonzero multiplier.

Equations (9.19) and (9.20) are followed by an integer calculation. The private key is d, and the ephemeral private key is k:

$$e = td + k \quad \bmod r \tag{9.21}$$

and an elliptic curve calculation using the other side's ephemeral point R' and public key Q':

$$W = e(R' + t'Q'). \tag{9.22}$$

As before, the shared secret is the x component of the point W. If we expand the points in equation (9.22) to be multiples of the base point P, we find:

$$R' + t'Q' = (k' + t'd')P. \tag{9.23}$$

Putting equation (9.23) back into equation (9.22), along with equation (9.21), we see that both sides do compute the same point W as:

$$W = (k + td)(k' + t'd')P. \tag{9.24}$$

Comparison of equation (9.24) with equation (7.28) shows that the later version is much less complex than the earlier version. Furthermore, the later version uses only half the bits of the ephemeral key, instead of all of them, and none of the bits from the public key. This was done in the hope that the protocol would be made more efficient. In June 1998, Burt Kaliski pointed out that this put the MQV algorithm (as presented in the standard) in the position of being open to an esoteric attack [3]. The original algorithm presented in chapter 7 is immune from this problem.

In the process of improving efficiency, the standard has lost security. The standard may change, or it may be appended with extensions. Be prepared to change the following code to meet whatever standard is in place when you need to put this into your product.

9.4.1 MQV: normal basis version

The inputs to the MQV key sharing are the other side's public key, their_W; the other side's ephemeral key, their_V; our side's EC_KEYPAIR my_first; our side's ephemeral key pair, my_second; and the common elliptic curve parameter's Base.

Inside the routine we need several variables. We need to mask off some of the inputs, and we need several storage locations for integer variables. The curve order is assumed to be an integer of the form used in chapter 2; if you use a different integer package, that structure will change. We need to do things to our side's data and their side's data (our side knows the private key and the ephemeral key) before we're all done, so there are several temporary storage variables as well.

```
void onb_mqv( Base, my_first, my_second,
                      their_first, their_second,
                      shared_secret)
EC_PARAMETER *Base;
EC_KEYPAIR *my_first, *my_second;
POINT         *their_first, *their_second;
FIELD2N       *shared_secret;
{
        BIGINT        my_x_value;
        BIGINT        my_secret, my_ephemeral;
        FIELD2N       my_half_x, their_half_x;
        BIGINT        temp1, quotient, temp2;
        BIGINT        cfactor, point_order;
        FIELD2N       e_value;
        POINT         Temp, Common;
        INDEX         i, limit, half_msb;
        ELEMENT       mask;
```

The first value to be determined is h in equation (9.18). I call it limit for lack of any better name. Once we decide how many bits to keep, a mask is created to null out unwanted bits, and the correct number of WORDSIZE chunks is zeroed out. The factor 2^h

is added by setting a bit (marked with `half_msb`). The result is converted to an integer for our side's data and left as is for their side. That's because the elliptic multiply routine takes the integer in FIELD2N format. Both sides have this done to their ephemeral (second) key.

```
/*  convert x component of my ephemeral key to an integer modulo
        2^h where h is half the size of the order of the base point.
        Since we are using curves with order almost equal to the
        field size, the value of h is about half NUMBITS.
        Change limit to meet the specs for your application.
*/

        limit = NUMBITS / 2;
        half_msb = limit % WORDSIZE;
        mask = ~(~0 << half_msb);
        limit = limit/WORDSIZE + ( half_msb ? 1 : 0);
        copy( &my_second->pblc_key.x, &my_half_x);
        for( i=0; i<limit; i++) my_half_x.e[i] = 0;
        my_half_x.e[i] &= mask;
        my_half_x.e[i] |= 1L << half_msb;
        field_to_int( &my_half_x, &my_x_value);

/*  get half the other sides ephemeral key  */

        copy( &their_second->x, &their_half_x);
        for( i=0; i<limit; i++) their_half_x.e[i] = 0;
        their_half_x.e[i] &= mask;
        their_half_x.e[i] |= 1L << half_msb;
```

The next major calculation is equation (9.21). I first convert the values of the local side's secrets into integers. These are then multiplied and added to the above half value of the *x* component of the ephemeral point to get the value *e* of equation (9.21). The resultant multiplication and sum are reduced modulo the base point order. This is converted back to a FIELD2N value for the next step.

```
/*  compute multiplier from my secrets and x component  */

        field_to_int( &my_first->prvt_key, &my_secret);
        field_to_int( &my_second->prvt_key, &my_ephemeral);
        field_to_int( &Base->pnt_order, &point_order);
        int_mul( &my_x_value, &my_secret, &temp1);
        int_add( &temp1, &my_ephemeral, &temp1);
        int_div( &temp1, &point_order, &quotient, &temp2);

/*  convert integer to equivelent compressed value for
        elliptic multiply. */
        int_to_field( &temp2, &e_value);
```

The final calculation is an elliptic curve multiply. The other side's half *x* value is already a field component, so we can call the elliptic multiply routine directly. Adding in the other side's ephemeral key point, and then performing the multiply of the above e value, gives us the shared secret. That is copied to the storage area specified on entry, and the routine is finished.

```
/*  use other sides public points to create their
        portion of the secret.  */

        elptic_mul( &their_half_x, their_first, &Common, &Base->crv);
        esum( their_second, &Common, &Temp, &Base->crv);
        elptic_mul( &e_value, &Temp, &Common, &Base->crv);

/*  take output from common point  */

        copy( &Common.x, shared_secret);
}
```

Here is an example of the above code using the normal basis library of routines. I picked a curve from table 6.1 in chapter 6, which has NUMBITS of 113 bits and is a Type II ONB. The example is contrived to show how to use the subroutine. In the real world, the permanent keys need to be stored, the private keys need to be generated by the user, and lots of communication takes place.

```
main()
{
        EC_PARAMETER            Base;
        EC_KEYPAIR              side1_perm, side2_perm;
        EC_KEYPAIR              side1_ephem, side2_ephem;
        BIGINT                  prime_order;
        POINT                   temp;
        FIELD2N                 side1_secret, side2_secret;
        char string1[MAXSTRING] ="5192296858534827627896703833467507";

#ifdef TYPE2
        genlambda2();
#else
        genlambda();
#endif

        random_seed = 0xFEEDFACE;

/*  compute curve order from Koblitz data  */

        ascii_to_bigint(&string1, &prime_order);
        int_to_field( &prime_order, &Base.pnt_order);
        null( &Base.cofactor);
        Base.cofactor.e[NUMWORD] = 2;

/*  create Koblitz curve  */

        Base.crv.form = 1;
        one(&Base.crv.a2);
```

```
            one(&Base.crv.a6);
            print_curve("Koblitz 113", &Base.crv);

/*   create base point of known order with no cofactor   */

            rand_point( &temp, &Base.crv);
            edbl( &temp, &Base.pnt, &Base.crv);
            print_point(" Base point ",&Base.pnt);

/*   Create each sides public keys.   These are the permenent
        versions which can be saved in a data base.
*/

            printf("permenent keys\n");
            ECKGP( &Base, &side1_perm);
            print_field("side 1 secret key", &side1_perm.prvt_key);
            print_point("side 1 public key", &side1_perm.pblc_key);
            ECKGP( &Base, &side2_perm);
            print_field("side 2 secret key", &side2_perm.prvt_key);
            print_point("side 2 public key", &side2_perm.pblc_key);

/*   Create each sides ephemeral keys.   These are destroyed
        after each link is established.
*/

            printf("ephemeral keys\n");
            ECKGP( &Base, &side1_ephem);
            print_field("side 1 secret key", &side1_ephem.prvt_key);
            print_point("side 1 public key", &side1_ephem.pblc_key);
            ECKGP( &Base, &side2_ephem);
            print_field("side 2 secret key", &side2_ephem.prvt_key);
            print_point("side 2 public key", &side2_ephem.pblc_key);

/*   Each side exchanges both sets of public keys.   Then they
        both perform the same calculations with the other sides
        data to find the same shared secret.
*/

            onb_mqv( &Base, &side1_perm, &side1_ephem, &side2_perm.pblc_key,
                            &side2_ephem.pblc_key, &side1_secret);
            print_field("side 1 secret value", &side1_secret);
            onb_mqv( &Base, &side2_perm, &side2_ephem, &side1_perm.pblc_key,
                            &side1_ephem.pblc_key, &side2_secret);
            print_field("side 2 secret value", &side2_secret);
}
```

The output of the above routine looks like this:

```
Koblitz 113
form = 1
a2 :    1ffff ffffffff ffffffff ffffffff
a6 :    1ffff ffffffff ffffffff ffffffff

 Base point
```

```
x :      16c80 3abc107c 188da158 67fa62d4
y :      de1e 607f7da5 8e4a1858 a8ba7c60

permenent keys
side 1 secret key :      698a 82651d65 5d7a9d36 7d395bac
side 1 public key
x :      4f7b 1ef82cb4 30f49db9 eaaaa5c9
y :      1070c 4970bfb7 d5249488  9e2de55

side 2 secret key :      e4a9 bb1e2000 b2f7442c 63ef1517
side 2 public key
x :      8ba7 f0fda3d5 ad175059 a194245b
y :      2e6b  4910445 ef070de5 e54e93f7

ephemeral keys
side 1 secret key :      969a 62161ada afe4520c 5069aa30
side 1 public key
x :      a054 e5673fe9 ad44367d 2f58bf67
y :      9a8a edd679fa 470547bf 262ddc7d

side 2 secret key :      9e83 7eb9919d ffc5f077 60603c64
side 2 public key
x :      ec60 b027e877 43066855 7e9f2524
y :      d035 6a466f72 e740fd5f f7812002

side 1 secret value :      a91a 39bf08c2 c5d578be 6fdb9b94
side 2 secret value :      a91a 39bf08c2 c5d578be 6fdb9b94
```

Clearly the math works. This is an exceptionally useful protocol; it will be interesting to see what (if any) patents are given for it.

9.4.2 MQV: polynomial basis version

Here are copies of the previous routines for a polynomial basis version. It really is the same code with just the lower-level calls to polynomial basis library routines replacing the calls to normal basis routines.

```
void poly_mqv( Base, my_first, my_second,
                    their_first, their_second,
                    shared_secret)
EC_PARAMETER *Base;
EC_KEYPAIR      *my_first, *my_second;
POINT        *their_first, *their_second;
FIELD2N      *shared_secret;
{
        BIGINT          my_x_value;
        BIGINT          my_secret, my_ephemeral;
        FIELD2N         my_half_x, their_half_x;
        BIGINT          temp1, quotient, temp2;
        BIGINT          cfactor, point_order;
        FIELD2N         e_value;
        POINT           Temp, Common;
```

```
        INDEX           i, limit, half_msb;
        ELEMENT         mask;

/*  convert x component of my ephemeral key to an integer modulo
        2^h where h is half the size of the order of the base point.
        Since we are using curves with order almost equal to the
        field size, the value of h is about half NUMBITS.
        Change limit to meet the specs for your application.
*/

        limit = NUMBITS / 2;
        half_msb = limit % WORDSIZE;
        mask = ~(~0 << half_msb);
        limit = limit/WORDSIZE + ( half_msb ? 1 : 0);
        copy( &my_second->pblc_key.x, &my_half_x);
        for( i=0; i<limit; i++) my_half_x.e[i] = 0;
        my_half_x.e[i] &= mask;
        my_half_x.e[i] |= 1L << half_msb;
        field_to_int( &my_half_x, &my_x_value);

/*  get half the other sides ephemeral key  */

        copy( &their_second->x, &their_half_x);
        for( i=0; i<limit; i++) their_half_x.e[i] = 0;
        their_half_x.e[i] &= mask;
        their_half_x.e[i] |= 1L << half_msb;

/*  compute multiplier from my secrets and x component  */

        field_to_int( &my_first->prvt_key, &my_secret);
        field_to_int( &my_second->prvt_key, &my_ephemeral);
        field_to_int( &Base->pnt_order, &point_order);
        int_mul( &my_x_value, &my_secret, &temp1);
        int_add( &temp1, &my_ephemeral, &temp1);
        int_div( &temp1, &point_order, &quotient, &temp2);

/*  convert integer to equivelent compressed value for
        elliptic multiply.  */

        int_to_field( &temp2, &e_value);

/*  use other sides public points to create their
        portion of the secret.  */

        poly_elptic_mul( &their_half_x, their_first, &Common, &Base->crv);
        poly_esum( their_second, &Common, &Temp, &Base->crv);
        poly_elptic_mul( &e_value, &Temp, &Common, &Base->crv);

/*  take output from common point  */

        copy( &Common.x, shared_secret);
}
```

Here is an example of how to use it.

```
main()
{
        EC_PARAMETERBase;
        EC_KEYPAIR      side1_perm, side2_perm;
        EC_KEYPAIR      side1_ephem, side2_ephem;
        BIGINT                  prime_order;
        POINT                   temp;
        FIELD2N                 side1_secret, side2_secret;
        FIELD2N                 roots[3];
        INDEX                   error;
        char string1[MAXSTRING] = "32451855365842672311495757233574l";

        random_seed = 0xBEEFACED;

        if (!irreducible(&poly_prime)) return(0);
        print_field("poly_prime = ", &poly_prime);

        if (error = init_poly_math())
        {
                printf("Can't initialize S matrix, row = %d\n", error);
                return(-1);
        }

/*  compute curve order from Koblitz data  */

        ascii_to_bigint(&string1, &prime_order);
        int_to_field( &prime_order, &Base.pnt_order);
        null( &Base.cofactor);
        Base.cofactor.e[NUMWORD] = 8;

        printf("create Base curve and point\n\n");

        Base.crv.form = 0;
        null(&Base.crv.a2);
        poly_gf8(&poly_prime, roots);
        copy( &roots[1], &Base.crv.a6);
        print_curve("Public curve", &Base.crv);

        rand_point(&temp, &Base.crv);
        poly_elptic_mul(&Base.cofactor, &temp, &Base.pnt, &Base.crv);
        print_point("Base point", &Base.pnt);


/*  Create each sides public keys.  These are the permenent
        versions which can be saved in a data base.
*/

        printf("permenent keys\n");
        poly_ECKGP( &Base, &side1_perm);
        print_field("side 1 secret key", &side1_perm.prvt_key);
        print_point("side 1 public key", &side1_perm.pblc_key);
        poly_ECKGP( &Base, &side2_perm);
        print_field("side 2 secret key", &side2_perm.prvt_key);
        print_point("side 2 public key", &side2_perm.pblc_key);
```

```
/*  Create each sides ephemeral keys.  These are destroyed
        after each link is established.
*/

        printf("ephemeral keys\n");
        poly_ECKGP( &Base, &side1_ephem);
        print_field("side 1 secret key", &side1_ephem.prvt_key);
        print_point("side 1 public key", &side1_ephem.pblc_key);
        poly_ECKGP( &Base, &side2_ephem);
        print_field("side 2 secret key", &side2_ephem.prvt_key);
        print_point("side 2 public key", &side2_ephem.pblc_key);

/*  Each side exchanges both sets of public keys.  Then they
        both perform the same calculations with the other sides
        data to find the same shared secret.
*/

        poly_mqv( &Base, &side1_perm, &side1_ephem, &side2_perm.pblc_key,
                          &side2_ephem.pblc_key, &side1_secret);
        print_field("side 1 secret value", &side1_secret);
        poly_mqv( &Base, &side2_perm, &side2_ephem, &side1_perm.pblc_key,
                          &side1_ephem.pblc_key, &side2_secret);
        print_field("side 2 secret value", &side2_secret);
}
```

Other than the type of curve and setting up the coefficients to generate the correct curve order, the example is identical to the normal basis version. Here is the output from the above code.

```
poly_prime =  :     8000        0        0     401
create Base curve and point

Public curve
form = 0
a6 :    5b85 d9a7e747 7e0c9615 7fb27dc6

Base point
x :     76e0 9d92192a f3140efe 224fcb21
y :     2966 26293730  61ba21f b5532ae0

permenent keys
side 1 secret key :       744 6856f094 1f67961f f4174aea
side 1 public key
x :     33e8 79b2f236 21960c50  f2656cd
y :     4bee 4fc23eb3 9c3e399f  fb417da

side 2 secret key :  /    d2b aa9e3d91 aefc908f c6f67c85
side 2 public key
x :     704b 99376f93 12394480 e684cc88
y :     716b b2b4512e cd567b1f e76719ff

ephemeral keys
side 1 secret key :       6aa 28de931b ec4a214d 5311773a
```

```
side 1 public key
x :     125b ad686c6a c68d47b5 c041a8a4
y :     6e34 b2c350da a3b74488 ca11f106

side 2 secret key :      577  5ce7c60 9c399a75 c40b19ae
side 2 public key
x :      ed8 3bd68256 19ec6009 88aa47fc
y :     7741 efb3c6af 2c666378 603b693f

side 1 secret value :    3462 6d3e7913 51f6960e 6d41e523
side 2 secret value :    3462 6d3e7913 51f6960e 6d41e523
```

Again, we see that the underlying math really works. If you try to follow the bit-flipping for a while (say by printing out intermediate values within a multiply routine), you begin to appreciate how awesome the perfection of this math is.

The Massey-Omura and MQV algorithms described in this chapter are very useful in many applications for sharing a secret key. While the examples given were done using a slow 40-MHz processor, they still only took a minute to compute. An attacker would require on the order of 10^{17} elliptic curve calculations to crack one message, and the protocols can be used to create a new secret for every message. With very few bits you get very high security. With contemporary processors near 1000 MHz, these calculations are reduced to milliseconds. Adding a few more bits of security makes the attacker's effort exponentially more difficult and requires fewer additional resources for the cryptographer.

The final protocols to look at are signatures. These require just about every trick used in the book. Take a break before diving into the next chapter. I think I'll take that advice myself!

9.5 References

1 C. R. Wylie, *Advanced Engineering Mathematics*, 4th ed. (New York: McGraw-Hill, 1975).

2 N. Koblitz, "CM—Curves with Good Cryptographic Properties," *CRYPTO '91* (New York: Springer-Verlag, 1992), 279.

3 B. Kaliski, "MQV Vulnerability," posting to stds-p1363-discussion@major-domo.ieee.org and x9f1@x9.org, June 17, 1998.

CHAPTER 10

Advanced protocols, signatures

10.1 Introduction to digital signatures 256

10.2 Message hash 259

10.3 Nyberg-Rueppel signature scheme 260

10.4 Digital Signature Algorithm (DSA) 271

10.5 Signatures: a summary 282

10.6 References 282

10.1 Introduction to digital signatures

The purpose of a digital signature is the same as a written signature: to prove that a particular individual represents a document to be valid. The data in the document are not hidden, but electronically we want to be sure they have not been altered. A signature may have to last for many years, so a high degree of security is usually required. For an excellent discussion about signature protocols see [1].

Only two elliptic curve signature schemes are given in the IEEE P1363 standard. They are similar in overall security. Supposedly the Nyberg-Rueppel version is patented, but U.S. patent number 5600725 patents the discrete log version and not the elliptic curve version as an explicit claim. The Digital Signature Algorithm (DSA) version is not patented at all. Schneier [1] gives a long list of discrete log signature schemes, which could all be converted to elliptic curve versions if someone is so inclined.

All signature schemes require a hash of a document that is to be signed. As shown in figure 10.1, the starting point of this chapter is a message hashing algorithm. The hash function is taken from chapter 8 and the output converted to integer for use within the signature algorithms. A new signature structure is defined, and then the mathematics of the Nyberg-Rueppel signature scheme is described. Following the code and examples for this scheme is the mathematics of the elliptic curve DSA. Both polynomial and normal basis versions of the code are given, along with test output.

Because there are so many routines used by the signature subroutines, I couldn't fit all the subroutine names in one page of schematic. The subroutine schematic for this chapter does not show the polynomial routines, but the subroutine structure is identical and the sources are from the same previous chapters.

For elliptic curve signatures the public key parameters include a curve, a base point, the order of the base point, and the user's private key. As usual, the public key is the private key times the base point. Depending on how the data are distributed, you can choose a single curve and base point for many users, or have each person choose his or her own curve and base point for documents. The size of the public key data block (and the associated structures) depends on these decisions. The IEEE standard is vague about this on purpose; set up the elliptic curve parameters to suit your needs.

For the following examples, we'll assume that a single public curve, base point, and private key have been previously generated. The public point for an individual signature will be used by the verification process, so it too must be available. This could be from a public database or it could be attached to the document. Wherever they are stored, I'll assume these values have been gathered together to feed into the following routines.

The first step is to compute a hash of the document to be signed. The standard suggests SHA-1, defined by NIST, or RIPEMD-160, defined by the ISO/IEC. The point

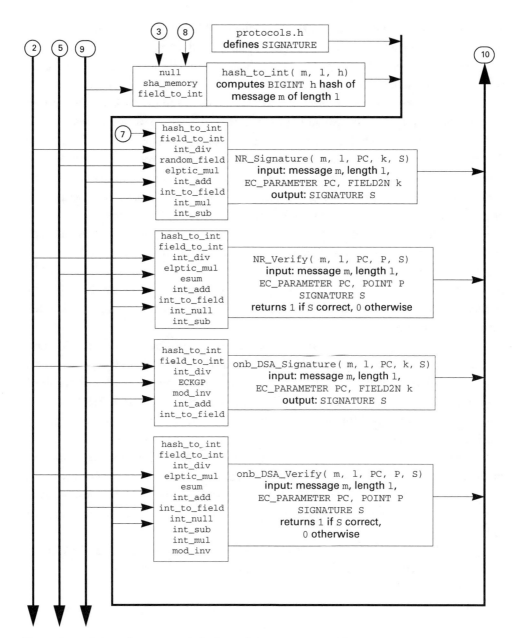

Figure 10.1   Subroutine schematic (polynomial versions omitted)

of the hash algorithm is to make it impossible (or nearly so) to find a match between the real input and some minor changed version that would give the same hash value. The problem is considered exceptionally difficult to solve with the above hash algorithms.

This hash value of the document is then its "digest." Mathematically we have to somehow combine the hash with the author's key to bind the document to its creator.

The second step is to compute two numbers, which will be defined as the "signature." The computation mixes a random bit pattern, the signer's private key, and the hash data to create these two numbers. The base point of the public key is also multiplied by the combination of hash and key to create the elliptic curve connection.

Once a signature to a document has been created, it must be verifiable by anyone. To verify a signature, the first step is to compute the hash of the document. The second step is to recover the original hash using the two numbers generated by the signature and the signer's public key. If the message hash matches the computed hash, the document is original. If not, the document is an altered version and should not be trusted.

The hash function's sensitivity to its input has a number of practical consequences. Some kinds of transmission quietly remove spaces or empty lines. This is fatal to a cryptographic scheme. As soon as a single bit is changed—even one utterly irrelevant to the content humans read—the signature the hash function produces will fail to verify. The applications that follow assume the developer takes responsibility for ensuring the fidelity required for correct use.

As I said previously, the two signature schemes described in the IEEE P1363 standard are called Nyberg-Rueppel and DSA. The security of both schemes depends on the order of the base point being a large prime number. Both signature schemes require a hash function, large integer math, and elliptic curve math over a Galois Field. In addition, random bits are used for each document to help create a unique signature for any individual document.

Fortunately, we've seen all those subroutines in this book. The implementation of these signature schemes is straightforward. The signer's private key is combined with the hash of the message and a random number, which are then multiplied against a public base point. This combination is different for the two schemes, but the security appears to be similar.

Each scheme outputs two numbers. I combine these two values into a single structure called SIGNATURE. It has just two FIELD2N values:

```
typedef struct
{
        FIELD2N         c;
        FIELD2N         d;
} SIGNATURE;
```

The name of each element comes from the November 1997 draft of P1363. The names are different from draft to draft, but it really doesn't matter. The first number is derived from the x component of the random public point, and the second number is an integer calculation modulo the order of the base point. The two numbers are derived differently for each scheme, so they must be used differently for the verification process.

Before describing the two schemes, let's look at one common subroutine. Calculation of hash values is common to all the schemes. It's useful to understand this clearly before examining the mathematics.

10.2 Message hash

The IEEE P1363 standard suggests that the signature scheme be generalized so that several possible subroutines can be called. It defines these as primitives and then describes the general calling algorithm. I have combined specific calls to the SHA-1 hash subroutine (chapter 8) with a check to ensure that the result fits into a FIELD2N variable. This meets the standard as a minimum. It should not be too hard to add another hash function to generalize the following subroutine.

Once the hash has been found, it is converted to FIELD2N variable mdtemp. If there are more than 160 bits in the FIELD2N variable, the entire hash is loaded into the least significant bits of mdtemp. If there are fewer than 160 bits, mdtemp is loaded with the most number of machine words possible.

```
void hash_to_int( Message, length, hash_value)
char                *Message;
unsigned long       length;
BIGINT              *hash_value;  /*  then to an integer  */
{
        unsigned long  message_digest[5]; /* from SHA-1 hash function  */
        FIELD2N        mdtemp;   /* convert to NUMBITS size (if needed) */
        INDEX          i, count;

/*   compute hash of input message   */

        sha_memory( Message, length, message_digest);

/*   convert message digest into an integer */

        null ( &mdtemp);
        count = 0;
        SUMLOOP (i)
        {
                mdtemp.e[ NUMWORD - i] = message_digest[ 4 - i];
                count++;
                if (count > 4) break;
```

Note that this particular code (count > 4) was hard wired for 32-bit words (the value of 4 = 160/32 − 1). This must change for different machine architectures. A better way might have been 160/WORDSIZE-1, but life gets complicated for 64-bit machines (and larger), since it is no longer an even multiple.

After the hash is copied the most significant bits are masked off. This will be meaningless if your FIELD2N size is greater than 160 bits.

```
    }
    mdtemp.e[0] &= UPRMASK;
    field_to_int( &mdtemp, hash_value);
}
```

The returned value from this subroutine is a large integer. This value will be added to other large integers or compared with them to verify a signature.

Let's construct the Nyberg-Rueppel scheme first and then the Digital Signature Algorithm for elliptic curves. These bring together all the subroutines you've already seen in this book. While that's a lot to keep in mind simultaneously, keep the schematics in front of you, and you'll always know where you are.

10.3 Nyberg-Rueppel signature scheme

Let's start with some math. Let e be the hash value of the document, E be the elliptic curve that satisfies equation 6.1, P be the base point for the public key, n the order of the base point, and s the signer's private key.

The signer's public key is:

$$Q = sP. \tag{10.1}$$

The standard assumes the order of P is n, and proceeds as follows. First generate a random bit string, k, and compute:

$$R = kP. \tag{10.2}$$

The next step looks weird: Using the x component of R as an integer, compute:

$$c = x + e \quad \bmod n \tag{10.3}$$

and finally compute the term:

$$d = k - sc \quad \bmod n. \tag{10.4}$$

The pair (c,d) is the signature for the document hashed into the value e. To verify that this is indeed the correct hash, the standard says to first compute:

$$R' = dP + cQ. \tag{10.5}$$

Then, using the x component of R', compute:

$$e' = c - x' \mod n.$$ (10.6)

As long as the value of e' computed in equation (10.6) matches the hashed value of the document, everything verifies.

First, let's see how all that math actually works. The signature scheme relies on the similarity of modular arithmetic and elliptic curve math, just as with the key agreement schemes of the previous chapter.

The random value k is multiplied by the base point P to give R. The x component of the point R is a random value as well. Adding x as an integer to the hash value e modulo the order of P effectively hides the hash. The trick of verification is to recover this hidden hash without leaking any information that would allow an attacker to alter the document and hash to make it appear correct. The calculation of equation (10.4) combines the random data and the user's private key—again, using modular arithmetic. Since the modulus is the order of the base point, we can do the same math on the curve.

To see this, let's compute cP instead of the value c for equation (10.3):

$$cP = xP + eP$$ (10.7)

over the curve E. We can also multiply the base point into the equation for d, equation (10.4):

$$dP = kP - s(cP).$$ (10.8)

The verification process includes equation (10.8) as the first term in equation (10.5). The second term of equation (10.5) is similar to multiplying equation (10.7) by s, the signer's private key. But the public only knows Q, the hidden version of the private key. This means the second term in equation (10.5) is:

$$cQ = c(sP)$$ (10.9)

which, when added to equation (10.8), gives the original point R back. The x component of this term then gets subtracted from the signature value c to recover the hash value e. This last step is equation (10.6). As long as this value of the hash agrees with a freshly computed hash, then the binding is complete. The owner of the private key s is the only one who could have generated the signature.

10.3.1 Nyberg-Rueppel signature: normal basis

The inputs to the signature subroutine are the message, its length, the public curve data, and the signer's private key. The output is the signature for the message. Obviously there is a great deal more that must be done. For example, converting the signature to ASCII and attaching it to the message is pretty basic. One might also attach the public key or an e-mail address about where to get it.

Here's the beginning of the code. After variable definitions, the first step is to compute the hash of the input message. This value is then reduced modulo the order of the base point. For field sizes greater than 160 bits this reduction can be removed.

```
void NR_Signature( Message, length, public_curve, secret_key, signature)
char *Message;
unsigned long length;
EC_PARAMETER *public_curve;
FIELD2N *secret_key;
SIGNATURE *signature;
{
        BIGINT              hash_value;
        FIELD2N             random_value;
        POINT               random_point;
        BIGINT              x_value, k_value, sig_value;
        BIGINT              temp, quotient;
        BIGINT              key_value, point_order;
        INDEX               i, count;

/*  compute hash of input message  */

        hash_to_int( Message, length,  &temp);
        field_to_int( &public_curve->pnt_order, &point_order);
        int_div( &temp, &point_order, &quotient, &hash_value);
```

Once the integer version of the hash value of the message has been determined, the next step is to generate a random value and associated point to help hide it. The following code calls a random bit generator and the elliptic curve multiply routine. The x component of the random point is used as in equation (10.3) to create the first signature term.

```
/*  create random value and generate random point on public curve  */

        random_field( &random_value);
        elptic_mul( &random_value, &public_curve->pnt,
                                &random_point, &public_curve->crv);

/*  convert x component of random point to an integer and add to message
        digest modulo the order of the base point.
*/

        field_to_int( &random_point.x, &x_value);
        int_add( &x_value, &hash_value, &temp);

        int_div( &temp, &point_order, &quotient, &sig_value);
        int_to_field( &sig_value, &signature->c);
```

The last step is to combine the signer's private key with the above signature and the random value, modulo the order of the base point. This requires converting the private key and the random value into integers, performing the multiply, finding the remainder modulo the order, and subtracting this from the random value. Since the routines in chapter 2 assume positive inputs, I ensure the output integer is positive before I convert it back to a FIELD2N variable.

```
/*  final step is to combine signer's secret key with random value
            second number = random value - secret key * first number
            modulo order of base point
*/

        field_to_int( &random_value, &k_value);
        field_to_int( secret_key, &key_value);
        int_mul( &key_value, &sig_value, &temp);
        int_div( &temp, &point_order, &quotient, &sig_value);

        int_sub( &k_value, &sig_value, &sig_value);
        while( sig_value.hw[0] & 0x8000)
            int_add( &point_order, &sig_value, &sig_value);
        int_div( &sig_value, &point_order, &quotient, &temp);
        int_to_field( &sig_value, &signature->d);
}
```

The verification code is even simpler. The inputs are almost identical to the inputs of the signature function. Instead of using the signer's private key, we use the signer's public key. The inputs are left in the same order as before, with the only change being a point instead of a field in the second to last input parameter.

The verification code returns a value of 1 if the signature corroborates the message and 0 if there is a failure to verify. The standard suggests that a test of the signature should include a verification that the value of the input for the signature should be less than the order of the base point. I don't make that check here, but it is easy to add.

```
int NR_Verify( Message, length, public_curve, signer_point, signature)
char                *Message;
unsigned long       length;
EC_PARAMETER        *public_curve;
POINT               *signer_point;
SIGNATURE           *signature;
{
        BIGINT                  hash_value;
        POINT                   Temp1, Temp2, Verify;
        BIGINT                  x_value, c_value;
        BIGINT                  temp, quotient;
        BIGINT                  check_value, point_order;
        INDEX                   i, count;

/*  find hidden point from public data  */
```

```
elptic_mul( &signature->d, &public_curve->pnt,
                    &Temp1, &public_curve->crv);
elptic_mul( &signature->c, signer_point, &Temp2, &public_curve->crv);
esum( &Temp1, &Temp2, &Verify, &public_curve->crv);
```

On entry, I first compute equation (10.5). The code uses the variable `Verify` to hold the value of R in that equation. This recovers the x component of the random point used to hide the hash. The next two lines convert this value of x from a `FIELD2N` variable to an integer.

```
/*  convert x value of verify point to an integer and first signature value too
*/

        field_to_int( &Verify.x, &x_value);
        field_to_int( &signature->c, &c_value);
```

The next step is to compute the signed message digest by executing equation (10.6). Again, I make sure the output from this subtraction is positive before attempting to do modular reduction. In most cases the modular reduction is not necessary. However, we have to account for every possible outcome.

```
/*  compute resultant message digest from original signature  */

        field_to_int( &public_curve->pnt_order, &point_order);
        int_sub( &c_value, &x_value, &temp);
        while( temp.hw[0] & 0x8000) /* ensure positive result */
                int_add( &point_order, &temp, &temp);
        int_div( &temp, &point_order, &quotient, &check_value);
```

The last step is to compute the raw message digest of the input message and convert it to an integer. I use exactly the same code as found in the signature scheme. This is subtracted from the computed message digest integer form. If the result of that subtraction is not 0, then the message is not the same as the original.

```
/*  generate hash of message and compare to original signature  */

        hash_to_int( Message, length, &temp);
        int_div( &temp, &point_order, &quotient, &hash_value);

        int_null(&temp);
        int_sub( &hash_value, &check_value, &temp);
        while( temp.hw[0] & 0x8000) /*  ensure positive zero */
                int_add( &point_order, &temp, &temp);

/*  return error if result of subtraction is not zero  */

        INTLOOP(i) if (temp.hw[i]) return(0);
        return(1);
}
```

The routine returns the correct value by scanning every element in the subtracted result. If any term is not 0, there is definitely a problem. This routine does not attempt to figure out what the problem is; it only reports that the source message does not belong to the signature.

Here is an example using the above subroutines. In the real world there is a great deal of time and space between a signature and a verification. But this gives you an idea of how the above routines can be used within a program that provides signatures to documents.

```
main()
{
        EC_PARAMETER            Base;
        EC_KEYPAIR              Signer;
        SIGNATURE               signature;
        BIGINT                  prime_order;
        POINT                   temp;
        INDEX                   i, error;
        char                    Message[1024];
        char string1[MAXSTRING] ="5192296858534827627896703833467507";/*N 113
*/

#ifdef TYPE2
        genlambda2();
#else
        genlambda();
#endif

        random_seed = 0xFEEDFACE;

/*  compute curve order from Koblitz data  */

        ascii_to_bigint(&string1, &prime_order);
        int_to_field( &prime_order, &Base.pnt_order);
        null( &Base.cofactor);
        Base.cofactor.e[NUMWORD] = 2;

/*  create Koblitz curve  */

        Base.crv.form = 1;
        one(&Base.crv.a2);
        one(&Base.crv.a6);
        print_curve("Koblitz 113", &Base.crv);

/*  create base point of known order with no cofactor  */

        rand_point( &temp, &Base.crv);
        print_point("random point", &temp);
        edbl( &temp, &Base.pnt, &Base.crv);
        print_point(" Base point ",&Base.pnt);

/*  create a secret key for testing.
```

```
            Note that secret key must be less than order.
            The standard implies that the field size which
            can be used is one bit less than
            the length of the public base point order.
    */

            ECKGP( &Base, &Signer);
            print_field("Signer's secret key", &Signer.prvt_key);
            print_point("Signers public key", &Signer.pblc_key);

    /*  create a message to be signed  */

            for (i=0; i<1024; i++) Message[i] = i;

    /*  call Nyberg_Rueppel signature scheme  */

            NR_Signature( Message, 1024, &Base, &Signer.prvt_key, &signature);
            print_field("first component of signiture", &signature.c);
            print_field("second component of signiture", &signature.d);

    /*  verify message has not been tampered.
            Need public curve parameters, signers
            public key, message, length of message,
             and order of public curve parameters
            as well as the signature. If there is a
            null response, message is not same as
            the orignal signed version.
    */
            error = NR_Verify( Message, 1024, &Base, &Signer.pblc_key,
                    &signature);
            if (error) printf("Message Verifies");
            else printf("Message fails!");
    }
```

As you can see, this is very similar to the examples in the previous chapter. The message is simply several blocks of bytes counting from 0 to 255. The output of the above code appears as follows:

```
Koblitz 113
form = 1
a2 :    1ffff ffffffff ffffffff ffffffff
a6 :    1ffff ffffffff ffffffff ffffffff

random point
x :     f6ac c2ba5d4e a49b8cc4  6b3cf47
y :     64e5 db3ee3ce 49a3c318 70ee8584

 Base point
x :     16c80 3abc107c 188da158 67fa62d4
y :     de1e 607f7da5 8e4a1858 a8ba7c60

Signer's secret key :      698a 82651d65 5d7a9d36 7d395bac
Signers public key
```

```
x :       4f7b 1ef82cb4 30f49db9 eaaaa5c9
y :       1070c 4970bfb7 d5249488  9e2de55
```

```
first component of signiture :    e8a7 aef82fb1 56aef1de  153555f
second component of signiture :    a176 7ee75d97 8a51ae99 76269fac
Message Verifies
```

The signature seems like garbage. Even as a decimal number it seems like garbage. But the math works. It took more tries than I care to admit to get the last message correct. There is not a whole lot to see in terms of numbers or field values—either you have a valid signature or you don't.

10.3.2 Nyberg-Rueppel: polynomial basis

The following code is essentially identical to the normal basis routines shown previously. Copy whichever set of libraries is appropriate for your application. The important aspect is initialization of each math package. The rest of these functions all follow the same math and only require different elliptic curve subroutines.

Without further ado, here's the signature generation code.

```
void poly_NR_Signature( Message, length, public_curve, secret_key, signature)
char *Message;
unsigned long length;
EC_PARAMETER *public_curve;
FIELD2N *secret_key;
SIGNATURE *signature;
{
        BIGINT                  hash_value;
        FIELD2N                 random_value;
        POINT                   random_point;
        BIGINT                  x_value, k_value, sig_value;
        BIGINT                  temp, quotient;
        BIGINT                  key_value, point_order;
        INDEX                   i, count;

/*  compute hash of input message  */

        hash_to_int( Message, length, &temp);
        field_to_int( &public_curve->pnt_order, &point_order);
        int_div( &temp, &point_order, &quotient, &hash_value);

/*  create random value and generate random point on public curve  */

        random_field( &random_value);
        poly_elptic_mul( &random_value, &public_curve->pnt,
                                &random_point, &public_curve->crv);

/*  convert x component of random point to an integer and add to message
        digest modulo the order of the base point.
*/
```

```
            field_to_int( &random_point.x, &x_value);
            int_add( &x_value, &hash_value, &temp);

            int_div( &temp, &point_order, &quotient, &sig_value);
            int_to_field( &sig_value, &signature->c);

/*  final step is to combine signer's secret key with random value
            second number = random value - secret key * first number
            modulo order of base point
*/

            field_to_int( &random_value, &k_value);
            field_to_int( secret_key, &key_value);
            int_mul( &key_value, &sig_value, &temp);
            int_div( &temp, &point_order, &quotient, &sig_value);

            int_sub( &k_value, &sig_value, &sig_value);
            while( sig_value.hw[0] & 0x8000)
                    int_add( &point_order, &sig_value, &sig_value);
            int_div( &sig_value, &point_order, &quotient, &temp);
            int_to_field( &temp, &signature->d);
}
```

And here is the polynomial basis signature verification code.

```
int poly_NR_Verify( Message, length, public_curve, signer_point, signature)
char                    *Message;
unsigned long           length;
EC_PARAMETER            *public_curve;
POINT                   *signer_point;
SIGNATURE               *signature;
{
        BIGINT                  hash_value;
        POINT                   Temp1, Temp2, Verify;
        BIGINT                  x_value, c_value;
        BIGINT                  temp, quotient;
        BIGINT                  check_value, point_order;
        INDEX                   i, count;

/*  find hidden point from public data  */

        poly_elptic_mul( &signature->d, &public_curve->pnt,
                                        &Temp1, &public_curve->crv);
        poly_elptic_mul( &signature->c, signer_point,
                                        &Temp2, &public_curve->crv);
        poly_esum( &Temp1, &Temp2, &Verify, &public_curve->crv);

/*  convert x value of verify point to an integer
        and first signature value too  */

        field_to_int( &Verify.x, &x_value);
        field_to_int( &signature->c, &c_value);

/*  compute resultant message digest from original signature  */
```

```
        field_to_int( &public_curve->pnt_order, &point_order);
        int_sub( &c_value, &x_value, &temp);
        while( temp.hw[0] & 0x8000) /* ensure positive result */
                int_add( &point_order, &temp, &temp);
        int_div( &temp, &point_order, &quotient, &check_value);

/* generate hash of message and compare to original signature */

        hash_to_int( Message, length, &temp);
        int_div( &temp, &point_order, &quotient, &hash_value);

        int_null(&temp);
        int_sub( &hash_value, &check_value, &temp);
        while( temp.hw[0] & 0x8000) /* ensure positive zero */
                int_add( &point_order, &temp, &temp);

/* return error if result of subtraction is not zero */

        INTLOOP(i) if (temp.hw[i]) return(0);
        return(1);
}
```

Here is a sample routine that calls the above subroutines. I chose the same curve as in the previous chapter.

```
main()
{
        FIELD2N         roots[3];
        EC_PARAMETER    Base;
        EC_KEYPAIR      Signer;
        SIGNATURE       signature;
        BIGINT          prime_order;
        POINT           temp;
        INDEX           i, error;
        char            Message[1024];
        char string1[MAXSTRING] = "32451855365842672311495757233574l";

        random_seed = 0x9ef1b325;

        if (!irreducible(&poly_prime)) return(0);
        print_field("poly_prime = ", &poly_prime);

        if (error = init_poly_math())
        {
                printf("Can't initialize S matrix, row = %d\n", error);
                return(-1);
        }

/* compute curve order from Koblitz data */

        ascii_to_bigint(&string1, &prime_order);
        int_to_field( &prime_order, &Base.pnt_order);
        null( &Base.cofactor);
        Base.cofactor.e[NUMWORD] = 8;
```

```
        printf("create Base curve and point\n\n");

        Base.crv.form = 0;
        null(&Base.crv.a2);
        poly_gf8(&poly_prime, roots);
        copy( &roots[0], &Base.crv.a6);
        print_curve("Public curve", &Base.crv);

        rand_point(&temp, &Base.crv);
        poly_elptic_mul(&Base.cofactor, &temp, &Base.pnt, &Base.crv);
        print_point("Base point", &Base.pnt);

/*   create a secret key for testing.
     Note that secret key must be less than order.
     The standard implies that the field size which
     can be used is one bit less than
     the length of the public base point order.
*/

        poly_ECKGP( &Base, &Signer);
        print_field("Signer's secret key", &Signer.prvt_key);
        print_point("Signers public key", &Signer.pblc_key);

/*   create a message to be signed   */

        for (i=0; i<1024; i++) Message[i] = i;

/*   call Nyberg_Rueppel signature scheme   */

        poly_NR_Signature( Message, 1024, &Base, &Signer.prvt_key, &signature);
        print_field("first component of signature", &signature.c);
        print_field("second component of signature", &signature.d);

/*   verify message has not been tampered.
     Need public curve parameters, signers
     public key, message, length of message,
     and order of public curve parameters
     as well as the signature. If there is a
     null response, message is not same as
     the orignal signed version.
*/
        error = poly_NR_Verify( Message, 1024,
                            &Base, &Signer.pblc_key, &signature);
        if (error) printf("Message Verifies");
        else printf("Message fails!");
}
```

As usual, it took longer than I expected to get the routines to work correctly. Here is the output from the above example.

```
poly_prime =  :      8000        0       0      401
create Base curve and point

Public curve
```

```
form = 0
a6 :        8da 4bbca9b3 37df45ae 9dd58ba8

Base point
x :        1346 f5bf6af0 f1715064 62bfd7ca
y :        73b5 baef0ba9 5b64547f cf751d68

Signer's secret key :        fb5 a0da0953 b3a23918 e2bd68a3
Signers public key
x :        c38 714a2554 2469d8d7 3136008f
y :        549a 371cc14d 30b3249 16069681

first component of signature :        be9 7c6ff2c 2a0cb8e5 4cc95b8d
second component of signature :        933 46aea539 9972a519 5630c426
Message Verifies
```

While this is not very exciting to read about, if properly used, a signature scheme can increase the trust of who says what on the Net. An electronic signature can be tied to who (or what) owns the private key. Because real signatures can be falsified, it is probably safe to assume that electronic signatures can be falsified as well. However, it is a far more difficult task and requires both advanced mathematical skills and computer resources.

10.4 Digital Signature Algorithm (DSA)

It seems that digital signatures are clearly important to the authors of the IEEE P1363 draft. They have included two schemes for elliptic curves that look amazingly similar. As with the previous scheme, the DSA version uses a random EC_KEYPAIR, along with the signer's private key, to create a random value for the signature. In the DSA scheme the inverse of the random value is used to hide the message hash. Another difference is in the verification: You use the hash to compute one of the key parameters, which must match the original signature.

As before, let P be the base point with order n on curve E, which satisfies equation (6.1). I'll call the signer's private key s and the public key $Q = sP$, as in equation (10.1). Similar to equation (10.2), I'll take a random value k and random point $R = kP$. The message hash is e and has been generated to be less than n. The first step in DSA is to take the x component of R modulo the order of the curve to get the first signature component:

$$c = x \mod n. \tag{10.10}$$

The second component is then computed as:

$$d = k^{-1}(e + sc).$$ (10.11)

According to the IEEE standard, the process of verifying the signature from equations (10.10) and (10.11) requires computation of three values after computing the hash of the message (called e' here):

$$h = d^{-1} \quad \text{mod } n$$
$$h_1 = e'h \quad \text{mod } n$$
$$h_2 = ch \quad \text{mod } n.$$ (10.12)

These values are used to compute a point on the public elliptic curve with the formula:

$$R' = h_1 P + h_2 Q.$$ (10.13)

If the x component of equation (10.13) does not equal equation (10.10), the message is assumed to be different from the original signed document. Let's see why.

The first equation in equation (10.12) can be rewritten with equation (10.11):

$$h = k(e + sc)^{-1}.$$ (10.14)

With this, the last two equations in equation (10.12) expand to:

$$h_1 = e'k(e + sc)^{-1}$$
$$h_2 = ck(e + sc)^{-1}.$$ (10.15)

Putting the above fully expanded terms into equation (10.13) gives:

$$R' = e'k(e + sc)^{-1}P + sck(e + sc)^{-1}P$$ (10.16)

where I have also substituted equation (10.1) (the signer's public key) for Q. Clearly there are common terms, which reduce down to:

$$R' = k(e' + sc)(e + sc)^{-1}P.$$ (10.17)

The middle factors will cancel only if the hash of the original message, the signer's key, and the published signature are correct. In some sense the math is self-descriptive, because the random point is used to compute itself. It would be interesting to see an analysis of any possible attacks that could take advantage of this self-reference, but I suspect the mathematics would be horrendous.

10.4.1 DSA in normal basis

The DSA signature scheme requires the same inputs as the Nyberg-Rueppel signature scheme. The output has the same structure, but the calculations to derive it are different. The start of the DSA signature routine should look familiar:

```
void onb_DSA_Signature( Message, length, public_curve, secret_key, signature)
char                    *Message;
unsigned long           length;
EC_PARAMETER            *public_curve;
FIELD2N                 *secret_key;
SIGNATURE               *signature;
{
        BIGINT                  hash_value;      /*  then to an integer  */
        EC_KEYPAIR              random_key;
        BIGINT                  x_value, k_value, sig_value, c_value;
        BIGINT                  temp, quotient;
        BIGINT                  key_value, point_order, u_value;
        INDEX                   i, count;

/*  compute hash of input message  */

        hash_to_int( Message, length, &hash_value);

/*  create random value and generate random point on public curve  */

        ECKGP( public_curve, &random_key);
```

After computing the message hash, I call the key generating subroutine. This forces the random value into the range of the base point order. This is important, because we have to compute the inverse modulo the order of the base point, and I want to be sure there will be no surprises. Note also that this is the only reference to elliptic curve mathematics in the entire routine. The polynomial version (included below) is identical except for this line.

```
/*  convert x component of random point to an integer modulo
        the order of the base point.  This is first part of
        signature.
*/

        field_to_int( &public_curve->pnt_order, &point_order);
        field_to_int( &random_key.pblc_key.x, &x_value);
        int_div( &x_value, &point_order, &quotient, &c_value);
        int_to_field( &c_value, &signature->c);
```

Calculating the first term is easy; just convert to an integer and divide by the order of the point to get the proper-size remainder. Converting to a FIELD2N value is just to save space. I then proceed to compute the second number for the signature. First, con-

vert the private key to an integer and then multiply by the first number—*c* in equation
(10.11). Add in the message hash and reduce modulo the order of the base point.

```
/*      multiply that  by signers private key and add to message
        digest modulo the order of the base point.
        hash value + private key * c value
*/

        field_to_int( secret_key, &key_value);
        int_mul( &key_value, &c_value, &temp);
        int_add( &temp, &hash_value, &temp);
        int_div( &temp, &point_order, &quotient, &k_value);
```

Finally, I compute the inverse of the random value, multiply this by the above
result, and again reduce modulo the order of the base point. This gives the second signature value, and the algorithm is complete.

```
/*  final step is to multiply by inverse of random key value
              modulo order of base point.
*/

        field_to_int( &random_key.prvt_key, &temp);
        mod_inv( &temp, &point_order, &u_value);
        int_mul( &u_value, &k_value, &temp);
        int_div( &temp, &point_order, &quotient, &sig_value);
        int_to_field( &sig_value, &signature->d);
}
```

Verification of the above signature is also straightforward using the integer math
routines previously described. There are a few more calls to elliptic curve math in this
subroutine. The routine returns 1 if the signature matches the message and 0 otherwise.

```
int onb_DSA_Verify( Message, length, public_curve, signer_point, signature)
char                    *Message;
unsigned long           length;
EC_PARAMETER            *public_curve;
POINT                   *signer_point;
SIGNATURE               *signature;
{
        BIGINT                  hash_value;
        POINT                   Temp1, Temp2, Verify;
        BIGINT                  c_value, d_value;
        BIGINT                  temp, quotient, h1, h2;
        BIGINT                  check_value, point_order;
        INDEX                   i, count;
        FIELD2N                 h1_field, h2_field;

/*  compute inverse of second signature value  */

        field_to_int( &public_curve->pnt_order, &point_order);
        field_to_int( &signature->d, &temp);
```

```
mod_inv( &temp, &point_order, &d_value);
```

The first equation in equation (10.12) is computed above; this is just the inverse of the second signature value. The second equation of equation (10.12) multiplies this with the hash of the message. The third equation in equation (10.12) is the multiple of the two signature values reduced modulo the order of the curve.

```
/*   generate hash of message   */

        hash_to_int( Message, length, &hash_value);

/*   compute elliptic curve multipliers:
        h1 = hash value * d_value, h2 = c * d_value
*/

        int_mul( &hash_value, &d_value, &temp);
        int_div( &temp, &point_order, &quotient, &h1);
        int_to_field( &h1, &h1_field);
        field_to_int( &signature->c, &c_value);
        int_mul( &d_value, &c_value, &temp);
        int_div( &temp, &point_order, &quotient, &h2);
        int_to_field( &h2, &h2_field);
```

The integer values from the above calculations are converted to FIELD2N values and used to multiply the base point and signer's public key, respectively. These two points are summed to compute equation (10.13).

```
/*   find hidden point from public data   */

        elptic_mul( &h1_field, &public_curve->pnt, &Temp1,
                    public_curve->crv);
        elptic_mul( &h2_field, signer_point, &Temp2, &public_curve->crv);
        esum( &Temp1, &Temp2, &Verify, &public_curve->crv);
```

Converting the *x* component of the result to an integer and again reducing modulo the order of the base point should give the same value as originally given for the first number in the signature. If not, return a 0 result.

```
/*   convert x value of verify point to an integer modulo point order */

        field_to_int( &Verify.x, &temp);
        int_div( &temp, &point_order, &quotient, &check_value);

/*   compare resultant message digest from original signature   */

        int_null(&temp);
        int_sub( &c_value, &check_value, &temp);
        while( temp.hw[0] & 0x8000) /*   ensure positive zero */
                int_add( &point_order, &temp, &temp);
```

```
/*  return error if result of subtraction is not zero  */

        INTLOOP(i) if (temp.hw[i]) return(0);
        return(1);
}
```

Testing the above routines is identical to testing the Nyberg-Rueppel scheme. Here is an example.

```
main()
{
        EC_PARAMETER            Base;
        EC_KEYPAIR              Signer;
        SIGNATURE               signature;
        BIGINT                  prime_order;
        POINT                   temp;
        INDEX                   i, error;
        char                    Message[1024];
        char string1[MAXSTRING] ="519229685853482762789670383346750 7";/*N 113
*/

#ifdef TYPE2
        genlambda2();
#else
        genlambda();
#endif

        random_seed = 0xFACED0FF;

/*  compute curve order from Koblitz data  */

        ascii_to_bigint(&string1, &prime_order);
        int_to_field( &prime_order, &Base.pnt_order);
        null( &Base.cofactor);
        Base.cofactor.e[NUMWORD] = 2;

/*  create Koblitz curve  */

        Base.crv.form = 1;
        one(&Base.crv.a2);
        one(&Base.crv.a6);
        print_curve("Koblitz 113", &Base.crv);

/*  create base point of known order with no cofactor  */

        rand_point( &temp, &Base.crv);
        print_point("random point", &temp);
        edbl( &temp, &Base.pnt, &Base.crv);
        print_point(" Base point ",&Base.pnt);

/*  create a secret key for testing.
        Note that secret key must be less than order.
        The standard implies that the field size which
        can be used is one bit less than
```

```
        the length of the public base point order.
*/


        ECKGP( &Base, &Signer);
        print_field("Signer's secret key", &Signer.prvt_key);
        print_point("Signers public key", &Signer.pblc_key);

/*  create a message to be signed  */

        for (i=0; i<1024; i++) Message[i] = i;

/*  call DSA signature scheme  */

        onb_DSA_Signature( Message, 1024, &Base, &Signer.prvt_key,
                    &signature);
        print_field("first component of signature", &signature.c);
        print_field("second component of signature", &signature.d);

/*  verify message has not been tampered.
        Need public curve parameters, signers
        public key, message, length of message,
        and order of public curve parameters
        as well as the signature. If there is a
        null response, message is not same as
        the orignal signed version.
*/
        error = onb_DSA_Verify( Message, 1024, &Base,
                                &Signer.pblc_key, &signature);
        if (error) printf("Message Verifies");
        else printf("Message fails!");
}
```

The output of this test is just as boring but just as important as the previous descriptions.

```
Koblitz 113
form = 1
a2 :    1ffff ffffffff ffffffff ffffffff
a6 :    1ffff ffffffff ffffffff ffffffff

random point
x :    7d17 b7423658 5f8dae64 d624d542
y :    100a4 823ec133 6f1d883c a95f43ac

 Base point
x :    1f43c 6942b1a4 9aaaac4a b572fdbf
y :    10145 c084d629 96208f8e 44d9f291

Signer's secret key :     1988 296d3d8c a8d08ecf 91ff45bf
Signers public key
x :    282b a9e578b1  bcd0319 24bdb6fc
y :    2950 906bb03b 415e5ad8 4bd2c559

first component of signature :    c0c2 421b5284 57235894 76f9862a
```

second component of signature :   8ca2 a1dccee5 7cde9114 a74ff0a3
Message Verifies

10.4.2 DSA: polynomial basis

As I said previously, this is identical to the above with changes made only in the lower-level libraries calling polynomial basis routines instead of normal basis routines. The integer math and hash functions are the same. Everything is included here: Copy what you need and go!

```
void poly_DSA_Signature( Message, length, public_curve, secret_key, signature)
char *Message;
unsigned long length;
EC_PARAMETER *public_curve;
FIELD2N *secret_key;
SIGNATURE *signature;
{
        BIGINT                  hash_value;     /*  then to an integer  */
        EC_KEYPAIR      random_key;
        BIGINT                  x_value, k_value, sig_value, c_value;
        BIGINT                  temp, quotient;
        BIGINT                  key_value, point_order, u_value;
        INDEX                   i, count;

/*  compute hash of input message  */

        hash_to_int( Message, length, &hash_value);

/*  create random value and generate random point on public curve  */

        poly_ECKGP( public_curve, &random_key);

/*  convert x component of random point to an integer modulo
        the order of the base point.  This is first part of
        signature.
*/

        field_to_int( &public_curve->pnt_order, &point_order);
        field_to_int( &random_key.pblc_key.x, &x_value);
        int_div( &x_value, &point_order, &quotient, &c_value);
        int_to_field( &c_value, &signature->c);

/*      multiply that  by signers private key and add to message
        digest modulo the order of the base point.
        hash value + private key * c value
*/

        field_to_int( secret_key, &key_value);
        int_mul( &key_value, &c_value, &temp);
        int_add( &temp, &hash_value, &temp);
        int_div( &temp, &point_order, &quotient, &k_value);
```

```
/*  final step is to multiply by inverse of random key value
            modulo order of base point.
*/

        field_to_int( &random_key.prvt_key, &temp);
        mod_inv( &temp, &point_order, &u_value);
        int_mul( &u_value, &k_value, &temp);
        int_div( &temp, &point_order, &quotient, &sig_value);
        int_to_field( &sig_value, &signature->d);
}
```

The verification uses the polynomial elliptic curve routines.

```
int poly_DSA_Verify( Message, length, public_curve, signer_point, signature)
char                  *Message;
unsigned long length;
EC_PARAMETER*public_curve;
POINT                 *signer_point;
SIGNATURE       *signature;
{
        BIGINT                hash_value;
        POINT                 Temp1, Temp2, Verify;
        BIGINT                c_value, d_value;
        BIGINT                temp, quotient, h1, h2;
        BIGINT                check_value, point_order;
        INDEX                 i, count;
        FIELD2N               h1_field, h2_field;

/*  compute inverse of second signature value  */

        field_to_int( &public_curve->pnt_order, &point_order);
        field_to_int( &signature->d, &temp);
        mod_inv( &temp, &point_order, &d_value);

/*  generate hash of message  */

        hash_to_int( Message, length, &hash_value);

/*  compute elliptic curve multipliers:
        h1 = hash value * d_value, h2 = c * d_value
*/

        int_mul( &hash_value, &d_value, &temp);
        int_div( &temp, &point_order, &quotient, &h1);
        int_to_field( &h1, &h1_field);
        field_to_int( &signature->c, &c_value);
        int_mul( &d_value, &c_value, &temp);
        int_div( &temp, &point_order, &quotient, &h2);
        int_to_field( &h2, &h2_field);

/*  find hidden point from public data  */

        poly_elptic_mul( &h1_field, &public_curve->pnt, &Temp1,
                    &public_curve->crv);
```

```
        poly_elptic_mul( &h2_field, signer_point, &Temp2, &public_curve->crv);
        poly_esum( &Temp1, &Temp2, &Verify, &public_curve->crv);

/*  convert x value of verify point to an integer modulo point order */

        field_to_int( &Verify.x, &temp);
        int_div( &temp, &point_order, &quotient, &check_value);

/*  compare resultant message digest from original signature   */

        int_sub( &c_value, &check_value, &temp);
        while( temp.hw[0] & 0x8000) /*  ensure positive zero */
                int_add( &point_order, &temp, &temp);

/*  return error if result of subtraction is not zero   */

        INTLOOP(i) if (temp.hw[i]) return(0);
        return(1);
}
```

The test routine is similar to the Nyberg-Rueppel test of polynomial basis routines.

```
main()
{
        FIELD2N             roots[3];
        EC_PARAMETER        Base;
        EC_KEYPAIR          Signer;
        SIGNATURE           signature;
        BIGINT              prime_order;
        POINT               temp;
        INDEX               i, error;
        char                Message[1024];
        char string1[MAXSTRING] = "32451855365842672311495757233 5741";

        random_seed = 0x9e25f1b3;

        if (!irreducible(&poly_prime)) return(0);
        print_field("poly_prime = ", &poly_prime);

        if (error = init_poly_math())
        {
                printf("Can't initialize S matrix, row = %d\n", error);
                return(-1);
        }

/*  compute curve order from Koblitz data   */

        ascii_to_bigint(&string1, &prime_order);
        int_to_field( &prime_order, &Base.pnt_order);
        null( &Base.cofactor);
        Base.cofactor.e[NUMWORD] = 8;

        printf("create Base curve and point\n\n");
```

```
        Base.crv.form = 0;
        null(&Base.crv.a2);
        poly_gf8(&poly_prime, roots);
        copy( &roots[1], &Base.crv.a6);
        print_curve("Public curve", &Base.crv);

        rand_point(&temp, &Base.crv);
        poly_elptic_mul(&Base.cofactor, &temp, &Base.pnt, &Base.crv);
        print_point("Base point", &Base.pnt);

/*  create a secret key for testing.
        Note that secret key must be less than order.
        The standard implies that the field size which
        can be used is one bit less than
        the length of the public base point order.
*/

        poly_ECKGP( &Base, &Signer);
        print_field("Signer's secret key", &Signer.prvt_key);
        print_point("Signers public key", &Signer.pblc_key);

/*  create a message to be signed  */

        for (i=0; i<1024; i++) Message[i] = i;

/*  call DSA signature scheme  */

        poly_DSA_Signature( Message, 1024, &Base, &Signer.prvt_key,
                        &signature);
        print_field("first component of signiture", &signature.c);
        print_field("second component of signiture", &signature.d);

/*  verify message has not been tampered.
        Need public curve parameters, signers
        public key, message, length of message,
        and order of public curve parameters
        as well as the signature. If there is a
        null response, message is not same as
        the orignal signed version.
*/
        error = poly_DSA_Verify( Message, 1024, &Base,
                                    &Signer.pblc_key, &signature);
        if (error) printf("Message Verifies");
        else printf("Message fails!");
}
```

Just to be different though, in the above test I used a different root to the solution of the coefficient for a_6. The output of the above test was as follows:

```
poly_prime =  :      8000         0         0      401
create Base curve and point

Public curve
form = 0
```

```
a6 :     5b85 d9a7e747 7e0c9615 7fb27dc6

Base point
x :     747b 489729a1 98dac66c 8eb26273
y :     26d8 d21f0c55 d9641d89 36dbc0c4

Signer's secret key :     685 43c6fffc e02152ec 87fd5959
Signers public key
x :     42cf 1f83ee86 335ecc23 9b9297d6
y :     803 df98aac2 4b5d338c ac2097af

first component of signiture :     981 35edc001 42c9905b 5ffccf50
second component of signiture :     80d bf5693d2 45cff70d b31937bc
Message Verifies
```

10.5 Signatures: a summary

Implementing digital signatures is easy once the underlying mathematical subroutines are available. If you decide to use other integer math packages, you will need to convert their storage method to and from a FIELD2N type variable. The choice of normal basis or polynomial basis math for the low-level fields depends more on what curves you decide to pick and on what kind of throughput you need. With polynomial bases you have a wider variety of field sizes to choose from. The most important decision is an estimate of the level of security you require and the number of signatures you need to perform. Higher security means fewer signatures per second.

To help increase throughput, let's return to normal basis inversion in the next chapter and look at a really fast implementation. Now that we have the basics and lots of applications, we can take a look at refinements of the low-level math routines.

10.6 References

1   B. Schneier, *Applied Cryptography*, 2d ed. (New York: John Wiley & Sons, 1996).

C H A P T E R   1 1

The bleeding edge

11.1   High-speed inversion for ONB   284

11.2   Faster inversion, preliminary subroutines   288

11.3   Security from cryptography   297

11.4   Counting points   298

11.5   Polynomials: base p 299

11.6   Hyperelliptic curves   299

11.7   References   300

This chapter contains several routines that don't fit elsewhere in the book. The first topic is a very fast inversion technique, recently discovered, which combines optimal normal basis with polynomial basis. The subroutine schematic is shown in figure 11.1. Then I'd like to discuss a few unrelated things such as compression and hyperelliptic curves.

11.1 High-speed inversion for ONB

The following routine combines polynomial basis and optimal normal basis to implement a very high speed inversion algorithm. Most research into elliptic curve crypto systems over the past few years has concentrated on finding mathematical tricks to increase

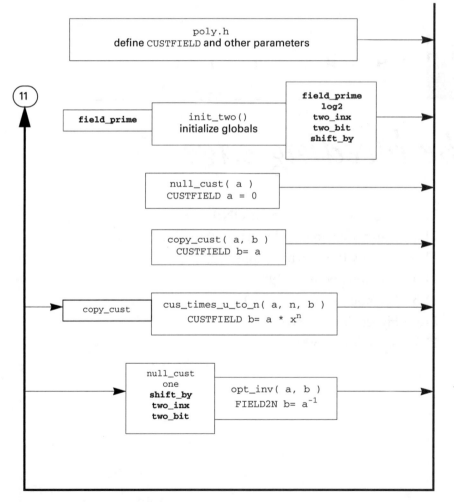

Figure 11.1 Subroutine schematic

throughput. Many of these tricks rely on the structure of certain fields. Others rely on finding specific irreducible polynomials.

The routine presented here was first developed by Dave Dahm [1]. While it has been "published" on the Internet, I don't believe it has been documented elsewhere. Because this inversion routine is as fast as an optimal normal basis multiply, it is faster than any other routine described in the literature. Most inversion routines require two to five times as long as a multiply. An ONB multiply may take longer than a specialized polynomial basis multiply, but the overall throughput may be better for the ONB. It will take some testing to see which method is best for any particular application.

Dahm's inversion algorithm is based on [2] for the "almost inverse algorithm" and on [3] for the irreducible polynomial, which converts from Type I and Type II ONB to polynomial basis. The "almost inverse algorithm" is based on Euclid's algorithm, but it leaves a final factor of x^k, which has to be divided out. Fortunately, this is a trivial operation for ONB, so the conversion to and from polynomial basis and the elimination of the final factor turns out to be much faster than the inversion algorithm described in chapter 4.

The basic idea of the almost inverse algorithm is the same as polynomial inversion, described in chapter 3. We keep the following formula constant:

$$B \cdot F + C \cdot G = 1 \quad \mod M \tag{11.1}$$

where M is the prime polynomial. For an ONB the prime polynomial is very specific; I'll describe it later.

The almost inverse algorithm is initialized with:

$$
\begin{aligned}
B &= 1 \\
C &= 0 \\
F &= \text{Source Polynomial} \\
G &= M = \text{Prime Polynomial} \\
k &= 0.
\end{aligned}
\tag{11.2}
$$

The variables B, C, F, and G are polynomials, and k is an integer. The algorithm proceeds by repeating the following steps:

While the last bit of F is 0:

        shift F right   (divide by x)
        shift C left   (multiply by x)
        increment k by 1.

If $F = 1$, return B, k.

If degree (F) < degree (G), then exchange F, G and B, C.

$F = F + G.$

$B = B + C.$

Repeat entire loop.

The reason this is an "almost" inverse routine is that we have the final result with an extra factor of x^k, which must be divided out. For optimal normal basis this factor is very easy to find, and we don't need a full-scale multiply to remove it.

There are additional tricks that Schroeppel et al. [2] include in their paper to help speed up the algorithm. These include using two separate loops rather than exchanging polynomials, using registers, and expanding structures to explicitly named variables. Many of these tricks reduce portability but increase throughput.

The major contribution that Dahm reported is the conversion between an ONB representation and a polynomial representation. In [3] an irreducible polynomial for a Type II optimal normal basis, for which 2 is primitive in Z_{2n+1}, is:

$$M_2 = 1 + x + x^2 + \ldots + x^{2n}.$$

(11.3)

It follows (and Dahm has proved it as well) that for a Type I ONB (with 2 primitive in Z_m) an irreducible polynomial is given by:

$$M_1 = 1 + x + x^2 + \ldots + x^{m-1}.$$

(11.4)

For the Type II optimal normal basis, for which 2 generates the quadratic residues, the polynomial in equation (11.3) has two factors, so it is not irreducible. Fortunately, the almost inverse algorithm will still work. This is due to the requirement that the source polynomial (F) be relatively prime to the basis polynomial (M). This will always be the case for sources of Type II ONB. I leave it to the mathematicians to prove it.

Let's first look at how Dahm converts a Type I normal basis representation to a polynomial basis representation. Each term in a normal basis is of the form:

$$a_i x^{2^i}.$$

(11.5)

But since 2 is a generator modulo m, we can also write this term as:

$$a_i x^k.$$

(11.6)

If we assume the prime polynomial of equation (11.4), then we can move the ith coefficient of Type I ONB to the $k = \log_2(i)$ position to convert from normal to polynomial basis. This is just a permutation of all the bits, and we only have to move the ones that are set.

The only problem we have is when $i = m - 1$. This term is not represented in the polynomial basis, because it has the power of the most significant coefficient in equation (11.4). In the normal basis case, there is no representation for x^0. For this case, we map the coefficient of the most significant bit of the ONB to the least significant bit of the polynomial representation, and nothing is lost. I'm sure the mathematicians can prove this is true, because the code works!

Here is Dahm's explanation for the more mathematically inclined: As vector spaces, the basis vectors are exactly the same (except for order) at all places except 1. Each set of basis vectors contains $x, x^2, x^3, \ldots, x^{m-2}$. The only difference is that ONB contains x^{m-1} and polynomial contains 1. In the Type I field these two representations are related by:

$$1 + x + x^2 + \ldots + x^{m-1} = 0.$$

(11.7)

For a Type II optimal normal basis, things are almost as easy. The polynomial basis is twice as long as the normal basis. For each bit in the ONB we will have 2 bits in the polynomial basis. It turns out that the 2 bits are palindromes; if bit i is set, then so is bit $2n + 1 - i$.

In chapter 4, near equation (4.25), I took the basis to be of the form:

$$\gamma + \gamma^{-1} = \beta.$$

(11.8)

The combination of these two terms created a new one, which was the basis for the Type II ONB. Using this, along with the polynomial of equation (11.3), we can derive a simple conversion scheme to go from Type II ONB to polynomial representation and back by flipping just 2 bits in a known permutation. Since the permutation is pre-defined for any ONB, we can create a lookup table at initialization, along with the creation of the multiplication vectors.

Let's rewrite equation (4.27). For simplicity, let $p = 2n + 1$. Since we're doing base 2 field math, we have:

$$\left(\gamma + \gamma^{-1}\right)^{2^i} = \gamma^{2^i} + \gamma^{-2^i} = \gamma^{2^i} + \gamma^{p - 2^i}.$$

(11.9)

Just as with the Type I ONB, we have a permutation from the coefficient of each term to a corresponding one in the polynomial representation. But there are now 2 bits that we have to map: one that maps 2^i to k and one that maps $p - 2^i$ to $p - k$. By creating the permutation map as a set of indices and bit masks, the conversion is very fast. The almost inverse algorithm is then simple to invoke. The whole process is identical for both Type I and Type II (other than the number of bits needed).

11.2 *Faster inversion, preliminary subroutines*

There are several steps to creating a faster inversion routine. The first is a pair of tables used in the conversion from normal basis to polynomial and back. Another is the multiplication of x^{-k} as the final step in the almost inverse algorithm. Then there is the inversion routine itself. The latter has been expanded using some of the suggestions in [2].

Let's start with some new constants, which are defined in a header file:

```
#define LONGWORD    (field_prime/WORDSIZE)
#define LONGSHIFT   ((field_prime-1)%WORDSIZE)
#define LONGBIT     (1L<<(LONGSHIFT-1))
#define LONGMASK    (~(-1L<<LONGSHIFT))
```

These are used to create the polynomial basis representation, as we'll see below. LONGWORD is the number of ELEMENTS needed to hold the polynomials we'll be using. LONGSHIFT is the number of left shifts needed to get to the most significant bit in the most significant ELEMENT of the polynomial representation. LONGBIT is the most significant bit we'll need in the polynomial basis, and LONGMASK is a mask that keeps the most significant bits in the most significant ELEMENT of the polynomial basis.

Next comes some additional initialization code, which needs to be called only once. I've copied it directly from [1]. The initializations are for the following arrays, which need to be added to the onb.c file (chapter 4 subroutines):

```
static INDEX          log2[field_prime+1];
static INDEX          two_inx[field_prime];
static ELEMENT        two_bit[field_prime];
static unsigned char  shift_by[256];
```

The variable log2 is the same; it's just global for use in the conversion process. The two arrays two_* are used to find specific bits. Rather than save the bit position, as in the log2 array, Dahm saves the ELEMENT index and bit offset within an ELEMENT. This speeds execution with only a minor increase in memory requirements. The array shift_by is used as one of the speed enhancements. Instead of shifting the *F* polynomial only once and incrementing *k* as stated in the algorithm, Dahm does several shifts at once if possible.

We have seen the genlambda routines before; the only change there is the removal of variable log2, because it is now global. The routine init_two fills in the arrays two_inx and two_bit. It's pretty simple too.

```
static void init_two(void)
{
        INDEX n, i, j;

        j = 1;
```

```
        n = (field_prime-1)/2;
          for ( i=0;  i<n;  i++ )
          {
              two_inx[i] = LONGWORD-(j / WORDSIZE);
              two_bit[i] = 1L << (j % WORDSIZE);
              two_inx[i+n] = LONGWORD-((field_prime-j) / WORDSIZE);
             two_bit[i+n] = 1L << ((field_prime-j) % WORDSIZE);
             j = (j << 1) % field_prime;
          }
          two_inx[field_prime-1] = two_inx[0];
       two_bit[field_prime-1] = two_bit[0];

          for ( i=1;  i<256;  i++ )
              shift_by[i] = 0;
          shift_by[0] = 1;
          for ( j=2;  j<256;  j+=j )
           for ( i=0;  i<256;  i+=j )
              shift_by[i]++;
}
```

The variable `shift_by` is really simple. By masking the last 8 bits of a FIELD2N ELEMENT, and using that as an index into the array, it tells us how many bits are clear. Watch it work with a debugger; you'll agree it's clever code.

The initialization code, which was put in the main routine in the previous chapters, is now combined with the above initialization routine. This is similar to the polynomial initialization and just cleans up the main routine.

```
void init_opt_math()
{

#ifdef TYPE2
        genlambda2();
#else
        genlambda();
#endif
        init_two();
}
```

Dahm introduces yet another type of variable. It is used to hold double-size arrays for Type II optimal normal basis conversions to "customary" polynomial basis representations. For Type I optimal normal basis, it is the same size as FIELD2N, but this makes the code more general.

```
typedef struct {
        ELEMENT e[LONGWORD+1];
} CUSTFIELD;
```

Basic operations on this structure are similar to operations on FIELD2N and DBLFIELD structures. To copy values from one CUSTFIELD to another, we use the following code segment:

```
void copy_cust (a,b)
CUSTFIELD *a,*b;
{
       INDEX i;

       for (i=0; i<=LONGWORD; i++)  b->e[i] = a->e[i];
}
```

And to clear out a variable, the following routine is used:

```
void null_cust(a)
CUSTFIELD *a;
{
     INDEX i;

       for (i=0; i<=LONGWORD; i++)  a->e[i] = 0;
}
```

The last step of the almost inverse algorithm is the multiplication of the extra factor x^{-k}. Dahm's code performs this step as follows. It's not clear to me that it is fully speed enhanced; I think there are some mathematical tricks that can be used to eliminate this step completely. The reason for this conjecture is that the final multiply is only a shifting of the bits, and instead of shifting we can just change how we do look ups. But I'll leave that for another programmer; the point here is that speed improvements are not only possible but that much more work needs to be done to find even more enhancements. Now, let's see how this routine works.

```
/* set b  = a * u^n, where n>0 and n <= field_prime */

void cus_times_u_to_n(CUSTFIELD *a, int n, CUSTFIELD *b)
{
#define SIZE           (2*LONGWORD+2)
       ELEMENT         w, t[SIZE+1];
       INDEX           i, j, n1, n2, n3;
```

The constant SIZE is used here to make the dimension of the array t hold twice as many bits as the normal basis representation. The check for n being equal to field_prime is robust code; in practice, it should never happen.

```
       if ( n == field_prime )
       {
           copy_cust(a, b);
           return;
       }
```

The next line of code clears the t array. Since this array is special, this could be done with a pointer, too. The variables n1 and n2 determine the index into the t array and the bit within an ELEMENT of that array. The offset is from the end of the array rather than the start—this is why SIZE - n1 appears everywhere.

```
for ( j=0; j<=SIZE; j++ ) t[j] = 0;

n1 = n / WORDSIZE;
j = SIZE-n1;
n2 = n & (WORDSIZE-1);
```

The next block of code then shifts every word of the input. If the bit position is 0, then whole ELEMENTS can be moved. Otherwise, the variable n3 is used to shift a word up a portion, and n2 is used to shift a word down a portion. Each word is put into t shifted by the amount SIZE − n1. Note that j is decremented after being used as the subscript, so that the second line in the for loop uses the previous value of j.

```
if ( n2 )
{
    n3 = WORDSIZE-n2;
    for ( i=LONGWORD; i>=0; i-- )
    {
        t[j--] |= a->e[i] << n2;
        t[j] |= a->e[i] >> n3;
    }
}
else
{
        for ( i=LONGWORD; i>=0; i-- )
        {
                t[j--] |= a->e[i];
        }
}
```

At this point we have actually multiplied the input by x^n (presumably the value for n was computed modulo field_prime). This is just a shift by n bit positions, since each coefficient is multiplied by its appropriate power of x.

The next block of code then shifts the upper portion by the correct amount to account for the fact that the field size does not fill a complete word.

```
n3 = LONGSHIFT+1;
i = SIZE-LONGWORD;
for ( j=SIZE; j>=SIZE-n1; j-- ) {
    t[j] |= t[i--] >> n3;
    t[j] |= t[i] << (WORDSIZE-n3);
}
```

This moves the upper portion of an ELEMENT at an offset, which holds the most significant bits of the result back to the least significant ELEMENT position. The code works because:

$$x^p - 1 = (x - 1)M \qquad (11.10)$$

where M is given by either equation (11.3) or (11.4). What equation (11.10) tells us is that every power of x^{p+k} reduced modulo M will simply be x^k. To see this, rewrite equation (11.10) as:

$$x^p = 1 + (x-1)M.$$ (11.11)

Multiply both sides by x^k and reduce modulo M (which eliminates the second term), and we have the relationship:

$$x^{p+k} = x^k.$$ (11.12)

The final step is to move the data from the t array to the output array. This includes one important check: If the coefficient to x^{p-1} is set, we can reduce this power by adding in the rest of M (since $M = 0 \bmod M$). This is just all bits set, and the variable w is used to contain these bits for each ELEMENT.

```
        w = t[SIZE-LONGWORD] & (1L << LONGSHIFT ) ? ~0 : 0;
        for ( i=0; i<=LONGWORD; i++ )
            b->e[i] = t[i+SIZE-LONGWORD] ^ w;
        b->e[0] &= LONGMASK;

#undef SIZE
}
```

Finally, the upper bits are cleared to complete the operation and clean up the output. (The term SIZE was previously defined at the beginning of the routine. Since the name is common, I think Dahm wanted to limit the scope.)

11.2.1 Faster inversion, the code

The fast inversion algorithm does not translate into pretty code. The following code works and has been tested. It uses all the methods described previously, including the conversion from optimal normal basis to polynomial basis and back using equations (11.3) or (11.4). The almost inverse algorithm is included, along with several speed ups mentioned in [2]. To really understand this requires some study with a debugger.

```
/* This algorithm is the Almost Inverse Algorithm of Schroeppel, et al. given
   in "Fast Key Exchange with Elliptic Curve Systems" [SOM]
*/

void opt_inv(FIELD2N *a, FIELD2N *dest)
{
        CUSTFIELD       f, b, c, g;
        INDEX           i, j, k, m, n, f_top, c_top;
        ELEMENT         bits, t, mask;

        /* f, b, c, and g are not in optimal normal basis format: they are held
```

in 'customary format', i.e. a0 + a1*u^1 + a2*u^2 + ...; For the
comments in this routine, the polynomials are assumed to be
polynomials in u. */

The first thing Dahm does is initialize G to the prime polynomial M, as in the algorithm of equation (11.2). This is all bits set, including 1 extra bit past the defined limit of LONGSHIFT.

```
/* Set g to polynomial (u^p-1)/(u-1) */

for ( i=1; i<=LONGWORD; i++ )
    g.e[i] = ~0;
g.e[0] = LONGMASK | (1L << LONGSHIFT);
```

The next chunk of code converts the input value a from normal basis to polynomial basis using the predefined offset and bit masks created in init_two. For a Type II normal basis we need 2 bits set.

```
/* Convert a to 'customary format', putting answer in f */

null_cust(&f);
j = 0;
for ( k=NUMWORD; k>=0; k-- )
{
    bits = a->e[k];
    m = k>0 ? WORDSIZE : UPRSHIFT;
    for ( i=0; i<m; i++ )
    {
        if ( bits & 1 )
        {
            f.e[two_inx[j]] |= two_bit[j];
#ifdef TYPE2
            f.e[two_inx[j+NUMBITS]] |= two_bit[j+NUMBITS];
#endif
        }
        j++;
        bits >>= 1;
    }
}
```

After initializing the remaining variables of equation (11.2), Dahm then eliminates powers of x (which he calls u), as stated in the first step of the almost inverse algorithm. The variables c_top and f_top are used to track the unused (zeroed out) ELEMENTS in b, c and f, g, respectively. This also helps speed up the code, since it eliminates loop executions, which have null results.

```
/* Set c to 0, b to 1, and n to 0 */

null_cust(&c);
null_cust(&b);
```

```
        b.e[LONGWORD] = 1;
        n = 0;

        /* Now find a polynomial b, such that a*b = u^n */

        /* f and g shrink, b and c grow.  The code takes advantage of this.
        c_top and f_top are the variables which control this behavior */

        c_top = LONGWORD;
        f_top = 0;
        do
        {
            i = shift_by[f.e[LONGWORD] & 0xff];
            n+=i;
/* Shift f right i (divide by u^i) */
            m = 0;
            for ( j=f_top; j<=LONGWORD; j++ )
            {
                bits = f.e[j];
                f.e[j] = (bits>>i) | ((ELEMENT)m << (WORDSIZE-i));
                m = bits;
            }
        } while ( i == 8 && (f.e[LONGWORD] & 1) == 0 );
```

Everything is now initialized, and we're ready for the main loop. If $F = 1$, then the routine is finished. This will happen on occasion if you enter with a single bit set; the above code shifts the bit down and the main routine would not be needed. Dahm checks for that here.

```
        for ( j=0; j<LONGWORD; j++ )
            if ( f.e[j] ) break;
        if ( j<LONGWORD || f.e[LONGWORD] != 1 )
          {
```

Assuming F is not equal to 1, we enter the "almost inverse algorithm's" main loop.

```
        /* There are two loops here: whenever we need to exchange f with g and
            b with c, jump to the other loop which has the names reversed! */
        do
        {
        /* Shorten f and g when possible */
            while ( f.e[f_top] == 0 && g.e[f_top] == 0 ) f_top++;
        /* f needs to be bigger - if not, exchange f with g and b with c.
            (Actually jump to the other loop instead of doing the exchange)
            The published algorithm requires deg f >= deg g, but we don't
            need to be so fine */
                if ( f.e[f_top] < g.e[f_top] ) goto loop2;
loop1:
        /* f = f+g, making f divisible by u */
                for ( i=f_top; i<=LONGWORD; i++ )
                    f.e[i] ^= g.e[i];
        /* b = b+c */
```

```
                     for ( i=c_top; i<=LONGWORD; i++ )
                         b.e[i] ^= c.e[i];
                     do
                     {
                         i = shift_by[f.e[LONGWORD] & 0xff];
                         n+=i;
    /* Shift c left i (multiply by u^i), lengthening it if needed */
                         m = 0;
                         for ( j=LONGWORD; j>=c_top; j-- )
                         {
                             bits = c.e[j];
                             c.e[j] = (bits<<i) | m;
                             m = bits >> (WORDSIZE-i);
                         }
                         if ( m ) c.e[c_top=j] = m;

    /* Shift f right i (divide by u^i) */
                         m = 0;
                         for ( j=f_top; j<=LONGWORD; j++ )
                         {
                             bits = f.e[j];
                             f.e[j] = (bits>>i) | ((ELEMENT)m << (WORDSIZE-i));
                             m = bits;
                         }
                     } while ( i == 8 && (f.e[LONGWORD] & 1) == 0 );
    /* Check if we are done (f=1) */
                         for ( j=f_top; j<LONGWORD; j++ )
                             if ( f.e[j] ) break;
                     } while ( j<LONGWORD || f.e[LONGWORD] != 1 );
```

There are two loops here that are identical; only the variable names have been flipped to do the correct operations. The last step in the loop is to check to see if $F = 1$. If it is, then the above while loop ends. Note that if we exit the loop this way, the value of j will always be equal to LONGWORD. The use of goto's may violate most C programming styles, but it is very useful here.

```
          if ( j>0 )
          goto done;
          do
          {
          /* Shorten f and g when possible */
            while ( g.e[f_top] == 0 && f.e[f_top] == 0 ) f_top++;
          /* g needs to be bigger - if not, exchange f with g and b with c.
             (Actually jump to the other loop instead of doing the exchange)
             The published algorithm requires deg g >= deg f, but we don't
             need to be so fine */
                if ( g.e[f_top] < f.e[f_top] ) goto loop1;
loop2:
          /* g = f+g, making g divisible by u */
                for ( i=f_top; i<=LONGWORD; i++ )
                        g.e[i] ^= f.e[i];
          /* c = b+c */
```

```
                for ( i=c_top; i<=LONGWORD; i++ )
                    c.e[i] ^= b.e[i];
            do
            {
                i = shift_by[g.e[LONGWORD] & 0xff];
                n+=i;
    /* Shift b left i (multiply by u^i), lengthening it if needed */
                m = 0;
                for ( j=LONGWORD; j>=c_top; j-- )
                {
                    bits = b.e[j];
                    b.e[j] = (bits<<i) | m;
                    m = bits >> (WORDSIZE-i);
                }
                if ( m ) b.e[c_top=j] = m;

    /* Shift g right i (divide by u^i) */
                m = 0;
                for ( j=f_top; j<=LONGWORD; j++ )
                {
                    bits = g.e[j];
                    g.e[j] = (bits>>i) | ((ELEMENT)m << (WORDSIZE-i));
                    m = bits;
                }
            } while ( i == 8 && (g.e[LONGWORD] & 1) == 0 );
    /* Check if we are done (g=1) */
                for ( j=f_top; j<LONGWORD; j++ )
                    if ( g.e[j] ) break;
        } while ( j<LONGWORD || g.e[LONGWORD] != 1 );
        copy_cust(&c, &b);
    }
```

The guts of the routine are straightforward executions of the almost inverse algorithm. The variables c_top and f_top are both adjusted along the way to reduce the number of execution loops as the procedure progresses. If we exit the last loop, then we have to swap b and c so we can finish the algorithm correctly. The shifting is done using the least significant byte of f or g as an index into the shift_by array. Instead of calling a subroutine, Dahm has made the code inline for this shift, so we see it a lot.

The final stage is to multiply b by the appropriate power of x and then convert that value back to normal basis so we'll get the right answer.

```
done:
    /* Now b is a polynomial such that a*b = u^n, so multiply b by u^(-n) */
    cus_times_u_to_n(&b, field_prime - n % field_prime, &b);

    /* Convert b back to optimal normal basis form (into dest) */

if ( b.e[LONGWORD] & 1 )
    one(dest);
else
    null(dest);
```

```
        j = 0;
        for ( k=NUMWORD; k>=0; k-- )
        {
            bits = 0;
            t = 1;
            mask = k > 0 ? ~0 : UPRMASK;
            do
            {
                if ( b.e[two_inx[j]] & two_bit[j] ) bits ^= t;
                j++;
                t <<= 1;
            } while ( t&mask );
            dest->e[k] ^= bits;
        }

} /* opt_inv */
```

This version of the inverse algorithm requires about as much time to compute as a normal basis multiply. This is faster than any other method I have seen for normal basis. However, special polynomial bases can be made much faster in general. The problem is then using the routines of chapter 6 to find the square root and quadratic solution matrices to help embed data onto an elliptic curve.

As an example of run time, the Nyberg-Rueppel example in the previous chapter took over a minute to run with the original inversion routine described in chapter 5 and only five seconds to run with the above routine on the same processor. This routine is at least ten times faster. So, although it looks messy, it is much quicker to execute. As usual, it takes up more code space to reduce run time, but inversion is called by every elliptic sum or doubling. It is extremely useful to use this if you have ROM to spare.

11.3 Security from cryptography

To create a secure system using cryptographic primitives is not easy. I repeat again that cryptography is not security. A very important aspect of security is to understand the data flow. Where does the secret key get generated? Where does the private key get generated? How do we keep track of many keys? For a secure system to work, questions such as these must be answered.

Another aspect completely left out of this book is the concept of compression. The simplest way to reduce the probability that an attacker can understand the data being transmitted is to remove any duplication of data. This duplication is extremely useful to cryptanalysis. Searching for patterns in data and having a clue as to what might be there will make cracking a code with computers fairly simple. By using a very good compression scheme before encrypting the data, you can ensure that the cryptanalyst's task will be far more difficult.

Never underestimate the ability of another person to crack a code. If you know the security level of your choice of cryptographic parameters, it is good practice to underestimate the time it takes to recover data. For example, a 40-bit key was known in 1997 to be crackable in three hours using the resources of a university. A 56-bit key requires the resources of several thousand computers on the Internet and about a month's time. This does not mean that 40 bits is useless. For a cell phone conversation that lasts minutes and has consequences over a period of an hour, a 40-bit key is perfectly adequate. Depending on the situations you need to cover for, plan to use the minimum resources that get the job done.

This book has tried to describe the least amount of mathematics required to help you create state-of-the-art cryptographic software. Now, I'd like to mention a few things that have not been discussed. I hope to spur some interest in this field, so that even more secure software can be developed some time in the future.

11.4 Counting points

The difficulty of counting points on elliptic curves has been reduced in recent years. The mathematics is far beyond the scope of this book. However, it should be noted that there are many papers in the public domain ([4], for example) that help mathematicians. For most business applications, random curves are perfectly adequate. This is because most businesses do not have an army of mathematicians at their disposal to create the software that implements the mathematics described in the above-mentioned papers, let alone the computer resources needed to crack random curves.

There are many governments that do have an army of mathematicians at their disposal. If you must protect your data from this level of threat, then it is a good idea to pick known curves (such as those mentioned in chapter 6) or to go through the calculations yourself to find a good curve and a point of known order on that curve. This will give the maximum security possible.

The IEEE P1363 draft standard has several methods for counting the points on elliptic curves. The simplest to implement is Weil's Theorem. The most difficult to understand (for me anyway) is the Complex Multiplication (CM) method. The CM method was used by Koblitz to derive the curves in chapter 6, and Solinas [5] extended that work. As long as the security levels already exist, the best choice is known curves. As time goes on, counting points on random elliptic curves will become simpler.

11.5 Polynomials: base p

Throughout this book I have assumed that all polynomials are base 2. Mathematicians don't usually assume this; it just happens that computers are base 2 and so it makes the effort at the bit level much easier. But this is not completely necessary.

An example of one practical use of base p polynomials is Crandall's patent (U.S. number 5159632) for Diffie-Hellman key exchange. The idea is to use modular mathematics for each coefficient of the polynomial. The polynomial equation:

$$a_n x^n + \ldots + a_1 x + a_0 = P \tag{11.13}$$

can have the values a_k take on any value in the range 0 to $p - 1$ for modular arithmetic. The mathematics described in chapter 3 applies. Addition of like powers of x^k is straightforward: We just sum coefficients mod p. Similarly, multiplication proceeds with a shift and add of coefficients, but now everything is done mod p.

This might seem to be very difficult. The Crandall patent uses some very special values of p to make the division process painless. This can be ignored if one uses a processor that has remainder as part of the division algorithm. A great example is the Motorola 680x0 series of microprocessors. Since this series is used as part of many embedded systems, simple calculations can create very complex mathematical structures.

11.6 Hyperelliptic curves

One possible structure that may be used in the future of cryptography is hyperelliptic curves. These are no more hyperelliptic than elliptic curves are ellipses. Rather, this refers to a class of mathematical curves that appears as follows:

$$y^2 = x^m + a x^{m-1} + \ldots + z. \tag{11.14}$$

The value of m is assumed odd and greater than 3. There may be more cross-terms on the left-hand side as well, but the point is that instead of a third-order equation we now use an mth-order equation.

It turns out that these curves can also be used to create an algebra. The number of operations is much higher to sum two points to get a third that lies on equation (11.14), but the mathematicians have shown that it is possible to do. At the present time, this type of mathematics is not practical.

But, in the late 1980s, elliptic curve public key cryptography was not practical either. Today it is very practical and, in fact, is state of the art. By 2010 hyperelliptic curves may also be practical. The jump from integer modular exponentiation to elliptic curves may seem difficult, but, once made, the next step to hyperelliptic curves won't be so bad. The basic foundations are now available in code; it is simply a matter of putting the code to work.

Unfortunately, it may turn out that the structure of hyperelliptic curves allows them to be more easily attacked than the lowest-level elliptic curve. This is an interesting field of mathematics and a great deal more work will be done by the cryptographic community. Several proposals for using hyperelliptic curves have been presented in the literature. More work is needed to be sure these proposals are as secure as the authors believe them to be. As more is learned about the higher levels of math, the basic code presented in this book can change to incorporate it. I hope that you have enjoyed learning the math as much as I have.

11.7 References

1 D. Dahm, private communication and sci.crypt postings, September 1997.

2 R. Schroeppel, H. Orman, and S. O'Mally, "Fast Key Exchange with Elliptic Curve Systems," TR-95-03 (Tucson, AZ: University of Arizona, Computer Sciences Department, 1995). (Also appears in *CRYPTO '95* [New York: Springer-Verlag, 1995].)

3 R. C. Mullin, I. M. Onyszchuk, S. A. Vanstone, and R. M. Wilson, "Optimal Normal Bases in GF (p^n)," in *Discrete Applied Math*, vol. 22 (Amsterdam: Elsevier Science Publishers/ North-Holland, 1988), 149–161.

4 R. Lercier and F. Morain, "Counting the Number of Points on Elliptic Curves over Finite Fields: Strategies and Performances," in *EUROCRYPT '95* (Berlin: Springer-Verlag, 1995).

5 J. A. Solinas, "An Improved Algorithm for Arithmetic in a Family of Elliptic Curves," in *CRYPTO '97* (New York: Springer-Verlag, 1997).

C H A P T E R   1 2

A simple application

12.1   Personal security example   302
12.2   Security analysis   305
12.3   Putting it all together   305
12.4   References   307

12.1 Personal security example

Security is such an inclusive subject that complete analysis of even a single application can fill an entire book. Perhaps the most important single aspect of engineering a secure system is judging its design tradeoffs. This chapter gives you a flavor for the challenges this presents by examining the design decisions for a simple example. Most of the chapters in this book have concentrated on delivering code you can use. In this chapter, the focus is on the thought process behind the code.

The simple application I'll work with is "personal security." The purpose of this sample utility is to allow users with no knowledge of crypto to have secure e-mail with a few friends. As programmers we will make all the decisions and build the security into the code.

Cryptographic zealots scorn this approach. They argue that end users should have control over the operating parameters of a crypto system, such as key length, hashing method, and so on. This is similar to automotive performance enthusiasts, who insist on manual transmissions and chokes in their cars. Most drivers, though, focus simply on a safe arrival at their destinations and are content to leave technical details to Ford or Toyota. In a similar way, the overwhelming majority of e-mail users want their messages to arrive securely, while they focus on priorities other than the entire body of cryptographic theory that supports the applications they use.

Our responsibility as programmers to make design choices on behalf of end users is even clearer, in one way, than in the automotive case. Drivers must simply trust that engineers built the right power curve into their transmissions. When we distribute our work in the form of source code, however, it's open for inspection. Anyone with sufficient technical knowledge can verify for himself or herself its accuracy and applicability.

The criteria for this simple utility are given in the following list:

1 No plain text ever touches nonvolatile memory. The user's files will be compressed and encrypted before saving. This protects users in case their hard drives are stolen.

2 A built-in editor will manipulate data in RAM. For some operating systems this may be difficult, but the idea is to prevent plain text information from being stored on disk. This limits the utility severely but simplifies security since there is only one source of data.

3 Users share keys directly. As a simple utility there is no need for key servers. Any two people who want to talk securely have to exchange their keys and find their own way to verify them.

To create this utility we need an editor that works out of RAM. By making certain OS system calls we can lock down large chunks of RAM for use with this editor. Anywhere from 256 KB to 1 MB should be more than sufficient for most users' e-mail messages.

Once the user is finished editing a message, the utility takes over. The text (and possibly binary data) is first compressed. A compression algorithm such as Arithmetic Coding might be used (see [1], chapters 5 and 6). The compressed data must also be locked down in RAM and not swapped out.

There are many choices of compression routines. The main purpose of compression is to remove redundancy from the data. This eliminates a character frequency analysis and makes an attacker's task more difficult. The better the compression algorithm, the slower it runs. The benefit is slightly better security than a weaker compression algorithm. Because users spend most of their time in the editor, speed is not a constraint for this application. Therefore, I suggest the more advanced technique of Arithmetic Coding.

The main problem is next: What level of crypto security? For this utility we want the ability to digitally sign a message. So we need to pick a curve of known order. There are three very good curves in chapter 6 that we could use for reasonably high security. These are field sizes 163 (table 6.1), 158 (table 6.3), and 177 (table 6.6). Field size 158 gives about 2^{75} for brute-force security. (As explained in chapter 1, that means an attacker needs 2^{75} operations before he or she finds the key.) It is also a Type II optimal normal basis. This makes the crypto portion a bit faster to calculate, but it is also slightly faster for the attacker. However, it will take computer speed enhancements until the year 2050 before large corporations or universities will have the resources to attack this problem.

All the tools are given in this book to choose the other curves. The `poly_gf8()` routine in chapter 9 can be used to determine the possible coefficients to the largest field size of 177. This has a security level of about 2^{85}. It will take until somewhere around the end of the twenty-first century before this level of crypto security will be crackable by large organizations.

A minor, but very important, point is to force users to create a pass phrase before they can use the utility. The pass phrase must never be stored for long. Only the hash of the pass phrase should be kept in the program's locked down RAM data space. The hash of the pass phrase should *never* touch a disk, because it is the user's secret key.

To make the program easily usable, the pass phrase should be entered when the utility starts. The phrase is hashed, and this secret value is accessible to the program whenever it needs it. To help protect the user, the absence of keyboard activity after some reasonable time (e.g., ten minutes) should exit the program. This can be done gracefully to save all entered data in compressed and encrypted format. It's vital that the user's manual emphasize basic precautions to take to help prevent data from being stolen or accessed improperly. While a user interface with such protections as a ten-minute time-out helps, much of the responsibility for security remains with the user.

Once the user has entered the secret key, the application regenerates the corresponding public key to verify its correctness. This is accomplished by multiplying the secret key by the base point to get the public key. If it fails, we can be nice and ask for the pass phrase again—or we can be mean and exit. Being mean is more secure, because it slows down dictionary attacks. Remember that the manual for this application must train users to pick good pass phrases.

Another section of the utility is the storage of other users' public keys. A method of transmitting and absorbing public keys, as well as picking them out for future use, is required. The PGP style "web of trust" is also a good idea. Keys can be signed and traded to help prevent spoofing.

The basic protocols we need to implement a "web of trust"–style key exchange might include the DSA signature scheme (chapter 10) and ElGamal secret sharing (chapter 7). In addition to the integer, ONB, and elliptic curve math packages, we'll need data exchange routines.

We can also choose a symmetric key algorithm for the encryption portion of the utility instead of the mask generation function of chapter 8. There are many choices for this type of algorithm. Among them are Blowfish, IDEA, and CAST (see [2] for descriptions). For simplicity we'll pick one of them and embed it in the utility. The application gives no choice to the end user in this matter. While crypto programmers eagerly argue the merits of the alternatives, most end users are indifferent. Any of these meet their requirements.

Using a symmetric key algorithm to encrypt all data allows saving the file with the symmetric key encrypted with the user's public key. If the user wants to send the file to different people later, the utility only has to recover the symmetric key using the user's private key and reencrypt the symmetric key using a friend's public key. This allows different, randomly generated symmetric keys to be used for every file, and, again, this makes any attacker's task much more difficult.

The final step is to convert the binary data into something that can be e-mailed through any network server. This requires a simple expansion routine, which converts four bytes of binary data into six bytes of ASCII. In PGP this is called "ASCII armor," and in some mail programs it is called "base 64." To preserve the simplicity of this utility, we'll pick one method, and all programs will know what to expect.

12.2 Security analysis

If we pick a symmetric key scheme such as CAST (because it's free and because I like the way the substitution boxes were designed), we have a 128-bit key to hide. But our public key scheme is only good to 75 bits (assuming we chose the 158-bit field size). This means that it is easier to attack the public key scheme than to attack the symmetric cipher. We have more than enough bits to hide the 128-bit key, and we can tack on another 30 bits of random noise to make the attacker's job harder.

What does this really mean? Any attack will have to solve the discrete log problem over elliptic curves for the 158-bit field. No one will bother to attempt to crack the symmetric key.

Since the utility is encrypting all files to the user, an attacker may be well motivated to crack the user's private key by brute-force. This would give the attacker access to all the files the user has created. For the purposes of this simple utility, this isn't too big a worry. But in some environments it will be well worth the effort to change pass phrases and public keys at regular intervals. If the effort to crack a public key is reasonably large, then only messages encrypted within some time frame will be susceptible to attack.

If we choose a different key exchange protocol, such as MQV or Massey-Omura, then a brute-force crack of a user's public key won't divulge that much information. However, we'll have to transmit a lot of data back and forth just to send an e-mail message. That is overkill for this application. It is better to explain to users through the manual that it is worth changing keys every so often if they are sending sensitive data that some large organization might be interested in.

The utility should make it easy for the user to have multiple public keys and to accept multiple public keys from others. If the user forgets his or her pass phrase, he or she will have to generate a new public key. There have to be reasonable limits on this too. Sixteen user keys and 256 public keys should be enough for most e-mail purposes. These types of limits are easily expanded if needed, but for our purposes it's a good place to start.

12.3 Putting it all together

Figure 12.1 shows most of the components mentioned previously. The routines to enter public keys into a file are part of the "public keys" box. The user's secret key only has to be generated once at program start up. The user's public key only has to be saved once, whenever a new one is generated. If no public key for the user exists, the program should prompt for a pass phrase.

The application uses the hash algorithm (SHA-1 in chapter 8, for example) in two situations. One is to create the user's secret key. In the second situation, it hashes every message to create the signature for that message. Instead of just tacking on the signature, we could compress and encrypt it. Details of the choice don't matter, as long as we can undo it the same way.

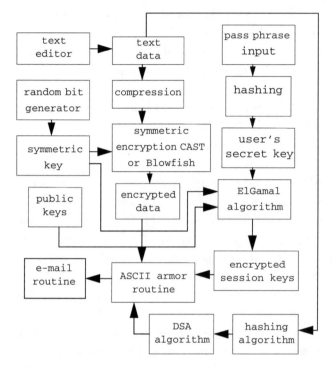

Figure 12.1 Simple utility, encryption direction

Figure 12.1 shows the half of the utility that composes a message and sends it out. We obviously have to do the same thing backwards to decrypt a message and display it on the screen. Users may not like the fact that we won't allow direct printing of the text. That's the idea behind security. Users can use the cut-and-paste options of most operating systems to bypass security and create plain text files. There's not much we can do about that except to warn them in the manual that this is not going to help their security unless they have a really good shredder.

To run the routine backwards is very straightforward. We just call most of the routines in reverse order. First, we unpack the signature and encrypted session key by removing the ASCII armor. Then we use our private key to extract the session key. Then we run the encrypted data through the symmetric algorithm to recover the plain text.

This can be dropped into the editor so the user can reply directly. We can even be fancy and put in ">" for quotes if we like.

Along the way, we can verify the signature and warn the user if a message doesn't check. Usually the message will be unreadable garbage and the user will notice. In any case, the program can only tell the user what it knows; it is up to the user to pay attention to the information presented.

I also don't show any disk storage activity in figure 12.1. The step labeled "e-mail routine" can also just save the data to disk for future access by the user. This method allows users to encrypt messages to themselves. To recover the session key, they use the same ElGamal protocol but with their own private key.

The nice aspect of this utility is that users do not have to remember anything but their own pass phrases. They can save messages to themselves—as well as send messages to others—all safely encrypted. By fixing all the code to work only one way, every user can easily talk to any other. The program is pretty much platform independent, so interoperability is fairly easy to achieve.

Users can also send multiple copies of a single message to many other people. This can be done all at once or, if the encrypted data are saved to disk, at different times. The session key can be recovered by the utility using the original user's private key, and this can be encrypted using any other user's public key. While not shown in figure 12.1, all the components are there to accomplish this.

I've already explained several of the limits this utility has. The point is that we, as crypto engineers, can design the system to be reasonably secure when used by reasonably well trained users (those who actually read the manual). There will always be some users who find ways to bypass security for their own immediate convenience. Rather than decorating the program with frills to help save users from every way they might compromise their own information, the best we can do is to help them understand the limits to the security this utility offers.

12.4 References

1 M. Nelson, *The Data Compression Book* (Redwood City, CA: M&T Books, 1992).
2 B. Schneier, *Applied Cryptography,* 2d ed. (New York: John Wiley & Sons, 1996).

index

A

addition
    elliptic curve 106
        normal basis 118
        over GF(2^n) 110
        over real numbers 107
        polynomial basis 49, 54, 115
    integer 14, 20
almost inverse algorithm 285
ascii_to_bigint 28
authen_secret 191, 194
avalanche 130

B

balanced form 122
BIGINT 17
bigint_to_ascii 28
binary representation 17

C

CARRY 16
Certicom 4
Certicom challenge 168
commutative cipher. See Massey-Omura.
complex multiplication method 298
compression 297
conversion 57
copy 57
copy_cust 290

copy_point 113
counting points 298
cracking. See cryptanalysis.
Crandall 299
cryptanalysis 132
    time to crack 4
cryptography 129
CURVE 113
cus_times_u_to_n 290
CUSTFIELD 289

D

Dahm. See inversion, fast.
DBLBITS 54
DBLFIELD 54
DBLLOOP 54
dblnull 56
DBLSHIFT 54
DBLWORD 54
degree 49, 60
degreeof 61
derivative 68
DERIVMASK 54, 69
DES 132
DH_gen_send_key 175
DH_key_share 176
DIEHARD 168
Diffie-Hellman 166, 174–180
digital signature 256–282
div_shift 59

division
  integer 14, 23
  polynomial 50, 58, 62
DSA 271–282

E

EC_KEYPAIR 224
EC_PARAMETER 212, 224
ECES_decrypt 217
ECES_encrypt 217
ECKGP 216, 225
edbl 119
ELEMENT 17, 52
ElGamal 166, 180–188
elliptic curve
  discrete logarithm problem 132
  embedding data 136
  nonsupersingular 110, 133
  order 108
  over $GF(2^n)$ 109
  over real numbers 104
  subtraction
      polynomial basis 117
  supersingular 110
elliptic curve equation 104
  Galois Fields 109
  real 104
elliptic curve mathematics 103–126
elptic_mul 123
embedding data 136
  normal basis 146
  polynomial basis 161
encryption 199
  Elliptic Curve Encryption Scheme 200
esub 120
esum 118
Euclid's algorithm 50, 66
example
  DSA 276, 280
  encryption 215, 218
  integer 27
  Massey-Omura 240, 242
  MQV 192, 194, 248, 251
  Nyberg-Rueppel 265, 269

exponential time 5, 6

F

factoring 5
Fermat's Theorem 39, 104
field conversion. See conversion.
field_prime 82, 85
field_to_int 222
FIELD2N 52
finite fields 40
fofx 147
freelip 14

G

Galois Fields 43
Gaussian elimination 227
gen_MO_pair 236
generator 43
      See also prime polynomial.
genlambda 82
genlambda2 90
GF. See Galois Field.
Gillogly, James 203
greatest common factor
  integer 30, 35
  polynomial 67

H

HALFSIZE 16
hash 259
hash_to_int 259
Hasse's Theorem 108, 133, 171
header
  bigint.h 16, 18
  eliptic.h 111
  field2n.h 18, 51
  poly.h 54
HIMASK 16
hyperelliptic curves 299

I

IDEA 132
identity element 40

IEEE P1363 131, 166, 200, 225, 244, 258, 271

INDEX 18, 52

init_opt_math 289

init_poly_math 153

init_two 288

initialization
    normal basis math 289
    polynomial math 153

int_add 20

int_copy 19

int_div 24

int_div2 34

int_gcd 35

int_mul 22

int_neg 20

int_null 19

int_onecmp 236

int_sub 21

int_to_field 224

integer representation 17

INTLOOP 18

INTMAX 16

inversion
    fast 284–297
    matrix, polynomial basis 150
    normal basis 97, 100, 292
    polynomial 66

irreducible 70

irreducible polynomial 49

isomorphic 76

K

key exchange 222

Knuth 34

Koblitz 4, 122, 136, 219, 226, 234, 298

Koblitz curves 133

L

Lambda 82

lambda matrix 79, 82, 87, 90

language 11

large integer math 14, 19, 27

lg2_m 82

LiDIA 14

linear equations 226

log_2 60

log2 288

LOMASK 16

LONGBIT 288

LONGMASK 288

LONGSHIFT 288

LONGWORD 288

M

man-in-the-middle attack 179

Marsaglia 168

mask generation function 202–212

mass
    hydrogen 6
    sun 6

Massey-Omura 222, 234–244

matrix 227
    diagonalize 231
    transpose 231

matrix_print 152

MAXBITS 51

MAXDBL 54

MAXLONG 16, 51

MAXSHIFT 51

MAXSTRING 16

Menezes-Qu-Vanstone 188–197, 222

Mentat 203

message hash 259

MGF_Hash 210

Miller 4

MIRACL 14

mod_exp 38

mod_inv 42

modular arithmetic
    exponentiation 38
    integer 29, 37
    inversion 41

modulus 41

Mother 169

MQV. See Menezes-Qu-Vanstone.

MSB 51

MSB_HW 16

mul_shift 55
mul_x_mod 69
multiplication
    elliptic curve 120
        normal basis 92, 122
        polynomial basis 125
    integer 14, 21
    normal basis 78, 94
    polynomial 49, 55, 57, 65, 69
multiplication table 79, 82

N

negation
    elliptic curve 110, 113
    integer 20
nist_guts 208
nonadjacent form 122
normal basis 75–102
    inversion 284–297
normal basis representation 76
NR_Signature 262
NR_Verify 263
null 56
null_cust 290
Null_Row 149
number theory 13–44
NUMBITS 16, 51
NUMWORD 16, 51
Nyberg-Rueppel 256, 260–271

O

onb_DSA_Signature 273
onb_DSA_Verify 274
onb_Massey_Omura_rcv 239
onb_Massey_Omura_send 238
onb_mqv 246
one 97
opt_embed 146
opt_inv 100, 292
opt_mul 94
opt_quadratic 141
optimal normal basis 76, 101
    Type I 80–84
    Type II 85–92

order 43
    See also Hasse's Theorem.
output 96

P

P1363. See IEEE P1363.
perfect forward secrecy 189
PGP 4, 5
Pinch 140
POINT 113
point at infinity 105
poly_div 62
poly_DSA_Signature 278
poly_DSA_Verify 279
poly_ECES_decrypt 214
poly_ECES_encrypt 213
poly_ECKGP 225
poly_ECKGP_0 213
poly_edbl 116
poly_embed 161
poly_esub 117
poly_esum 115
poly_fofx 161
poly_gcd 68
poly_gf8 230
poly_inv 66
poly_Massey_Omura_rcv 239
poly_Massey_Omura_send 238
poly_matrix_invert 150
poly_mqv 250
poly_mul 65
poly_mul_partial 57
poly_NR_Signature 267
poly_NR_Verify 268
poly_quadratic 158
polynomial basis 48
polynomial math 47–72
polynomial time 5
prime 30, 48
prime polynomial 49, 65, 68, 70
print_curve 114
print_field 96, 114
print_point 114
private key 130, 166

protocols 165–197
protocols. See Diffie-Hellman, ElGamal, Massey-Omura, Nyberg-Rueppel, DSA, Menezes-Qu-Vanstone, encryption.
public key 130, 166

Q

quadratic equation
    normal basis 141
    polynomial basis 148, 158
quadratic equations 137

R

rand_curve 172
rand_point 173
random bit generator 168
random_field 171
receive_elgamal 183, 186
remainder 49
rot_left 94
rot_right 94
rotate
    left 94
    right 94
RSA 5

S

schematic 15, 53, 77, 112, 142, 167, 201, 223, 257, 284
Schroeppel 292
secret key 130, 166
security 131, 297
send_elgamal 182, 185
sha_file 206
sha_memory 207
sha_stream 207
SHA-1 200, 202, 203, 259
shift
    left 55
    right 59
shift_by 288
SIGNATURE 258

signature 256–282
Smatrix 149
sngltodbl 57
solution vectors 229, 233
square root
    normal basis 141
    polynomial 160
squaring
    normal basis 78, 94
    polynomial 70
subexponential time 5
subtraction
    elliptic curve
        normal basis 120
        polynomial basis 117
    integer 21
    polynomial 50
SUMLOOP 52

T

test routine 96
time to crack 4
Tmatrix 149, 158
Trace 137, 138
Trace vector 139
Trace_Vector 149
twist 133
two_bit 288
two_inx 288
TYPE2 85

U

UPRBIT 52
UPRMASK 52
UPRSHIFT 16, 51
U.S. patent 5600725 256
    See also Nyberg-Rueppel.

V

vectors 229

W

WORDSIZE 14, 51

All source code for the examples presented in *Implementing Elliptic Curve Cryptography* is available to purchasers from the Manning Web site. The url `www.manning.com/Rosing` includes a link to the source code files.

Purchase of *Implementing Elliptic Curve Cryptography* also includes free author online support. For more information on this feature, please refer to page xiii. Each example is presented as a complete set of files which can be compiled and linked as a terminal application on any ANSI C compiler.